CRITICAL RACE THEORY IN MATHEMATICS EDUCATION

Critical Race Theory in Mathematics Education brings together scholarship that uses critical race theory (CRT) to provide a comprehensive understanding of race, racism, social justice, and experiential knowledge of African Americans' mathematics education. CRT has gained traction within the educational research sphere, and this book extends and applies this framework to chronicle the paths of mathematics educators who advance and use CRT. This edited collection brings together scholarship that addresses the racial challenges thrusted upon Black learners and the gatekeeping nature of the discipline of mathematics. Across the ten chapters, scholars expand the uses of CRT in mathematics education and share insights with stakeholders regarding the racialized experiences of mathematics students and educators. Collectively, the volume explains how researchers, practitioners, and policymakers can use CRT to examine issues of race, racism, and other forms of oppression in mathematics education for Black children and adults.

Julius Davis is Associate Professor of Mathematics Education in the Department of Teaching, Learning, and Professional Development at Bowie State University. His research critically examines Black students' mathematics experiences and how policies shape their experiences. His research also focuses on Black mathematics teachers' content and pedagogical knowledge, academic and professional experiences, and policies that shape their praxis, and critical race theory permeates throughout his scholarship.

Christopher C. Jett is Associate Professor of Mathematics Education in the Department of Mathematics at the University of West Georgia (UWG) in Carrollton, GA. In 2017, he became the first African American to earn tenure in UWG's College of Science and Mathematics. His research investigates the experiences of high-achieving African American male STEM majors at different institution types coupling critical race theory with qualitative methods. His current research project has been funded via the National Science Foundation's prestigious Early Career Development (CAREER) Award. Dr. Jett's research utilizing critical race theory has been published in the *Journal of Black Studies,* the *Journal of Urban Mathematics Education, Spectrum: A Journal on Black Men,* and the *Journal for Research in Mathematics Education* (in press). He is the 2019 Association of Mathematics Teacher Educators (AMTE) Early Career awardee, and he has a host of other distinguished accomplishments as an emerging mathematics education scholar.

CRITICAL RACE THEORY IN MATHEMATICS EDUCATION

Edited by Julius Davis and Christopher C. Jett

Routledge
Taylor & Francis Group

NEW YORK AND LONDON

First published 2019
by Routledge
52 Vanderbilt Avenue, New York, NY 10017

and by Routledge
2 Park Square, Milton Park, Abingdon, Oxon OX14 4RN

Routledge is an imprint of the Taylor & Francis Group, an informa business

© 2019 Taylor & Francis

The right of Julius Davis and Christopher C. Jett to be identified as the authors of the editorial material, and of the authors for their individual chapters, has been asserted in accordance with sections 77 and 78 of the Copyright, Designs and Patents Act 1988.

Library of Congress Cataloging-in-Publication Data
Names: Davis, Julius, editor. | Jett, Christopher C., editor.
Title: Critical race theory in mathematics education / edited by Julius Davis and Christopher C. Jett.
Description: New York, NY : Routledge, 2019. | Includes bibliographical references and index.
Identifiers: LCCN 2018055760| ISBN 9781138562660 (hardback : alk. paper) | ISBN 9781138562677 (pbk. : alk. paper) | ISBN 9781315121192 (ebook)
Subjects: LCSH: Mathematics--Study and teaching--United States--Social aspects. | African Americans--Education. | Racism in education--United States.
Classification: LCC QA13 .C75 2019 | DDC 371.829/00151--dc23
LC record available at https://lccn.loc.gov/2018055760

ISBN: 978-1-138-56266-0 (hbk)
ISBN: 978-1-138-56267-7 (pbk)
ISBN: 978-1-315-12119-2 (ebk)

Typeset in Bembo
by Taylor & Francis Books

CONTENTS

ILLUSTRATIONS

Figures

Tables

CONTRIBUTORS

Nathan N. Alexander is the James King, Jr. Visiting Professor in the Department of Mathematics at Morehouse College and the Associate Director of the Communicating TEAMs (Thinking Effectively in and About Mathematics) Initiative at the James King, Jr. Institute for Student and Faculty Engagement in the Division of Science and Mathematics. His research focuses on the intersections of race and mathematics teaching and learning in traditional schools, alternative spaces, and community-based settings. He received his Ph.D. in mathematics and education from Columbia University and bachelor's degrees in mathematics and sociology from the University of North Carolina at Chapel Hill.

Erika C. Bullock is Assistant Professor of Curriculum Studies and Mathematics Education at the University of Wisconsin-Madison. Dr. Bullock's work spans curriculum studies, urban education, and mathematics education. She uses theories from urban sociology, critical geography, literary theory, and science and technology studies to historicize issues and ideologies within mathematics and STEM education to examine how power operates within these disciplines to create and maintain inequities. Dr. Bullock is a 2017–2018 National Academy of Education/Spencer Foundation postdoctoral fellow. Her work has been published in outlets including *Educational Studies in Mathematics, The Journal of Education, Review of Research in Education*, and *Teachers College Record*. She has also been featured in *The Atlantic*. She was awarded the 2017 Taylor and Francis Publication Best Paper Award for "Only STEM can save us? Examining race, place, and STEM education as property," published in *Educational Studies*.

Floyd Cobb is Adjunct Faculty Member with the Morgridge College of Education at the University of Denver. There, he teaches courses in educational policy, curriculum and instruction and social inequality. In 2017, he was awarded the Ruth Murray Underhill Teaching Award, which is given annually to one adjunct faculty member for excellence in teaching at the University of Denver. Dr. Cobb holds almost 20 years of experience in the field of education spanning the P-20 continuum as both a teacher and educational leader. He is the author of the book *Leading While Black* (2017, Peter Lang), an autoethnography detailing his reflections on educational leadership. He is also the co-editor of the book *Interrogating Whiteness Relinquishing Power* (2016, Peter Lang) with Nicole Joseph and Chayla Haynes.

Toya Jones Frank is Assistant Professor in the Mathematics Education Leadership (MEL) and Secondary Education programs at George Mason University in Fairfax, Virginia. Her research interests include: access to advanced mathematics for under-represented secondary students, secondary mathematics teacher preparation, and exploring issues related to diversifying the STEM teacher workforce with respect to race and ethnicity. She is the Principal Investigator of *Examining the Trajectories of Black Mathematics Teachers: Learning from the Past, Drawing on the Present, and Defining Goals for the Future*, a 3-year project funded by the National Science Foundation. Dr. Frank is a former high school mathematics teacher and department chair who worked in Maryland and Florida public schools as well as a former educational consultant for clients including DC Public Schools and ACT, Inc.

Nicole M. Joseph is Assistant Professor of Mathematics Education in the Department of Teaching and Learning at Vanderbilt University. She is the recipient of the 2018 AERA Scholars of Color Early Career Contribution Award. Her research explores two lines of inquiry: (a) Black women and girls, their identity development, and their experiences in mathematics; and (b) Whiteness, White supremacy and how they operate and shape Black women's and girls' underrepresentation and retention in mathematics. Her scholarship has been published in top-tier journals such as the *Review of Research in Education* and *The Journal of Negro Education*. Her activist work includes founding the Tennessee March for Black Women in STEM, an event held every fall that seeks to bring together the Tennessee community to raise awareness about issues Black women and girls face in STEM learning, education, and industry.

Gregory V. Larnell is Associate Professor in the Department of Curriculum and Instruction at the University of Illinois at Chicago (UIC). His primary research and teaching interests center on mathematics education, urban education, and curriculum studies. More specifically, his research includes attention to mathematics curriculum, learning and identity, and teacher education. In 2017, Dr. Larnell was awarded the Special Interest Group (SIG)/Research in Mathematics Education (RME) Early Career Publication Award for his paper published in the *Journal for Research in Mathematics Education*.

Danny Bernard Martin is Professor of Education and Mathematics at the University of Illinois at Chicago (UIC). His research has focused on understanding the salience of race and identity in Black learners' mathematical experiences. He is author of the book *Mathematics Success and Failure Among African Youth* (2000, Erlbaum), editor of *Mathematics Teaching, Learning, and Liberation in the Lives of Black Children* (2009, Routledge), co-editor of *The Brilliance of Black Children in Mathematics: Beyond the Numbers and Toward New Discourse* (2013, Information Age), and co-author of *The Impact of Identity in K–8 Mathematics Learning and Teaching* (2013, NCTM).

Roxanne Moore is Doctoral Student in the Mathematics and Science Education program in the College of Education at Washington State University. She received her M.Ed. in secondary education with an emphasis in mathematics from Chaminade University of Honolulu, and a BA in Law, Letters, and Society with a minor in African & African American Studies from the University of Chicago. Ms. Moore is a former secondary mathematics teacher and K-8 school leader. Ms. Moore's work seeks to critically examine and productively expand the revolutionary action necessary to engage in the people's vocation, the humanization of all. Her areas of expertise include critical mathematics education, critical race theory, implementations of critical pedagogy, values/valuing in mathematics in Hawai'i, complexity theory in mathematics education, pragmatist epistemologies, and mixed methods research.

Paula Groves Price is Professor in the Cultural Studies and Social Thought program and the Associate Dean for Diversity and International Programs in the College of Education at Washington State University. She received her Ph.D. in the Social Foundations of Education from the University of North Carolina Chapel Hill, and BAs in Social Welfare and Interdisciplinary Field Studies with a minor in African American Studies from the University of California Berkeley. Dr. Price is the Editor in Chief of the *Western Journal of Black Studies* and the forthcoming *Oxford Research Encyclopedia of Race and Education*. She is also a section editor for the *Second International Handbook of Urban Education* (2017, Springer) and the *Handbook of Research in Social Foundations of Education* (2010, Routledge). Her areas of expertise include African American and Indigenous education, critical STEM, Black feminist epistemology, critical race theory, and qualitative research methodologies.

Celia Rousseau Anderson is Professor of Mathematics Education in the Department of Instruction and Curriculum Leadership at the University of Memphis. Her scholarly interests include equity in mathematics education, urban education, and critical race theory. Previous publications related to critical race theory have appeared in *Race, Ethnicity, and Education; Urban Education; Peabody Journal of Education;* and *Teachers College Record*. She also served as co-editor of the book, *Critical Race Theory in Education: All God's Children Got a Song* (2006, 2016, Routledge). Her scholarship in mathematics education includes publications in

Theory into Practice and the *Journal of Urban Mathematics Education* as well as a co-authored chapter in the *Compendium for Research in Mathematics Education*.

Editors

Julius Davis is Associate Professor of Mathematics Education in the Department of Teaching, Learning, and Professional Development at Bowie State University. His research critically examines Black students' mathematics experiences and how policies shape their experiences. His research also focuses on Black mathematics teachers' content and pedagogical knowledge, academic and professional experiences, and policies that shape their praxis, and critical race theory permeates throughout his scholarship.

Christopher C. Jett is Associate Professor of Mathematics Education in the Department of Mathematics at the University of West Georgia (UWG) in Carrollton, GA. In 2017, he became the first African American to earn tenure in UWG's College of Science and Mathematics. His research investigates the experiences of high-achieving African American male STEM majors at different institution types coupling critical race theory with qualitative methods. His current research project has been funded via the National Science Foundation's prestigious Early Career Development (CAREER) Award. Dr. Jett's research utilizing critical race theory has been published in the *Journal of Black Studies,* the *Journal of Urban Mathematics Education, Spectrum: A Journal on Black Men,* and the *Journal for Research in Mathematics Education* (in press). He is the 2019 Association of Mathematics Teacher Educators (AMTE) Early Career awardee, and he has a host of other distinguished accomplishments as an emerging mathematics education scholar.

ACKNOWLEDGMENTS

We would like to thank the contributors for seeing this project through until the very end. The contributors represent an eclectic group of education researchers with cutting-edge critical race/mathematics education research agendas, interests, and paradigms. Without your research specialties, this edited volume would not be possible. We are appreciative to William F. Tate, IV for his support of this edited volume and for his continuous guidance and words of wisdom throughout the years. We would also like to thank Marvin Lynn for writing the foreword for this edited volume and for his invaluable contributions to critical race theory in education. We wish to thank Catherine Bernard, Rachel Dugan, Matthew Friberg, and Karen Adler at the Taylor & Francis Group within Routledge for their guidance throughout this entire process. Finally, we would like to thank our respective villages for supporting our professorial efforts as we attempt to imagine new possibilities, forge new ground, and make distinctive contributions related to critical race theory in mathematics education.

FOREWORD

Mathematics education scholars have worked to illuminate the potential power that mathematics holds in the lives of racially marginalized people in the United States. These scholars have also helped bring attention to the way mathematics, as a discipline, has ignored the experiences of African Americans thereby making it difficult for African Americans to develop strong mathematics identities (Martin, 2000). Reading, and in many cases, re-reading the work of mathematics education scholars who are principally concerned about African Americans' experiences with mathematics has caused me to reflect on my own experiences as an African American who, in many ways, excelled academically but was still alienated by and from mathematics as a middle and high school student in under-resourced urban public schools in Chicago.

In the introduction, Davis and Jett remind us that William Tate introduced Critical Race Theory (CRT) to the field of education in his 1993 article, "Advocacy versus Economics: A Critical Race Analysis of the Proposed National Assessment in Mathematics." I am not a mathematics educator. As a result, I was first introduced to Tate's (1994) work when I read a piece he published entitled, "From the Inner City to the Ivory Tower" published in the journal, *Urban Education*. Tate would go on to publish several other articles which helped bring attention to the framework. In "From the Inner City to the Ivory Tower," Tate describes how the development of a strong mathematical foundation in a Catholic elementary school was what helped him become an excellent mathematics student in high school, which eventually led him to excel in high level mathematics and science classes in high school. Tate was brave enough to share his personal story at the beginning of his illustrious career. I'm encouraged to reflect on my own story at this point in my career.

Like Tate, I grew up on the Southside of Chicago. However, I was not consistently exposed to excellent mathematics instruction or a curriculum which introduced me to higher level mathematics. I viewed higher level mathematics as something foreign, something outside the realm of my experience. Even though I was considered gifted, in many ways, I was not necessarily expected to excel in mathematics beyond arithmetic. I recall two critical incidents in my schooling experience that shaped my belief that mathematics was essentially created by and "for White people" (Delpit, 2012).

From kindergarten through the beginning of fourth grade, I attended an all-Black public school in Englewood, the poorest and most racially segregated neighborhood in the City of Chicago. At Sherwood Elementary School, I had loving Black teachers who encouraged me to excel. I recall being encouraged to read and having teachers work with me to build a strong foundation for reading, writing, and mathematics. Since my parents lacked the ability to support the advancement of my mathematical knowledge at a high level, I was heavily teacher-dependent. Teachers at Sherwood took on the role of Other Mothers who took responsibility for the lives of their students. My teachers focused mostly on the development of literacy skills—teaching phonemic awareness and encouraging us to read books.

In the middle of fourth grade, I moved to the River West neighborhood, which is part of the West Town community, on the near north side of the city in close proximity to the downtown area also referred to as "the loop." Unlike Englewood, with its overcrowding and abundance of challenges due to the poverty status of the majority of its mostly Black residents, River West was a nearly uninhabited neighborhood full of abandoned factories (Maguire, 1991). By the time my family arrived in 1981, there were only a few apartment buildings and single family homes intermixed with old abandoned factories with the Kennedy Expressway on one end and the Chicago River on the other. My elementary school served students from the neighboring area who were largely Latinx with a small population of African Americans.

After a couple of years in my new school, I began to notice that I was not being served well by my teachers. I remember having a teacher who struggled to teach mathematics. I was frustrated by this because I desperately wanted to advance my own mathematical knowledge. I had mastered the basics. I was interested in learning higher order thinking and conceptual mathematics. Unfortunately, this was not available to me. I relegated my thirst for greater mathematical knowledge to the sidelines. I continued to be rewarded for my reading, writing, and analytical skills. I continued to excel in school, but I did not see myself as a mathematical thinker.

By the time I got to high school, I was taking accelerated courses across all areas. It quickly became evident that Honors Algebra would prove to be a challenge. I remember my teacher—a large White southern gentleman who had been teaching for many years. He was well-respected for his mathematical knowledge. I knew right away, however, that he did not like Black children. Suffice it to say, I hated that class. I did okay, despite my challenges with the teacher. The following year, I took Geometry with that same teacher. It didn't end well. Because I had built strong relationships with other teachers and counselors in the building, mostly due to my reputation as a student leader and participant in the gifted and talented program, I found a way through this challenge.

As I reflect on these unfortunate experiences with mathematics in middle and high school, I believe my opportunities to see myself as a mathematical thinker were squandered. In one sense, I had teachers who either lacked sufficient mathematical knowledge to teach me high level mathematics or did not believe that Black children could be mathematically literate. Tate's story reminds me that the lack of rigorous mathematics curriculum in the schools I attended was not necessarily something teachers could control. They were subject to a curriculum that focused almost exclusively on "the basics" and undermined the creativity of teachers who might have explored areas beyond the curriculum. This certainly reflected my experience as a teacher in a Direct Instruction classroom on the Westside of Chicago in the mid-1990s. As an African American teacher in a poor all-Black school, I was completely alienated from the curriculum and micromanaged by the administration in a way that I found stifling. My past experience as both a learner and a teacher in large urban public school systems has taught me that both students and teachers are alienated from good mathematics teaching and learning in these contexts. The research in this volume confirms this.

This important book draws on CRT as a tool to explore the range of studies that explore both the promise and peril of mathematics education in the United States—particularly as it pertains to African Americans. Davis and Jett note in the introduction, that while mathematics education scholars like Tate, Martin, Rousseau Anderson and others have been concerned about the field's inattention to the plight of the Black community, mathematics education has not figured prominently within the CRT in Education community. In fact, there are few content-related discussions about the profession of teaching, more specifically. My work on Critical Race Pedagogy explored the perspectives of teachers across a range of areas but did not include much discussion about the subject matter as related to classroom pedagogy.

This book provides a greater opportunity for scholars to draw on CRT as a tool for thinking deeply about the nature of teaching and learning that is subject-specific. It also gives authors, as in the case of Martin and colleagues, an important tool to look beyond CRT in search of other tools such as BlackCrit to advance a mathematics education that is sensitive to the needs of Black students, and perhaps teachers like mine who lacked the training and/or administrative support to provide Black children with a liberatory mathematics education. This book helps to fill an important void.

References

Delpit, L. D. (2012). *"Multiplication is for White people": Raising expectations for other people's children*. New York, NY: The New Press.

Maguire, M. (1991, November 3). Change is flowing into River West neighborhood. *Chicago Tribune*. Retrieved from https://www.chicagotribune.com/news/ct-xpm -1991-11-03-9104090074-story,amp.html.

Martin, D. B. (2000). *Mathematics success and failure among African-American youth: The roles of sociohistorical context, community forces, school influence, and individual agency*. Mahwah, NJ: Lawrence Erlbaum.

Tate, W. F. (1993). Advocacy versus economics: A critical race analysis of the proposed national assessment in mathematics. *Thresholds in Education*, 19(1–2), 16–22.

Tate, W. F. (1994). From inner city to ivory tower: Does my voice matter in the academy? *Urban Education*, 29(3), 245–269.

INTRODUCTION

Julius Davis and Christopher C. Jett

Background

In 2013, we presented our critical race theory (CRT) mathematics education scholarship at the Critical Race Studies in Education Association (CRSEA) conference at Vanderbilt University in Nashville, TN. Our presentations were organized into one strand focused on mathematics education, and we were the only two presenters in that particular strand. Chris's presentation focused on using CRT to investigate the experiences of African American male mathematics majors while Julius's presentation centered on providing a direction for critical race studies of Black students in mathematics education. Our presentations provided a forum for us to share our views, perspectives, and understandings of CRT and its use in mathematics education. The subsequent discussions allowed us to make connections across our scholarly interests regarding the use of CRT in mathematics education.

Over the course of the conference, we attended many sessions to learn more about the work of other CRT scholars. One of the things that became increasingly apparent to us was the low number of mathematics education scholars attending the conference. To our knowledge, only three other mathematics education scholars were present at the CRSEA conference: Ebony McGee, Celia Rousseau Anderson, and Bill Tate. As a faculty member at Vanderbilt University, Ebony played a role in helping to arrange the conference. Celia gave a presentation on her work entitled, "Consolidation, Charters, and Choice Interest Convergence and Divergence in Memphis and Shelby County Schools." In addition, Bill received the Derrick Bell Legacy Award for his scholarly contributions to CRT.

Prominent CRT scholar, Marvin Lynn, was also at the conference promoting and signing his co-edited book, the *Handbook of Critical Race Theory in Education* (Lynn & Dixson, 2013). We both purchased the text and later noticed that there were no chapters focused on mathematics education in the edited volume. In all fairness, there were no chapters in the book that focused on a specific content area per se. Hence, we imagined what a CRT-related, discipline-specific edited volume could contribute to the field as it pertains to promoting race-related scholarship in mathematics education, especially given that mathematics is often considered an objective and raceless discipline, whereby race is inextricably linked to the origins of mathematics in the United States and Europe (Anderson, 1990). Therefore, we proposed that such a volume could promote scholarship that addresses the racial challenges thrusted upon Black learners and the gatekeeping nature of our primary discipline of mathematics, among other things.

We introduce this volume in this manner because the initial conceptualization of the book, *Critical Race Theory in Mathematics Education* (*CRT(ME)*) originated at the CRSEA conference. We kept in contact and saw each other periodically at various conferences over the years. We communicated about collaborating on either an edited book or a special issue of a journal focused on CRT in mathematics education. In 2016, we reconnected with the deliberate intent to map out a detailed plan to move forward with the *CRT(ME)* edited book.

Our major goals for *CRT(ME)* are to build on extant CRT in mathematics education scholarship, share advances mathematics education scholars have made to CRT, and, in some cases, usher in a new generation of scholars advancing CRT in mathematics education. It is important to note that this book comes at a time when critical mathematics educators are being attacked for their scholarship and pedagogy that challenges Whiteness, White supremacy, and the status quo in mathematics, especially those in marginalized groups (Gutiérrez, 2017). Therefore, researchers who are doing CRT work should be aware of and prepared to fight any potential backlash against critical scholarship. However, we remain optimistic that this work can push the field forward in unique ways.

CRT Scholarship in Mathematics Education

CRT developed from legal scholarship, including the work of Derrick Bell, Kimberlé Crenshaw, Richard Delgado, Alan Freeman, Mari J. Matsuda, and Jean Stefancic. Derrick Bell is considered the father of CRT, and his impact concerning this theory has been well documented in the literature (Ladson-Billings & Tate, 2016). The genealogy of CRT in law and education has also been well documented in the literature (Delgado & Stefancic, 2000; Dixson & Rousseau, 2006; Ladson-Billings, 2010; Ladson-Billings & Tate, 1995; Lynn & Parker, 2006), but its genesis in mathematics education is known to a lesser degree (Davis, 2014; Lynn & Adams, 2002). As such, this edited volume presents CRT's roots in mathematics education, leverages the benefits of CRT's tenets for the field, and offers future directions for using CRT in mathematics education.

In preparing this volume, we scoured the literature to discover CRT's contributions to mathematics education. Although dissertations have been one of the main vehicles to use CRT in mathematics education (see, e.g., Corey, 2000; Snipes, 1997; Wilson, 2018), mathematics education scholars have also used CRT to advance knowledge through journal articles, book chapters, conference proceedings, and so on across different domains. Some scholars have used CRT to examine policies, laws, standards, and assessments (Cobb & Russell, 2015; Tate, Ladson-Billings & Grant, 1993). Other scholars have used CRT to ground culturally specific mathematics pedagogy and advance social/racial justice pedagogy (Larnell, Bullock, & Jett, 2016; Leonard, 2007; Terry, 2010, 2011). Mathematics educators have also used CRT to investigate the racialized and mathematical experiences of Black students and parents (Martin, 2006; McGee, 2013; Strutchens, & Westbrook, 2009). In addition, many mathematics education researchers have crossed disciplinary boundaries to collaborate with scholars outside of the field to use CRT to examine educational inequality (Dixson & Rousseau, 2006), teacher education (Anderson & Cross, 2013; Milner, Pearman & McGee, 2013), policy (Allen et al., 2018), mental health research (McGee & Stovall, 2015), and so on. The point is that CRT offers extraordinary potential for scholars to engage in interdisciplinary projects, and we hope that this volume unearths some of that potential for the betterment of mathematics education.

Overview of *CRT(ME)*

CRT(ME) is comprised of ten chapters, and each chapter in this volume distinctively expands the use of CRT in mathematics education. Chapter one begins with a tribute to Bill Tate for introducing CRT to mathematics education. It also includes an emailed interview questionnaire to provide an overview of Tate's thoughts about his contributions to CRT, CRT's connection to mathematics education, and his thoughts about the future of CRT in mathematics education. In chapter two, Celia Rousseau Anderson illuminates the boundaries of CRT in mathematics education using legal studies scholar, Devon Carbado's (2011) notion of "critical what what."

In the next chapter, Danny Bernard Martin, Paula Groves Price, and Roxanne Moore embrace CRT and use BlackCrit (Dumas, 2016; Dumas & ross, 2016) as a lens to conceptualize and describe a Black Liberatory Mathematics Education to combat the systematic violence against Black children. In chapter four, Nathan N. Alexander uses Derrick Bell's (1987, 1992) allegorical storytelling method to launch a discussion about Black futurity. He presents the case of Daija to situate Afrofuturism in the CRT canon to counter deficit narratives regarding Black specificity in mathematics education.

Erika C. Bullock takes us back in time with a CRT historical counter-story of mathematics education policies and Black mathematics teachers' advocacy for Black children in chapter five. She argues that contemporary mathematics education reform maintains a White institutional space through racial remediation. In chapter six, Toya Jones Frank continues the focus on educational policies and

Black mathematics teachers by using CRT to critique recruitment and retention efforts. She uses CRT's tenets of critique of liberalism, interest convergence, intersectionality, Whiteness as property, and the permanence of racism to argue that conversations and policy solutions regarding the limited presence of Black mathematics teachers must include race and racism. She posits that Black mathematics teachers need solutions that center and humanize them instead of serving the interests of policymakers.

Gregory V. Larnell shifts the focus to mathematical proficiency and standardized testing in mathematics education in chapter seven. He opens with a parable to bring the construct of mathematical proficiency to life and uses CRT to critique mathematical proficiency. Continuing with a focus on standardized testing in mathematics education, Nicole M. Joseph and Floyd Cobb build on arguments made in their collaborative article critiquing mathematics assessments (Cobb & Russell, 2015). In their chapter, Joseph and Cobb use four CRT tenets: racial realism, the social construction of race, the myth of meritocracy, and interest convergence to complicate standardized mathematics assessments, myths about Black intelligence, and unequal access to mathematics curriculum.

In chapter nine, Christopher C. Jett shares some of his personal and professional racialized experiences that capture his CRT journey in mathematics education thus far. He also explicates how CRT can be useful for the disciplinary field of mathematics education in general and for his scholarship with Black male students in particular. Finally, Julius Davis uses CRT's tenets of mathematical counter-stories, intellectual property, Whiteness as property, and interest convergence to describe how it can be used as pedagogical, theoretical, methodological, or analytical tools in the field for Black adults and children in urban environments. Taken together, these ten chapters provide a means of explaining how researchers, practitioners, and policymakers can use CRT to examine issues of race, racism, and other forms of oppression in mathematics education for Black children and adults, and we hope that this volume offers unique insights to amplify the use of CRT in mathematics education scholarship.

References

Allen, K., Davis, J., Garraway, R., & Burt, R. (2018). Every student succeeds (except for Black males) act. *Teachers College Record*, 120(13). Retrieved from http://www.tcrecord. org/Content.asp?ContentId=22352.

Anderson, C. R., & Cross, B. E. (2013). What is "urban"? A CRT examination of the preparation of K-12 teachers for urban schools. In M. Lynn & A. Dixson (Eds.), *Handbook of critical race theory in education* (pp. 406–416). New York, NY: Routledge.

Anderson, S. E. (1990). Worldmath curriculum: Fighting Eurocentrism in mathematics. *The Journal of Negro Education*, 59(3), 348–359.

Bell, D. (1987). *And we are not saved: The elusive quest for racial justice*. New York, NY: Basic Books.

Bell, D. (1992). *Faces at the bottom of the well: The permanence of racism.* New York, NY: Basic Books.

Carbado, D. W. (2011). Critical what what? *Connecticut Law Review, 43*(5), 1593–1643.

Cobb, F., & Russell, N. M. (2015). Meritocracy or complexity: Problematizing racial disparities in mathematics assessment within the context of curricular structures, practices, and discourse. *Journal of Education Policy, 30*(5), 631–649.

Corey, D. L. (2000). *An African American male student learning mathematics in a web-based environment: How the absence of traditional classroom cultural differences effects his learning* (Unpublished doctoral dissertation). Florida State University, Tallahassee, FL.

Davis, J. (2014). The mathematical experiences of Black males in a predominantly Black urban middle school and community. *International Journal of Education in Mathematics, Science and Technology, 2*(3), 206–222.

Delgado, R., & Stefancic, J. (Eds.). (2000). *Critical race theory: The cutting edge* (2nd ed.). Philadelphia, PA: Temple University Press.

Dixson, A. D., & Rousseau, C. K. (Eds.). (2006). *Critical race theory in education: All God's children got a song.* New York, NY: Routledge.

Dumas, M. J. (2016). Against the dark: AntiBlackness in education policy and discourse. *Theory Into Practice, 55*(1), 11–19.

Dumas, M. J., & ross, K. M. (2016). "Be real Black for me": Imagining BlackCrit in education. *Urban Education, 51*(4), 415–442.

Gutiérrez, R. (2017). Why mathematics (education) was late to the backlash party: The need for a revolution. *Journal of Urban Mathematics Education, 10*(2), 8–24.

Ladson-Billings, G. (2010). Race … to the top, again: Comments on the genealogy of critical race theory. *Connecticut Law Review, 43*(5), 1439–1457.

Ladson-Billings, G., & Tate, W. F. (1995). Towards a critical race theory of education. *Teachers College Record, 97*(1), 47–68.

Ladson-Billings, G., & Tate, W. F. (Eds.). (2016). *"Covenant keeper": Derrick Bell's enduring education legacy.* New York, NY: Peter Lang.

Larnell, G. V., Bullock, E. C., & Jett, C. C. (2016). Rethinking teaching and learning mathematics for social justice from a critical race perspective. *Journal of Education, 196*(1), 19–29.

Leonard, J. (2007). *Culturally specific pedagogy in the mathematics classroom: Strategies for teachers and students.* New York, NY: Routledge.

Lynn, M., & Adams, M. (2002). Introductory overview to the special issue critical race theory and education: Recent developments in the field. *Equity & Excellence in Education, 35*(2), 87–92.

Lynn, M., & Dixson, A. D. (Eds.). (2013). *Handbook of critical race theory in education.* New York, NY: Routledge.

Lynn, M., & Parker, L. (2006). Critical race studies in education: Examining a decade of research on U.S. schools. *The Urban Review, 38*(4), 257–290.

Martin, D. B. (2006). Mathematics learning and participation as racialized forms of experience: African American parents speak on the struggle for mathematics literacy. *Mathematical Thinking and Learning, 8*(3), 197–229.

McGee, E. O. (2013). Growing up Black and brilliant: Narratives of two mathematically high-achieving college students. In J. Leonard & D. B. Martin (Eds.), *The brilliance of Black children in mathematics: Beyond the numbers and toward new discourse* (pp. 247–272). Charlotte, NC: Information Age.

McGee, E. O., & Stovall, D. (2015). Reimagining critical race theory in education: Mental health, healing, and the pathway to liberatory praxis. *Educational Theory, 65*(5), 491–511.

Milner, H. R., Pearman, F. A., & McGee, E. O. (2013). Critical race theory, interest convergence, and teacher education. In M. Lynn & A. Dixson (Eds.), *Handbook of critical race theory in education* (pp. 359–374). New York, NY: Routledge.

Snipes, V. (1997). *Examination of the mathematical education of African Americans in North Carolina and Louisiana utilizing critical race theory of education* (Unpublished doctoral dissertation). Florida State University, Tallahassee, FL.

Strutchens, M. E., & Westbrook, K. (2009). Opportunities to learn geometry: Listening to the voices of three African American high school students. In D. B. Martin, *Mathematics teaching, learning, and liberation in the lives of Black children* (pp. 249–264). New York, NY: Routledge.

Tate, W. F., Ladson-Billings, G., & Grant, C. (1993). The Brown decision revisited: Mathematizing social problems. *Educational Policy, 7*(3), 255–275.

Terry, C. L. (2010). Prisons, pipelines, and the president: Developing critical math literacy through participatory action research. *Journal of African American Males in Education, 1*(2), 73–104.

Terry, C. L. (2011). Mathematical counterstory and African American male students: Urban mathematics education from a critical race theory perspective. *Journal of Urban Mathematics Education, 4*(1), 23–49.

Wilson, J. A. (2018). *"Ain't I a woman?": Black women negotiate and resist systemic oppression in undergraduate engineering and mathematics disciplines* (Unpublished doctoral dissertation). University of South Florida, Tampa, FL.

1

INSERTING MATHEMATICS INTO CRITICAL RACE THEORY IN EDUCATION

An Exploration of William F. Tate's Scholarship

Julius Davis and Christopher C. Jett

Two years before Gloria Ladson-Billings and Bill Tate's (1995) seminal article "Toward a Critical Race Theory of Education" was published, Tate (1993) used critical race theory (CRT) in his article "Advocacy Versus Economics: A Critical Race Analysis of the Proposed National Assessment in Mathematics." Later, Lynn and Adams (2002) proclaimed: "[Tate] not only introduced CRT to the education community, [but] he also utilized it as a tool to expose the racist underpinnings of standardized testing in the United States" (p. 88). This particular example demonstrates one of the many ways in which Tate's work has caused a shift in the way race-related scholarship is proliferated within the field. As such, Tate's scholarship is largely responsible for linking mathematics and CRT as evidenced by his many publications that have combined these two intellectual domains (e.g., Tate, Ladson-Billings, & Grant, 1993; Tate, 1994c, 1995a), and his scholarly contributions have been influential in shaping our thinking about this edited volume, *Critical Race Theory in Mathematics Education (CRT(ME))*. With that being so, this first chapter's purpose is twofold: 1) to explore Tate's contributions to CRT within the mathematics education realm and 2) to share portions of an interview with him about his scholarship in this area.

An Exploration of Tate's Scholarship Conjoining CRT and Mathematics Education

This section provides a brief trajectory of Tate's CRT scholarship. Early in his career, he began a scholarly exploration documenting CRT in education and adjoining CRT and mathematics education. He and his colleagues (Tate et al., 1993) connected CRT and mathematics in their article "The Brown Decision Revisited: Mathematizing Social Problems." They used prominent CRT scholar

Kimberlé Crenshaw's (1988) notion of expansive versus restrictive reform and a mathematical model to explicate the impact and hidden costs of the landmark *Brown vs. Board of Education* decision.

After that, Tate continued to develop his scholarship linking CRT and mathematics education (1994a, 1994b). He (1994a) used CRT's notion of voice to describe his lived experiences as he explained how CRT's notion of voice and his scholarship was marginalized in the academy because his colleagues thought the theory and storytelling lacked a theoretical and methodological basis and "it was [not] neutral or objective" (p. 262). In doing so, he discussed the philosophical precepts of how his elementary education was grounded in Afrocentricity. His elementary education led him to believe that it is essential for Black students to receive a mathematics education "based on the integration of the centric, conflict, and cognitive approaches" (p. 261) used by his elementary educators. In this same article, he also addressed issues of equity in mathematics education for urban Black students. In addition, he shared an example of how an African American priest who risked his career and life in the fight and struggle for equality prepared him to be successful in mathematics and for an academic career.

In 1995, Tate persisted in connecting CRT and mathematics education. He contributed a chapter "Economics, Equity, and the National Mathematics Assessment: Are We Creating a National Toll Road?" to the book, *New Directions for Equity in Mathematics Education* (Tate, 1995a). In this chapter, Tate continued to use Kimberlé Crenshaw's (1988) notion of expansive versus restrictive reform to critically examine mathematics education policy, the voluntary national mathematics assessment, and the impact on Black students in urban areas. He argued that the mathematics education community must prioritize fiscal equity in implementing mathematics standards, assessment, and reform. In another article "School Mathematics and African American Students: Thinking Seriously About Opportunity-to-Learn Standards," Tate (1995b) elicited CRT to investigate the political and conceptual underpinnings of "opportunity-to-learn standards" in the teaching and learning of mathematics for Black students. He critically examined the adequacy of standards to achieve equity in mathematics education for these students. Tate argued that issues of rapid changes in mathematics, instruction, culture, fiscal adequacy, and policy context must be understood and considered before teachers can successfully implement opportunity-to-learn standards for students.

Tate's seminal co-authored article "Toward a Critical Race Theory of Education" (Ladson-Billings & Tate, 1995) presented propositions to connect race and property rights to analyze educational inequities. Ladson-Billings and Tate argued that property rights "relate to education in explicit and implicit ways" (p. 53). They used CRT to address the persistent inequities and problems resulting from racism in education and the failure of legal and educational scholars to theorize race. In this article, they used the propositions as a guide to illustrate the usefulness of the following CRT tenets: intellectual property, Whiteness as property, storytelling, and voice. In doing so, they made connections between mathematics and property rights to discuss opportunity-to-learn standards, curriculum, and the quality and quantity of curriculum. Ladson-Billings and Tate asserted that real property (i.e., tax dollars) must support learning a form of intellectual property. They also critiqued the multicultural education paradigm and highlighted its tensions with CRT while calling for race as a central construct in equity discussions.

Tate (1997) published "Critical Race Theory and Education: History, Theory, and Implications"—a review of CRT in education research that explained the historical, philosophical, and theoretical significance of the framework. Tate connected the law to education by explaining "the role of race in education and the law" (p. 202). In this manuscript, he described how the law and educational research had been influenced by the inferior paradigm that shapes the academic and social lives of people of color. Tate discussed how this belief system legitimizes social frameworks, policies, and laws that result in educational inequity for people of color. He also explained the defining elements of CRT that were pertinent to understanding the political dimension of educational equity. Tate argued that CRT could not be fully understood without understanding critical legal studies and the paradigm shift away from this movement. He indicated that the CRT scholarship of Derrick Bell, Richard Delgado, and Kimberlé Crenshaw was crucial to understanding the theoretical underpinnings of the framework. More pointedly, Tate declared that Bell's scholarship was key to understanding CRT and critiques of civil rights laws and efforts.

Tate's scholarly works have also advanced knowledge of CRT and qualitative research methods. Tate (1999) wrote the conclusion for the book *Race is… Race isn't: Critical Race Theory and Qualitative Studies in Education*, sharing his perspective on the linkages between CRT and qualitative research and contributed to a special issue of a methodological journal unpacking Whiteness (2003). In addition, Tate (2005) used Derrick Bell's racial reform to examine ethics and engineering and to share his perspective on truth. Specifically, he rejected the argument that there is no truth and lamented the framing of relative truth in scholarly work. Tate's CRT scholarship is significantly influenced by Bell's work as evidenced in the edited book, *"Covenant Keeper": Derrick Bell's Enduring Education Legacy* (Ladson-Billings & Tate, 2016). His last planned contribution to CRT appeared in the *Peabody Journal of Education* where he and Hogrebe evaluated segregation from a critical spatial perspective (Tate & Hogrebe, 2018).

As his primary scholarly interests have shifted away from CRT, he views his former students as those who will carry the CRT torch. In particular, his former student and prominent CRT scholar Celia Rousseau Anderson is positioned well to lead the intellectual charge as it pertains to the future of CRT in (mathematics) education. Tate and Rousseau Anderson have collaborated on various projects and presented ways to advance CRT scholarship in the field (see, Anderson &

Tate, 2008, 2016; Rousseau & Tate, 2003; Tate, Anderson, & King, 2011; Tate & Rousseau, 2002, 2007). Relatedly, in chapter two of this volume, Rousseau Anderson outlines the boundaries of CRT in mathematics education. We now turn our discussion to the interview with Tate.

An Email Interview with Tate about CRT and Mathematics Education

In this section, we share Tate's responses to the questions we posed to him. One of the first things we wanted to know is what led him to use CRT in mathematics education. Tate provided the following response:

I entered the field of mathematics education in a period of awakening. Many very talented researchers provided an intellectual bridge to support the study of race and mathematics. In 1984, my doctoral advisor at the University of Maryland at College Park, Professor Martin Johnson, published "Blacks in Mathematics: A Status Report" in the *Journal for Research in Mathematics Education (JRME)*. In that same issue of *JRME*, Westina Matthews, Gilberto Cuevas, and many others provided a framework to explore the relationship between race, culture, language, and mathematics education. Cora Marrett, a professor at the University of Wisconsin, applied a sociological lens to issues related to mathematics credentialing and enrollment patterns. Another Wisconsin faculty member, Thomas Carpenter, in conjunction with Westina Matthews and Edward Silver, studied minority achievement trends as part of a broader study that analyzed data from the National Assessment of Educational Progress. Lee Stiff and William Harvey synthesized findings from the learning styles literature in an effort to better understand the conditions that fostered African American students' learning of mathematics. Uri Treisman's dissertation study and follow-up development efforts informed our understanding of race, mathematics learning, and collegiate settings. These scholarly contributions and those of other colleagues served as a scaffold to support my intellectual journey. The strength of these efforts included building on psychometrics and assessment to parse out comparative insight. One exception exists among this collection; Treisman's study incorporated anthropological methods to better understand the lived experiences of African American students. While comparable in many respects, his approach to understanding race and mathematics performance represents a breakthrough that challenged historical structures of opportunity to learn, stock stories, bias, and folk wisdom. Another important project at that time included the critique of the influence of Eurocentrism on mathematics by colleagues working in ethnomathematics (e.g., Ubiratan D'Ambrosio) and the history of mathematics (e.g., George Ghevarughese Joseph).

The scholars and scholarly works mentioned above provided an intellectual space to examine the relationship between race and mathematics education. Tate described why the background information was necessary. He continued:

I offer this history as background. It represents my recollection of the state of the field in terms of race and mathematics education as I started my term (1991–1992), as the Anna Julia Cooper Postdoctoral Fellow at the University of Wisconsin. Revisiting these foundational studies, I recognized a problem space that proved broader than mathematics education. The predominate traditions focused on race, education, and opportunity, while helpful, often included blind spots related to the potential interdependencies of broader social and political structures, law, public policy and finance, history, and the conditions experienced by people of color. A few years prior, Kimberlé Crenshaw through the William H. Hastie Fellowship, earned the LL.M. (Master of Laws) at the University of Wisconsin Law School. In 1988, her LL.M. research project appeared in a *Harvard Law Review* article titled "Race, Reform, and Retrenchment: Transformation and Legitimation in Anti-discrimination Law." The article extended trailblazing scholarship on race in law by Derrick Bell. Bell's scholarship focused on desegregation and repre-sented a transformative approach to interpreting that part of United States history. Professors Bell and Crenshaw opened a door to a clearer way of making sense of the underpinnings and limitations of neoconservative thought and critical legal propositions with respect to race and public policy. Their project offered the conceptual tools to examine race, antidiscrimina-tion law, and education.

Crenshaw's (1988) article was so influential that Tate (1994c) published an article entitled "Race, Retrenchment, and the Reform of School Mathematics" in *The Phi Delta Kappan* journal that borrowed from elements of her "Race, Reform, and Retrenchment: Transformation and Legitimization in Antidiscrimination Law" article published in the *Harvard Law Review*. The legal scholarship of Der-rick Bell and Kimberlé Crenshaw provided Tate with the conceptual lens to further examine the connection between race, law, and mathematics education. He shared:

They set the course for my next project, a conceptual review of desegrega-tion case history that used mathematizing as a driving metaphor. In 1993, my Wisconsin collaborators (Gloria Ladson-Billings and Carl A. Grant) and I published, "The Brown Decision Revisited: Mathematizing Social Pro-blems" in *Educational Policy*. In this article, my understanding of mathematics proved useful to the analysis. Moreover, the article provided a framework to initiate my future scholarship focused on second (1964–1983) and third (1983–present) generation desegregation problems (e.g., tracking in STEM fields, mathematics and science achievement, STEM assessment, STEM teacher quality, STEM workforce, and technology and industrial clusters in urban communities). I do not view my CRT project as a mathematics education project. Rather it provided me with the conceptual tools to examine the aftermath of the legal battles associated with desegregation. In my view, CRT represents a tool to examine the law, and in particular anti-discrimination law, and within my research program, intergenerational segregation and its effects serve as my central problem space.

In the next question, we asked Tate about his first CRT in education article focused on standardized testing and African American students in *Threshold in Education*. Tate disclosed:

> The *Threshold*'s paper appeared as part of a conference proceeding. It represented a work-in-progress. In 1995, a more mature version of the paper appeared in a book co-edited by my Wisconsin colleagues, Walter Secada, Elizabeth Fennema, and Lisa Byrd Adajian, titled "Economics, Equity, and the National Mathematics Assessment: Are We Creating a National Toll Road?" The essay captures my long-standing interest in how the government supports academic credentialing. The national assessment concept provided a problem space to explore the relationship between federal tax policy and education policy. In terms of the first critical race theory in education article, I submit that Derrick Bell earned that honor. In 1976, the *Yale Law Review* published a provocative article by Professor Bell titled, "Serving Two Masters: Integration Ideals and Client Interests in School Desegregation Litigation" that challenges civil rights orthodoxy in the area of school desegregation. It remains a must-read article!

Tate did not view his 1993 article as the first CRT in education publication. He asserted that Derrick Bell introduced CRT to the field of education in his challenge of civil rights approaches to desegregation, and Tate's scholarship seems to be significantly influenced by Bell's work. Be that as it may, Tate appears to be the first scholar to conceptualize CRT in mathematics education.

Our next question focused on the article "From Inner City to Ivory Tower: Does My Voice Matter in the Academy?" where Tate raised questions about his voice in mathematics education. We asked him if he believed his voice mattered and how he feels his voice has changed the academy. Tate responded:

> I grew weary of progressive rhetoric about depravity and lack of agency in inner-city communities. Assets and a spirit of self-help existed in my inner-

city community. We worked hard and strived to do well. So the article represented my effort to offer a counter-narrative. Anyone that seeks to discover the truth matters in the academy. I leave my status for others to decide. With respect to a change in voice, I certainly hope so. I have access to more methodological tools, better conceptual insight, a constantly growing understanding of policy and politics, and an expanded network of former students, brilliant colleagues, and wise mentors. Thus, I have much more informed ways to articulate my thoughts and ideas.

The subsequent question focused on his seminal article with Ladson-Billings. We asked what prompted him and Gloria Ladson-Billings to write the landmark article on CRT in education in *Teachers College Record* and what led them to incorporate practical and theoretical constructs related to mathematics education in the article. He expressed:

> The article grew out of earlier scholarly collaborations. We both saw the opportunity to frame the start of a conceptual project. The reference to mathematics in the article involves tracking, a strategy to segregate, implemented in the second and third generations of the desegregation era. Professor Ladson-Billings chronicles the history of CRT in Education in a 2011 *Connecticut Law Review* article titled "Race … to the Top, Again: Comments on the Genealogy of Critical Race Theory." An expansive response to your questions exists in her review. See http://uconn.lawreviewnetwork.com/files/documents/Billings.pdf.

The following question focused on CRT ideas that have not been addressed adequately by mathematics education scholars. More pointedly, we asked what key ideas have not been addressed adequately in critical race mathematics education scholarship. He maintained:

> This question presupposes the existence of a field of study referred to as critical race mathematics education. That presupposition warrants further examination. Is there a definitive article, book, or program of research that delineates a critical race theory of mathematics education? If so, I am unaware of its existence. Therefore, I cannot directly answer the question. "What key ideas have not been addressed adequately in critical race mathematics education scholarship?" No overarching theory focused strictly on mathematics education exists. Rather, I observe articles that layer CRT onto cases involving mathematics. The theoretical propositions rehearse one or more of the main themes in CRT, jump to examples from the case that aligned with the theme, and conclude that CRT adequately captures the project under study. Historical background and questions, alternative theoretical possibilities, deeper pushes into the social theories that inform CRT,

and critiques of the CRT project emerge rarely. As a consequence, much of the effort to date lacks maturity and the type of intellectual playfulness required for sustainability.

In *Betrayal: How Black Intellectuals have Abandoned the Civil Rights Movement*, Professor Houston Baker argued that the Black public intellectual mission of the present day "is not to do great things, but to do small, racially specific, analytical work in the interest of the Black majority" (p. 217). The analytical work to achieve a CRT project in mathematics education remains as an opportunity.

Given Tate's demarcation from CRT, we wanted to know how Tate viewed his scholarship. With this in mind, we asked him to describe his line of research. He responded:

> I continue to work on second and third generation desegregation problems. My research program focuses on the social determinants of mathematics performance. The co-edited book project titled, *Disrupting Tradition: Research and Practice Pathways in Mathematics Education* captures my interest in connecting researchers, policymakers, and practitioners to improve the opportunity to learn in mathematics education. STEM attainment represents another of my interests (Tate, Anderson, & King, 2011). Ongoing research projects include understanding the distal and social factors that predict STEM doctoral degree attainment defined broadly to include highly quantitative social sciences disciplines (e.g., economics). My co-edited book titled *Beyond Stock Stories and Folktales: African Americans' Paths to STEM Fields* captures the direction of this research program (Frierson & Tate, 2011). For over a decade, my research has focused on the development of epidemiological and geospatial models to explain the social determinants of educational attainment as well as health and developmental outcomes. I served as a member of For the Sake of All research team, a multidisciplinary group studying the health, development, and well-being of African Americans in the St. Louis region. My book project titled *Research on Schools, Neighborhoods, and Communities: Toward Civic Responsibility* reflects my interest in the geography of opportunity in metropolitan America (Tate, 2012).

In our doctoral programs, we were both encouraged to use CRT as a theoretical framework to guide our dissertation studies (Davis, 2010; Jett, 2009). We asked Tate about his perspective on some graduate students being discouraged from using CRT in their work. We also inquired about his thoughts on undergraduate students using CRT given the increasing popularity of undergraduate research in the academy. He proclaimed:

> The quality of graduate education varies widely. For example, Wisconsin and UCLA established very strong doctoral programs where social theory represents a distinct quality factor of the program offerings. Moreover, both

institutions have education and law faculty working on problems using critical race theory. I venture to say these students encounter sufficient support to pose research questions and problem spaces where faculty members understand well the strengths and limitations of critical race theory. This capacity does not exist across the academy. Any student lacking this program capacity risks generating an inferior project. This, of course, represents the case for many areas of study. So I have no problem with discouraging students from working in research spaces where the intellectual capacity in a program falls short of the mark.

In my opinion, undergraduate students require a sound knowledge of United States history, constitutional law, social theory, and its debates, psychology, education, and political institutions prior to engaging with critical race theory. Few undergraduate students possess this background knowledge. Undergraduate research in one of the background areas represents a great beginning.

Following that, we asked Tate about the role of CRT for both junior and senior scholars. He relayed:

> Scholarship in education should be driven by the literature, historical conditions, and pressing social problems. I see no relief with respect to second and third generation desegregation problems. That said, it remains unclear how critical race theory will evolve.

Conclusion

Mathematics education researchers who aspire to use CRT as a framework must read the work of the father of CRT, Derrick Bell. We posit that scholars must also read the influential scholarship of Tate given his explicit connections to our disciplinary field. As this chapter demonstrates, Tate has published widely and critically analyzed mathematics policies, curricula, instructional practices, and assessments. Furthermore, his scholarship has addressed the educational needs of Black students in urban areas, thereby uniquely positioning his scholarship as a significant contribution to the CRT canon with respect to Black mathematics education. We hope that this chapter, along with the others in this volume, provides mathematics educators with a firm foundation to move forward to build a robust body of knowledge conjoining CRT with mathematics education.

References

Anderson, C. R., & Tate, W. F. (2008). Still separate, still unequal: Democratic access to mathematics in U.S. schools. In L. English & D. Kirshner (Eds.), *Handbook of international research in mathematics education* (2nd ed., pp. 299–318). New York, NY: Routledge.

Anderson, C. R., & Tate, W. F. (2016). Toward a sociology of mathematics education: Examining democratic access in U.S. schools. In L. English & D. Kirshner (Eds.),

Handbook of international research in mathematics education (3rd ed., pp. 374–394). New York, NY: Routledge.

Baker, Jr., H. A. (2008). *Betrayal: How Black intellectuals have abandoned the ideals of the Civil rights era.* New York, NY: Columbia University Press.

Bell, D. A. (1976). Serving two masters: Integration ideals and client interests in school desegregation litigation. *The Yale Law Journal,* 85(4), 470–516.

Crenshaw, K. W. (1988). Race, reform, and retrenchment: Transformation and legitimation in antidiscrimination law. *Harvard Law Review,* 101(7), 1331–1387.

Davis, J. (2010). *A critical ethnography of Black middle school students' lived realities and mathematics education.* (Unpublished doctoral dissertation). Morgan State University, Baltimore, MD.

Frierson, H., & Tate, W. F. (Eds.). (2011). *Beyond stock stories and folktales: African Americans paths to STEM fields.* Bingley, UK: Emerald Group.

Jett, C. C. (2009). *African American men and college mathematics: Gaining access and attaining success.* (Unpublished doctoral dissertation). Georgia State University, Atlanta, GA.

Johnson, M. L. (1984). Blacks in mathematics: A status report. *Journal for Research in Mathematics Education,* 15(2), 145–153.

Ladson-Billings, G. (2011). Race … to the top, again: Comments on the genealogy of critical race theory. *Connecticut Law Review,* 43(5), 1439–1456.

Ladson-Billings, G., & Tate, W. F. (1995). Toward a critical race theory of education. *Teachers College Record,* 97(1), 47–68.

Ladson-Billings, G., & Tate, W. F. (Eds.). (2016). *"Covenant keeper": Derrick Bell's enduring education legacy.* New York, NY: Peter Lang.

Lynn, M., & Adams, M. (2002). Introductory overview to the special issue critical race theory and education: Recent developments in the field. *Equity & Excellence in Education,* 35(2), 87–92.

Rousseau, C., & Tate, W. F. (2003). No time like the present: Reflecting on equity in school mathematics. *Theory Into Practice,* 42(3), 210–216.

Tate, W. F. (1993). Advocacy versus economics: A critical race analysis of the proposed national assessment in mathematics. *Thresholds in Education,* 19(1–2), 16–22.

Tate, W. F. (1994a). From inner city to ivory tower: Does my voice matter in the academy? *Urban Education,* 29(3), 245–269.

Tate, W. F. (1994b). Mathematics standards and urban education: Is this the road to recovery? *Educational Forum,* 58(4), 380–390.

Tate, W. F. (1994c). Race, retrenchment, and the reform of school mathematics. *The Phi Delta Kappan,* 75(6), 477–484.

Tate, W. F. (1995a). Economics, equity, and the national mathematics assessment: Are we creating a national toll road? In E. Fennema, W. G. Secada, & L. Byrd (Eds.), *New directions for equity in mathematics education* (pp. 191–208). New York, NY: Cambridge University Press.

Tate, W. F. (1995b). School mathematics and African American students: Thinking seriously about opportunity-to-learn standards. *Educational Administration Quarterly,* 31(3), 424–448.

Tate, W. F. (1997). Critical race theory and education: History, theory, and implications. *Review of Research in Education,* 22(1), 195–247.

Tate, W. F. (1999). Conclusion. In L. Parker, D. Deyhle, & S. A. Villenas (Eds.), *Race is … race isn't: critical race theory and qualitative studies in education.* Boulder, CO: Westview Press.

Tate, W. F. (2003). The "race" to theorize education: Who is my neighbor? *International Journal of Qualitative Studies,* 16(1), 121–126.

Tate, W. F. (2005). Ethics, engineering and the challenge of racial reform in education. *Race Ethnicity and Education*, 8(1), 121–127.

Tate, W. F. (Ed.). (2012). *Research on schools, neighborhoods, and communities: Toward civic responsibility*. Lanham, MD: Rowman & Littlefield.

Tate, W. F., Anderson, C. R., & King, K. (Eds.). (2011). *Disrupting tradition: Pathways for research and practice in mathematics education*. Reston, VA: National Council of Teachers of Mathematics.

Tate, W. F., & Hogrebe, M. C. (2018). Show me: Diversity and inclusion indicators of spatial segregation within and across Missouri's school districts. *Peabody Journal of Education*, 93(1), 5–22.

Tate, W. F., Ladson-Billings, G., & Grant, C. A. (1993). The Brown decision revisited: Mathematizing social problems. *Educational Policy*, 7(3), 255–275.

Tate, W. F., & Rousseau, C. (2002). Access and opportunity: The political and social context of mathematics education. In L. English (Ed.), *International handbook of research in mathematics education* (pp. 271–300). Mahwah, NJ: Lawrence Erlbaum.

Tate, W. F. & Rousseau, C. (2007). Engineering change in mathematics education: Research, policy, and practice. In F. Lester (Ed.), *Second handbook of research on mathematics teaching and learning* (pp. 1209–1246). Charlotte, NC: Information Age.

2

"CRITICAL WHAT WHAT?" CRITICAL RACE THEORY AND MATHEMATICS EDUCATION

Celia Rousseau Anderson

> More than twenty years after the establishment of critical race theory (CRT) as a self-consciously defined intellectual movement, defining oneself as a critical race theorist can still engender the question: critical what what? When asked, the inquiry is not just about the appellation…. The query is about the whatness (or less charitably, the "there there") of CRT as well.
>
> *(Carbado, 2011, p. 1595)*

In 1997, I took a course in graduate school that forever changed the way that I looked at the world. The course was on critical race theory (CRT), and it was taught by Professor William Tate. At that time, only a few writings existed on critical race theory in education (see, e.g., Ladson-Billings & Tate, 1995). As a result, the readings for the course were almost exclusively from the legal literature on CRT. We read the work of Derrick Bell, Richard Delgado, Cheryl Harris, Kimberlé Crenshaw, Neil Gotanda, Charles Lawrence, and others. It was during this time that I came to recognize that my own understanding of race and racism aligned with the vocabulary and analytical framework offered by CRT. Borrowing a metaphor used by Derrick Bell (1996), I would say that CRT felt like a familiar song for which I knew the tune but was beginning to learn the words.

At the time that I began to learn the words of the song that is CRT, I was also in the process of completing a degree in mathematics education. However, if I am honest, I must confess that the study of mathematics education felt more like a means to an end rather than an end in itself. The "end" was the calling put forth by CRT scholars in legal studies. These scholars described CRT as motivated by a "desire to not merely understand the vexed bond between law and racial power but to *change* it" (Crenshaw et al., 1995, p. xiii). This was the song of CRT that had spoken to me.

After finishing my degree in mathematics education, I secured a faculty position in curriculum and instruction with a focus on mathematics education. I share this story to offer a disclaimer. I would not describe myself as a mathematics educator who uses critical race theory. Rather, I consider myself a critical race theorist who happens to also be a mathematics educator. While this distinction may seem minor, it is one reason why much of my scholarship on CRT does not focus specifically on mathematics education. It also explains the approach that I have taken in this chapter. Rather than focusing on the literature in mathematics education that has utilized CRT, I start from legal literature on CRT and suggest some possible intersections with mathematics education. This approach is both a result of my own "training" in CRT and a reflection of the influence of other CRT scholars in education.

Over 20 years ago, Ladson-Billings (1998) offered a word of caution about the possible trajectory of CRT in educational scholarship. Referencing the examples of "cooperative learning" and "multicultural education," she pointed to the history of "transmutation of theory" in educational scholarship. This transmutation happens when a theory becomes popular with scholars and is interpreted multiple times. The ideas and commitments on which the original theory was built become lost. She warned that CRT was in danger of following this path and asserted the need for educational scholars to "study and understand the legal literature in which [CRT] is situated" (p. 22) to avoid this loss of identity. This warning has always resonated with me. As a result, I have attempted in my own scholarship to situate my understanding of CRT within the legal scholarship before attempting to draw connections to education.

Thus, my exploration of the "critical what what?" question for mathematics education begins in the scholarship in legal studies. Specifically, I begin this chapter by describing a perspective on CRT scholarship in legal studies outlined by Devon Carbado (2011). I then describe how four of these core concepts from CRT in legal studies might be applied to mathematics education. Finally, I utilize a classroom vignette to illustrate what it might mean to apply these ideas within the context of mathematics education.

Critical What What?

The quote by Carbado (2011) used to open this chapter was an observation made in reference to the 20 years of CRT in legal studies. As Carbado asserts, the "critical what what?" inquiry does not simply reflect unfamiliarity with the name. With regard to CRT in legal studies, Carbado argues that the question is also about the *content* of CRT: "What is the genesis of CRT? What are the core ideas? What are its goals and aspirations? What intellectual work does the theory perform outside of legal discourse? What are the limitations of the theory? What is its future trajectory?" (p. 1595). According to Carbado, these questions reflect the need to outline the boundaries of CRT. He argues that there is a need to define where CRT has been and where it might go. He provides a roadmap of the work of CRT in legal studies by establishing some of these boundaries.

There are several core ideas of CRT in legal scholarship (Carbado, 2011). While it is beyond the scope of this chapter to describe these ideas in detail, I submit that it is important to understand the boundaries of CRT in legal studies in order to understand the potential "whatness" of CRT in educational scholarship in general and mathematics education in particular. The key ideas described by Carbado (2011) include the following: (a) CRT rejects the standard racial progress narrative in which the history of race relations in the U.S. is one of linear uplift and improvement; (b) CRT acknowledges the racial taxes and racial compensation that we inherit and intervenes to correct these unjust racial allocations; (c) CRT challenges the dominant narrative regarding color blindness and color consciousness; (d) CRT argues that race is socially constructed, and CRT examines the role of the law in the construction of race (including Whiteness); (e) CRT articulates racism as a structural phenomenon; (f) CRT views racism as endemic; (g) CRT recognizes that racism interacts with other social forces (e.g., patriarchy, classism, homophobia, etc.); (h) CRT highlights "the discursive frames legal and political actors have employed to disadvantage people of color" (p. 1615); (i) CRT is both pragmatic and idealistic.

In outlining these core ideas, Carbado (2011) notes the danger of creating exclusionary boundaries. However, this danger must be weighed with the potential to lose the "whatness" of CRT. As Carbado argues, "a theory without clear boundaries is hard to mobilize and describe as a theory" (p. 1602). Although these boundaries are subject to change and adjustment, they are available to define CRT and the work done under its name (Carbado, 2011).

Although this list of key ideas overlaps with other framings of CRT (see, e.g., Matsuda, Lawrence, Delgado, & Crenshaw, 1993; Delgado & Stefancic, 2001), I chose Carbado's (2011) outline for this chapter because it was offered as a reflection on the two decades of CRT scholarship in legal studies. Because we are at a similar point in education, I have found Carbado's summary useful as a touchstone for thinking about CRT in education more generally and mathematics education specifically. In the next section, I seek to connect these ideas with mathematics education.

CRT and Mathematics Education

What are the implications of these boundaries for those who seek to understand mathematics education through the lens of CRT? How do these core ideas potentially inform the application of CRT within mathematics education? Before offering my perspective on these questions, I would note that several of these ideas are reflected in the existing scholarship in mathematics education that has utilized CRT in some way. These include: the endemic nature of racism (Jett, 2012), the intersectionalities that reflect overlapping subordinations in society

(Berry, 2008), and CRT's identification of Whiteness as a normative baseline (Martin, 2009). Each of these key ideas has been used to interrogate race in mathematics education. Yet, there are important constructs from CRT scholarship in legal studies that have arguably been underexplored with regard to mathematics education. It is to these underexplored ideas that I now turn.

According to Carbado (2011), one of the core commitments of CRT is the interrogation of the structures of inequity. Specifically, he argues that a central focus of the CRT project is "to articulate racism as a *structural phenomenon* rather than as a problem that derives from the failure on the part of individuals and institutions to treat people formally the same" (p. 1613, emphasis added). In a similar manner, Delgado (2003) also highlighted this distinction between intent and structure when he described the difference between "idealist" and "realist" perspectives within CRT in legal studies. According to Delgado, "the idealist school holds that race and discrimination are largely functions of attitude and social formation" (p. 123). In contrast, while the "realist" view does not discount the role of attitude and intention, this perspective looks to the allocation of material resources to understand racism. Delgado and Stefancic (2001) outlined the following hypothetical story in order to highlight the distinctions between the two perspectives:

> Suppose a magic pill were invented or perhaps an enterprising entrepreneur developed The Ultimate Diversity Seminar, one so effective that it would completely eliminate unkind thoughts, stereotypes, and misimpressions harbored by its participants toward persons of other races. The president's civil rights advisor prevails on all the nation's teachers to introduce it into every K-12 classroom, and on the major television networks and cable network news to show it on prime time. Would life improve very much for people of color?
>
> *(p. 16)*

For the racial realist, the answer to this question is "no." In the absence of dramatic changes in the structures of society and the distribution of material resources, it is unlikely that life would improve very much for people of color.

I submit that this core idea from legal studies should also be a foundational commitment within CRT in mathematics education. Moreover, the history of CRT in legal studies suggests that this orientation must be intentionally maintained. In 2003, for example, Delgado lamented what he viewed as a shift in CRT scholarship. According to Delgado (2003), "critical race theory, after a promising beginning, began to focus almost exclusively on discourse at the expense of power, history, and similar material determinants of minority-group fortunes" (p. 122). Taking this as an admonition, I would urge scholars who seek to further the CRT project in mathematics education to remain true to the "realist" perspective and to ground research and scholarship in a structural understanding of racism. I argue that this should be one boundary of the CRT territory in mathematics education.

Part of this attention to the structural nature of racism involves recognition of the various benefits and costs of race. According to Carbado (2011):

> CRT repudiates the view that status quo arrangements are the natural result of individual agency and merit... Racial accumulation—which is economic (shaping both our income and wealth), cultural (shaping the social capital upon which we can draw), and ideological (shaping our perceived racial worth)—structure our life chances. CRT exposes these intergenerational transfers of racial compensation.
>
> *(p. 1608)*

Thus, a key feature of CRT scholarship is to identify and intervene on the various racial taxes and racial shelters that operate within the systems of our society. In particular, CRT highlights the unearned nature of the racial benefits of Whites and the intergenerational impact of the racial costs for persons of color. As an extension of the view of racism as a structural phenomenon, I also highlight this attention to racial accumulation as one of the recommended boundaries of a CRT space in mathematics education.

According to Carbado (2011), one way in which CRT challenges these intergenerational transfers of racial wealth is by calling into question two baseline assumptions of law and politics. The first principle holds that color blindness promotes race neutrality. The second principle is the converse—that color consciousness leads to racial preferences. Carbado notes that CRT challenges these principles by situating racial inequities in historical context. He asserts that CRT can, in fact, reverse the dominant narrative by "demonstrating how color blindness can produce racial preferences and how color consciousness can neutralize and disrupt embedded racial advantages" (p. 1609). I submit that scholarship in mathematics education seeking to utilize CRT would benefit from a similar focus on the operation of color blindness. Such attention to color blindness serves to challenge the taken-for-granted assumptions around mathematics and equity and helps to dispel the myth that a color blind perspective on mathematics promotes racial neutrality.

Color blindness is a primary example of what Carbado (2011) describes as "discursive frames." In addition to color blindness, Carbado points to other discursive frames that are utilized to normalize racism and disadvantage people of color. These discursive frames include: "reverse discrimination," "merit," "foreigner," "illegal alien," "citizenship," and so on. On their face, these frames can appear racially neutral. Yet, CRT calls these frames into question and highlights the ways that even the most revered legal frameworks can "function as repositories of racial power" (Carbado, 2011, p. 1615). I submit that one core commitment of CRT in mathematics education must be a similar attention to the discursive frames that are utilized to structure inequity in K-12 mathematics.

I highlight these four key features—the structural nature of racism, racial taxes and compensation, the problem with color blindness, and the interrogation of other discursive frames—as proposed boundaries of a CRT territory in mathematics education. These concepts would shape the ways that we make sense of mathematics in K-12 schools and determine the lens that we apply in the analysis of race and racism. To illustrate a potential CRT lens based on these key ideas, I borrow a vignette that William Tate and I (2016) utilized in a chapter for the *Handbook of International Research in Mathematics Education.* For this chapter, I offer three different perspectives or lenses through which to view this classroom episode. The differences between these lenses are significant, as they highlight where a CRT perspective might diverge from other perspectives that we often use in mathematics education.

A Classroom Vignette

There were 16 students in the classroom: 14 African American students and 2 Latino students. There were 9 girls and 7 boys. The students were arranged into groups of four and were completing a worksheet. The worksheet included two tables that the students were to fill in with the numbers of vertices, faces, and edges of prisms and pyramids. The students also had a reference sheet with drawings of prisms and pyramids.

As the activity progressed, several students raised their hands to ask questions of the teacher. In most cases, an individual student asked the teacher a question and the teacher responded directly to that individual, while the other students in the same small group continued working on the task. After getting the same question from multiple students, the teacher made an announcement to the entire class, "Remember that I told you not to do questions 3 and 6. Mark those off on your paper." The two questions that the teacher eliminated asked the students to use the cases they had recorded to make a generalization about the relationships between the vertices, faces, and edges of any prism or pyramid.

As students finished the task, several conferred with others sitting next to them to compare answers. Once students were confident that they had completed the task, they took out other assignments, often from a different class (e.g., several students pulled out novels assigned for an English class). Students in the same group did not necessarily finish the task at the same time. A few students were still working when the teacher announced that class was ending. She instructed the students to turn in their worksheets and told them that they would discuss the activity the next day. As the class ended, she said, "One thing I noticed is that many of you are still getting mixed up on the difference between vertices, faces, and edges. And some of you are not clear on the difference between a prism and a pyramid. We will go back over that tomorrow."

An interview with the teacher after the lesson revealed that she decided to omit the generalization questions because she believed that they would be too difficult for her students. She said that the students would either not know how to respond to the questions or would become frustrated and give up. For this reason, she believed that it was better to skip these questions. As she explained, her main goal was for the students to identify vertices, faces, and edges and have an idea of what different prisms and pyramids looked like. She thought that this was an appropriate goal for the students in her class. She also noted that the state standardized test included questions that only asked the students to identity whether a figure was a prism or pyramid and the number of vertices, faces, or edges. As a result, she thought it was more appropriate to focus on the content that was included on the test. The students in her classes had not been successful previously on the state standardized test. During the year prior to the observation, only 19% of students in the school tested at a level considered to be "proficient" or "advanced" on the test. This compared with a statewide rate of 47% proficient or advanced for the same year.

What Do You See?

One approach to analyzing this classroom episode would focus on the character-istics of classroom instruction and the interactions within this classroom. From this perspective, we note immediately that, although the classroom was organized into small groups, there was very little collaboration apparent among the students. Most students worked independently within their groupings. Additionally, although the task involved counting the vertices, faces, and edges of polyhedra, the students had only two-dimensional renderings of the prisms and pyramids for reference. An examination of the task itself revealed that the removal of the two generalization questions significantly altered the nature of the task. By removing these questions, the teacher had effectively changed the level of cognitive demand (Stein, Smith, Henningsen, & Silver, 2009) of the task, making it a procedural task involving counting. Additionally, the teacher's comments at the end of class focused on the students' identification of the parts of the polyhedra, rather than their understanding of relationships among these parts. This lens on the class-room, focused on the interactions among students, the nature of the classroom task, and the teacher's discourse, could be described as a teaching and learning lens (Rousseau Anderson, 2007). Through this lens, we would describe this classroom as lacking many characteristics that we associate with effective mathe-matics teaching and learning.

For many of us trained as mathematics educators, I suspect that our "default" lens focuses at the level of teaching and learning. This vignette was based on my own observations. And I must acknowledge that my initial focus was on the elements described above (i.e., the low demand of the task, the lack of colla-boration, the missed opportunity for discourse, etc.).

In addition, I also bring a related teacher education "lens." As a teacher educator, my next thoughts went to the nature of professional development that might be designed in an effort to support this teacher to improve in these identified areas. In addition, my lens was drawn to the deficit beliefs that appeared to influence this teacher's instructional decisions. In fact, a professional development intervention would likely center around the teachers' beliefs and the interaction of these beliefs with changes in teacher practice. As a mathematics educator, my focus on these areas comes naturally. Yet, I argue that this is not CRT territory. Even acknowledging that the class was populated by students of color does not get us to CRT territory.

In my view, to get to CRT territory, we must zoom out from this classroom. We must shift our attention to the larger patterns represented by what we observe in this case. To illustrate this shift in focus, I offer an adaptation of the hypothetical outlined by Delgado and Stefancic (2001). If we assume that the classroom in the vignette is representative of mathematics instruction in this school, we would likely conclude that there is a lack of opportunity-to-learn mathematics in this setting. The African American and Latino/a students in this school do not have the opportunity to learn mathematics with understanding. As I noted above, my first inclination, as a mathematics educator, is to focus on the teacher's beliefs about her students. However, let's imagine that a professional development seminar was offered at this school. Imagine that this seminar was exceptionally effective in removing all racial stereotypes and lowered expectations. Would the mathematical outcomes for students in this school (and other schools like it) dramatically improve? As a racial realist, my answer would be "no." This is not to discount the importance of teachers' beliefs and expectations. However, change in teacher expectations alone will arguably not improve the outcomes for students on a larger scale. These beliefs are situated within and supported by institutional structures. As Carbado (2011) reminds us, racism is a structural phenomenon. Changes in the teacher's beliefs would not lead to substantive improvements due to the "racial tax" imposed upon students in these schools with regard to mathematics.

If we envision the nature of instruction in the vignette classroom as representative of many of the schools serving students of color, our lens shifts to a larger territory characterized by inadequate mathematics instruction. Other observations in the same school and other schools in similar settings support this "racial cost" or "racial tax" with regard to mathematics learning. Students in these schools too often do not have access to effective mathematics instruction. This is the racial tax paid by students of color, relative to White students. This is not to suggest that all classrooms of students of color demonstrate instruction that fails to reflect opportunity-to-learn mathematics with understanding. Nor am I arguing that all classrooms of White students reflect such learning opportunities. However, my observations over the years point to this type of instruction as part of the racial cost levied on the classrooms and schools in which students of color are over-represented (Rousseau Anderson & Powell, 2009; Rousseau, 2004; Rousseau & Powell, 2005; Rousseau & Tate, 2003).

This racial cost is imposed, in part, through the ongoing effects of differential teacher quality. Students of color, particularly African American students, do not have the same access to qualified teachers as White students (Darling-Hammond, 2010; Rousseau Anderson & Tate, 2008; Tate, 2008). As Darling-Hammond (2010) argues, "in the United States, teachers are the most inequitably distributed school resource" (p. 40). In addition, schools serving students of color are more likely to experience high levels of teacher turnover (Frankenberg, 2006; Freeman, Scafidi, & Sjoquist, 2005; Ingersoll & Merrill, 2013). These higher levels of teacher turnover and lower levels of teacher quality are tied to lower student outcomes (Darling-Hammond, 2010; Ronfeldt, Loeb, & Wyckoff, 2013). This is the racial tax imposed upon students of color in mathematics education.

However, from a CRT perspective, it is also important to understand this tax across time. Tate (2008) argues that, "the pace of educational advancement depends on *multiple generations of children* attending good schools... Reform efforts targeted for students perceived as college capable merely accelerate the intergenerational resource value-added of largely White, middle-class, suburban students deemed college ready" (p. 954, emphasis added). Thus, as we view the inequitable distribution of high quality teachers across U.S. schools, we must consider these disparities in intergenerational terms. The impact of poor quality instruction is not felt simply by the students in the teacher's classroom at that moment. Teachers often teach in schools near those that they attended as a student (Loeb & Reininger, 2004). In this way, the racial tax of poor mathematics instruction is passed down from one generation to the next. According to Hill and Lubienski (2007), "schools that fail to adequately prepare teachers, in terms of mathematical knowledge, may suffer the consequences when these students return to teach in later years" (p. 764). The intergenerational cost is imposed through the reproduction of poor mathematics instruction and limited content knowledge. Thus, when we view settings such as the one in the vignette, I submit that a CRT lens directs us away from the individual classroom to the larger structures of teacher quality and the racial costs assessed across generations.

In addition to acknowledging the racial taxes imposed upon students of color, a CRT lens highlights the discursive frames that support the imposition of these costs. In the context of mathematics education, I submit that one of the primary frames utilized to this end is "accountability." Of course, under accountability is a subset of other frames that support it: assessment, value-added, data-driven, etc. As with the revered frameworks identified by Carbado (2011) in the law, the accountability frame is pervasive in education. It operates without overt color consciousness or discriminatory intent. Like other effective discursive frames, it almost seems benign. It is only logical that schools need "accountability." It can even be argued that "accountability" is necessary to promote equity in education. Yet, when we examine cases such as the one described in the vignette, we see that accountability operates to constrain opportunity-to-learn, particularly for students of color. "Accountability" has constructed the vignette school as in jeopardy of "failing." As such, the school and its teachers put a significant emphasis on preparing for the state mandated test. This focus on testing contributes to the lack of opportunity-to-learn with understanding. Thus, although "accountability" is ostensibly race neutral, it operates discursively to justify and institutionalize curriculum and instruction that disadvantages students of color. It is arguably one of the structures that would prevent (from a racial realist perspective) the magical professional development seminar from having the desired outcome, as the seminar would not remove the test-driven constraints of teachers and schools operating under accountability regimes.

In recognizing that certain discursive frames, such as accountability, can be utilized to paint inequity in mathematics education as color blind, the related process in CRT involves establishing color consciousness as the route to equity. In other words, once we acknowledge that mathematics education operates with "racial costs" and "racial compensation," we must then approach the re-allocation process in a race consciousness manner. For example, the issue of teacher quality cannot be left to standard market processes. A CRT perspective would direct us to intervene on this intergenerational resource with an intentional approach to correct race-based inequities.

My purpose in sharing the vignette has been to highlight the difference between the CRT lens and other lenses that are used in mathematics education. Table 2.1 provides a summary of these "lenses." I acknowledge that the "teaching

TABLE 2.1 The View Through Three Different Lenses

Which lens are you using?	*Where does this lens focus?*	*What does this lens reveal in this case?*
Teaching and learning lens	Focus on mathematics instruction and student learning.	• Low cognitive demand of the task • Lack of collaboration • Missed opportunity for discourse
Teacher education lens	Focus on interventions to strengthen instructional practice and student outcomes.	• The need for professional development to strengthen instructional practice • The need for professional development focused on teachers' beliefs about students
Critical race theory lens	Focus on the impact of racism as a structural phenomenon through racial taxes and the associated discursive frames that support these racial costs for student of color.	• Lack of opportunity-to-learn mathematics with understanding as a racial tax • Differential teacher quality as an intergenerational racial tax • Accountability as a discursive frame supporting ongoing racial taxation

and learning lens" and the "teacher education lens" are perspectives I have previously described or applied in my own work (e.g., Rousseau Anderson, 2007; Rousseau & Tate, 2003). My intent is not to suggest that either the "teaching and learning lens" or the "teacher education lens" and the associated perspectives are unimportant. Both are necessary in a search for equity in mathematics. Yet, I submit that the CRT lens is oriented differently than even an equity-focused view of teaching and learning or teacher education. In fact, the view through this CRT lens is not one that can be easily accommodated through the traditional paradigmatic boundaries of mathematics education scholarship. To look beyond individual classrooms to the larger racial cost of mathematics teaching and learning in contemporary schooling requires a different set of disciplinary lenses. To see the racial costs in an intergenerational manner requires attention to the distribution of high quality teachers and color-conscious strategies to accomplish a re-allocation of these human resources. It requires that we interrogate the ways that frames such as "accountability" serve to disadvantage students of color. These issues are not typically the purview of mathematics education (Rousseau Anderson & Tate, 2016). Yet, it is to this territory that we must train our lens if we seek to utilize CRT in mathematics education.

Looking Forward

In this chapter, I have attempted to outline several of the key ideas or potential "boundaries" of CRT in legal studies. In addition, I have sought to connect these key ideas to mathematics education. Yet, there is one remaining idea from CRT that I do not wish to overlook. Specifically, Carbado (2011) describes CRT as both pragmatic and idealistic. "It grapples with the immediacies of now without losing sight of the transformative possibilities of tomorrow" (p. 1615). Early writings on CRT in legal studies focused on the transformative aspirations of CRT. According to Matsuda and her colleagues (1993), CRT is "work that involves both action and reflection. It is informed by active struggle and in turn informs that struggle" (p. 3). I submit that the same should be true of CRT in mathematics education. Thus, one question for those who seek to utilize CRT would be: *How do we conceptualize the transformative possibilities of CRT in mathematics education?* We apply a CRT lens. What then?

In the process of answering this question, we must address another related query. How will we assess the impact of CRT in mathematics education? Carbado (2011) raises the same question with regard to CRT in legal studies:

> How should we assess the work that CRT has performed? The number of law review articles that reference the term? Cases that cite the work? Our numbers in the legal academy? The reach of the literature outside the law? Our engagement with communities outside of the academy? Who is our

primary constituency? Should we think of ourselves first and foremost as academics? In short, how do we know whether we are measuring up—and with respect to what standard? After twenty years, we have to begin asking ourselves—and answering—these questions.

(p. 1626)

While CRT does not truly have a 20-year history in mathematics education, it is worth raising these questions. What is the goal of utilizing CRT in mathematics education? How will we measure the success of CRT? Who is our primary constituency? Should we think of ourselves first and foremost as academics or advocates? Essentially, where are we going? Our students are paying a heavy racial tax in schools every day. What are we doing to alleviate that burden?

At this point, I must acknowledge that I have utilized more metaphors in this chapter than is probably advisable (CRT as a song, a lens, and a territory). In closing, I return to where I started: CRT as a song. In his book, *Gospel Choirs*, Professor Derrick Bell's (1996) alter ego closes one of the chapters singing James Cleveland's "I Don't Feel No Ways Tired." In the context of the story, it was a reminder that the history of racial equity is not one of linear progress. Rather, it is a history of incremental movement forward followed by forced steps backward—what Carbado (2011) refers to as the reform-retrenchment dialectic. It is this struggle to which Bell's character in *Gospel Choirs* was referring when he sang:

I don't feel no ways tired.
I've come too far from where I started from.
Nobody told me the road would be easy,
I don't believe He's brought me this far to leave me.

What is the road for CRT in mathematics education? In my view, the road forward involves utilizing the map established by CRT in legal studies. The work that legal scholars have done in understanding race and racism can (still) serve as a strong foundation for our research and scholarship in mathematics education. 20 years ago, Ladson-Billings (1998) warned:

It is very tempting to appropriate CRT as a more powerful explanatory narrative for the persistent problems of race, racism, and social injustice. If we are serious about solving these problems in schools and classrooms, we have to be serious about intense study and careful rethinking of race and education. (p. 22)

I think that her recommendation still holds true. We have a map. We should use it to engage in the intense study and careful rethinking of race in mathematics education.

In addition, we should remember the verses from Cleveland's song. At its core, CRT is a song of struggle. According to Ladson-Billings (1998), "adopting and adapting CRT as a framework for educational equity means that we will have to expose racism in education *and* propose radical solutions for addressing it" (p. 22, emphasis in original). As mathematics educators, we must identify what the site of our struggle will be. At the same time, we must also remember the other characteristic of CRT that is referenced by Bell's (1996) character. Namely, CRT is also a song of hope.

References

Bell, D. (1996). *Gospel choirs*. New York, NY: Basic Books.

Berry, R. (2008). Access to upper-level mathematics: The stories of successful African American middle school boys. *Journal for Research in Mathematics Education*, 39(5), 464–488.

Carbado, D. (2011). Afterword: Critical what what? *Connecticut Law Review*, 43, 1593–1643.

Crenshaw, K., Gotanda, N., Peller, G., & Thomas, K. (Eds.). (1995). *Critical race theory: The key writings that formed the movement*. New York, NY: Routledge.

Darling-Hammond, L. (2010). *The flat world and education: How our commitment to equity will determine our future*. New York, NY: Teachers College Press.

Delgado, R. (2003). Crossroads and blind alleys: A critical examination of recent writings about race. *Texas Law Review*, 82, 121–152.

Delgado, R., & Stefancic, J. (2001). *Critical race theory: An introduction*. New York: New York University Press.

Frankenberg, E. (2006). *The segregation of American teachers*. Retrieved from http://www.racialequitytools.org/resourcefiles/frankenberg.pdf.

Freeman, C., Scafidi, B., & Sjoquist, D. (2005). Racial segregation in Georgia public schools, 1994–2001: Trends, causes, and impact on teacher quality. In J. Boger & G. Orfield (Eds.), *School resegregation: Must the South turn back?* (pp. 143–163). Chapel Hill, NC: University of North Carolina Press.

Hill, H., & Lubienski, S. (2007). Teachers' mathematics knowledge for teaching and school context: A study of California teachers. *Educational Policy*, 21(5), 747–768.

Ingersoll, R., & Merrill, E. (2013). *Seven trends: The transformation of the teaching force, updated October 2013*. Retrieved from http://www.cpre.org/7trends.

Jett, C. C. (2012). Critical race theory interwoven with mathematics education research. *Journal of Urban Mathematics Education*, 5(1), 21–30.

Ladson-Billings, G. (1998). Just what is critical race theory and what's it doing in a nice field like education? *International Journal of Qualitative Studies in Education*, 11(1), 7–24.

Ladson-Billings, G., & Tate, W. (1995). Toward a critical race theory of education. *Teachers College Record*, 97(1), 47–68.

Loeb, S., & Reininger, M. (2004). *Public policy and teacher labor markets: What we know and why it matters*. Retrieved from http://education.msu.edu/epc/.

Martin, D. B. (2009). Researching race in mathematics education. *Teachers College Record*, 111(2), 295–338.

Matsuda, M., Lawrence, C., Delgado, R., & Crenshaw, K. (Eds.). (1993). *Words that wound: Critical race theory, assaultive speech, and the first amendment*. Boulder, CO: Westview Press.

Ronfeldt, M., Loeb, S., & Wyckoff, J. (2013). How teacher turnover harms student achievement. *American Educational Research Journal, 50*(1), 4–36.

Rousseau, C. (2004). Shared beliefs, conflict, and a retreat from reform: The story of a professional community of high school mathematics teachers. *Teaching and Teacher Education, 20*(8), 783–796.

Rousseau, C., & Powell, A. (2005). Understanding the significance of context: A framework for the examination of equity and reform in secondary mathematics. *The High School Journal, 88*(4), 19–31.

Rousseau, C., & Tate, W. (2003). No time like the present: Reflecting on equity in school mathematics. *Theory Into Practice, 42*(3), 211–216.

Rousseau Anderson, C. (2007). Examining school mathematics through the lenses of learning and equity. In G. Martin & M. Strutchens (Eds.), *The learning of mathematics: 2007 yearbook* (pp. 97–113). Reston, VA: National Council of Teachers of Mathematics.

Rousseau Anderson, C., & Powell, A. (2009). A metropolitan perspective on mathematics education: Lesson learned from a "rural" school district. *Journal of Urban Mathematics Education, 2*(1), 5–21.

Rousseau Anderson, C., & Tate, W. (2008). Still separate, still unequal: Democratic access to mathematics in U.S. schools. In L. English (Ed.), *Handbook of international research in mathematics education* (2nd ed., pp. 299–318). New York, NY: Routledge.

Rousseau Anderson, C., & Tate, W. (2016). Toward a sociology of mathematics education: Examining democratic access in U.S. schools. In L. English & D. Kirshner (Eds.), *Handbook of international research in mathematics education* (3rd ed., pp. 374–394). New York, NY: Routledge.

Stein, M. K., Smith, M., Henningsen, M., & Silver, E. (2009). *Implementing standards-based mathematics instruction: A casebook for professional development* (2nd ed.). New York, NY: Teachers College Press.

Tate, W. (2008). The political economy of teacher quality in school mathematics: African American males, opportunity structures, politics and method. *American Behavioral Scientist, 51*(7), 953–971.

3

REFUSING SYSTEMIC VIOLENCE AGAINST BLACK CHILDREN

Toward a Black Liberatory Mathematics Education

Danny Bernard Martin, Paula Groves Price and Roxanne Moore

> Violence is Black children going to school for 12 years and receiving 6 years' worth of education
>
> —*Julian Bond*

Introduction

Recent research on mathematics education for Black learners has contributed strong empirical evidence and robust theoretical framings showing that mathematics learning and participation can be characterized as racialized and gendered forms of experience; that is, as experiences in which the socially and politically constructed meanings for race and gender emerge as highly salient in intrapersonal and interpersonal contexts (see Berry, Ellis, & Hughes, 2014; Joseph, Hailu, & Boston, 2017; Martin, Anderson, & Shah, 2017 for related reviews). The emergence of this work helps to elucidate a more explicit sociopolitical framing (Gutiérrez, 2013) of mathematics learning and participation that foregrounds issues of power, race, and identity, and moves beyond perspectives which have historically been content with characterizing mathematics learning and participation as cognitive and cultural activities. We extend these racialized and gendered characterizations to show that mathematics learning and participation among Black learners can also be characterized by various forms of systemic violence—physical, symbolic, epistemological—that these students must negotiate in the contexts of their mathematical experiences. As noted in the quote above by Julian Bond, schooling is inherently violent for many Black children.

Given our specific concerns with the violence that is levied against Black children's bodies and minds, we first draw on recent theorizations of BlackCrit

(Dumas, 2016; Dumas & ross, 2016) to surface antiBlackness and the logic of the White racial imaginary that rationalizes and normalizes violence in the mathematical experiences of Black learners. Like Dumas and ross (2016), we see BlackCrit as theorizing within, and in response to, critical race theory (CRT) which has been increasingly employed in educational research (Lynn & Dixson, 2013; Taylor, Gillborn, & Ladson-Billings, 2015), including mathematics education (Martin, Anderson, & Shah, 2017). After our discussion of BlackCrit, we explore each form of systemic violence, in turn, highlighting theoretical considerations and pragmatic consequences. Although presented sequentially, we acknowledge the interlocking nature of these forms of violence.

Beyond surfacing the violence rooted in and brought to life in antiBlackness, we conclude with some thoughts about the potential for a Black Liberatory Mathematics education that would allow Black learners to flourish in their humanity (Mustaffa, 2017). Conceptualizing the seeds of a Black Liberatory Mathematics education requires us to engage in radical imagination (Kelley, 2002) and Black liberatory fantasy (Dumas & ross, 2016) of a new and different mathematics education in recognition of the fact that liberatory mathematics education for Black learners cannot exist within the current educational system, where White supremacy and antiBlackness are foundational. Martin (2013, in press) and other scholars (e.g., Anderson, 1970; Bullock, 2017; Chen & Buell, 2017; Groves Price & Moore, 2016; Gutstein, 2009; Vossoughi & Vakil, in press) have discussed how mainstream mathematics education has been put in service to political projects such as nationalism, xenophobia, militarism, and racial capitalism (Robinson, 1983) that are antithetical to Black liberation and progress. Liberation does not entail inviting Black learners to participate in antiBlack spaces that are made incrementally less dehumanizing as a result of reform or White benevolence (Martin, 2015). In offering the seeds of a Black Liberatory Mathematics education, we move beyond the present discourses and logics of mainstream mathematics education that emphasize college and career readiness, increased participation in science, technology, engineering, and mathematics (STEM), and the commodification of Black bodies in service to maintaining U.S. international competitiveness and national security. Black Liberatory Mathematics education is a form of Black life-making, in response to perpetual social death associated with antiBlackness (Mustaffa, 2017) and systemic violence.

BlackCrit and the Specificity of AntiBlackness

Dumas and ross (2016) take care to nuance BlackCrit *vis-à-vis* CRT, pointing out that as a theory of racism, CRT in education is more of a critique of White supremacy and liberal multiculturalism than it is a theorization of Blackness or the Black condition. While the basic tenets of CRT provide helpful framing elements to theorize the normalcy of institutional and structural racism (through critiques of liberalism and interest convergence) they are centered on Whiteness, rather than Blackness. Dumas and ross (2016) suggest that, "BlackCrit intervenes at the point of detailing how policies and everyday practices find their logic in, and reproduce Black suffering" (p. 429). Elaborating on these points, they further state:

> Understanding this distinction between a theory of racism and a theory of Blackness (in an antiBlack world) is key: whereas the former may invoke Black examples, and even rely on Black experience of racism in the formation of its tenets, only critical theorization of Blackness confronts the specificity of *antiBlackness*, as a social construction, as an embodied lived experience of social suffering and resistance, and perhaps most importantly, as an antagonism, in which the Black is a despised thing-in-itself (but not person for herself or himself) in opposition to all that is pure, human(e), and White (Gordon, 1997; Wilderson, 2010).
>
> *(pp. 416–417)*

Dumas and ross (2016) highlighted three foundational ideas in their formulation of BlackCrit. These ideas are helpful in supporting the main claims in this chapter regarding systemic antiBlack violence, and for envisioning a Black Liberatory Mathematics:

1. AntiBlackness is endemic to, and is central to sense-making of the social, economic, historical, and cultural dimensions of human life.
2. Blackness exists in tension with the neoliberal-multicultural imagination.
3. BlackCrit should create space for Black liberatory fantasy, and resist a revisionist history that supports dangerous majoritarian stories that disappear Whites from a history of racial dominance (Leonardo, 2004), rape, mutilation, brutality, and murder (Bell, 1987).

With respect to the first foundational idea, Dumas and ross (2016) state that "antiBlackness is not simply racism against Black people. Rather, antiBlackness refers to a broader antagonistic relationship between Blackness and (the possibility of) humanity" (p. 429). Elsewhere, Dumas (2016) stated:

> antiBlackness marks an irreconcilability between the Black and any sense of social or cultural regard. The aim of theorizing antiBlackness is not to offer solutions to racial inequality, but to come to a deeper understanding of the Black condition within a context of utter contempt for, and acceptance of violence against the Black.
>
> *(p. 13)*

AntiBlackness, therefore, is a transfiguring of Black people into something no longer human and without the possibility of becoming human, setting up the ontological obstacle of Blackness and the justification and normalization of willful and gratuitous violence. For us, antiBlackness is an appropriate explanatory context to consider systemic violence in mathematics education. We are not claiming that antiBlackness is unique to mathematics education, as it characterizes most aspects of Black education in public schools, including school discipline (Parker, 2017; Wun, 2016a, 2016b) and school policy (Dumas, 2016). Below we are able to point to specific forms of antiBlack violence in mathematics education.

In the context of so-called post-racialism and within the neoliberal-multicultural imagination, racism no longer exists. Dumas and ross (2016) note that, "BlackCrit proceeds with a wariness about multiculturalism (and its more current iteration, diversity)" (p. 430). In their view, and we share this view, multiculturalism is an "ideology that is increasingly complicit with neoliberalism in explaining away the material conditions of Black people as a problem created by Black people who are unwilling or unable to embrace the nation's 'officially anti-racist' multicultural future" (p. 430). Furthermore, they state:

> In this context, Black people become—or rather, remain—a problem, as the least assimilable to this multicultural imagination. The relative successes of some other groups of color are offered as evidence of the end of racism. Persistent joblessness, disparities in educational achievement, and high rates of incarceration are all seen as problems created by Black people, and problems of Blackness itself. Here, then, Black people are seen to stand in the way of multicultural progress, which is collapsed here with the advancement of the market, which in turn, under neoliberalism, is presumed to represent the interests of civil society and the nation-state.
>
> *(p. 430)*

In our view, the belief that Black people are responsible for the systemic oppression and violence that they experience helps to foster a belief about the expendability of Black children and the belief that violence against their bodies and minds is warranted. Yancy's (2015) "Dear White America," an open letter written in the New York Times (December 24, 2015), challenges the liberal "post-racial" imagination by asking White people to "not seek shelter from your own racism." Yancy suggests that it is the liberal imagination, rooted in denial, that prevents Whites from letting go of the White innocence which prevents them from reconciling "the lies that you tell yourself so that you don't feel the weight of responsibility for those who live under the yoke of Whiteness, your Whiteness." To White readers, he posed the following challenge:

> If you have young children, before you fall off to sleep tonight, I want you to hold your child. Touch your child's face. Smell your child's hair. Count the fingers on your child's hand. See the miracle that is your child. And then, with as much vision as you can muster, I want you to imagine that your child is Black.

Martin (in press) discusses how notions of equity and inclusion in mainstream mathematics education reforms represent delusions within liberal White imaginaries. Equity and inclusion have remained safe moral and intellectual spaces that have allowed Whites to profess their recognition of Black humanity while simultaneously supporting systemic violence against Black learners. Despite Yancy's (2015) appeal, we question whether Black liberation should rest on the contingency of White people seeing the humanity of Black people and Black children.

Third, Dumas and ross (2016) suggest that Black liberatory fantasy "is a fantasy of the eradication of a prison and the beginning of a necessary chaos. It represents the beginning of the end. It is the first taste of freedom" (p. 431). For our purposes, in fantasizing about a Black Liberatory Mathematics education, we are not advocating for continuing the ongoing pattern of slow, incremental changes in Black representation and achievement within the current system of mathematics education. This liberal commitment to incrementalism has the effect of metering out justice and putting Black liberation—from White supremacy and antiBlackness—on a schedule governed by White sensitivities and sensibilities. We see refusal of the invitation to participate in antiBlack spaces, and dismantling of those spaces, as necessary elements of liberatory fantasy. Recognizing that many children are ostensibly trapped and imprisoned by the dominant system of mathematics education, Martin (in press) suggests resistance in the forms of *refusal in* and *refusal of* this system. He notes that principled *refusal in* the system should ultimately result in principled *refusal of* the system. Liberatory fantasy within BlackCrit allows us to discuss the seeds of a new and different mathematics education for Black learners while considering how they must negotiate systemic violence within the current system.

Systemic Violence

In broadly characterizing systemic violence as a fundamental characteristic of Black children's mathematical experiences, we follow Epp and Watkinson (1997) who, in their examination of violence embedded in administrative and pedagogical practices, defined systemic violence as:

> Any institutionalized practice or procedure that adversely impacts on disadvantaged individuals or groups by burdening them psychologically, mentally, culturally, spiritually, economically, or physically. It includes practices and procedures that prevent students from learning, thus harming them. This may take the form of conventional practices and policies that foster a climate of violence, or policies and practices that appear neutral but result in discriminatory effects.
>
> *(p. 190)*

Systemic violence as a consideration in Black children's mathematical experience emerges from an understanding that mainstream mathematics education, as an institutional arm of the state, is not only a White institutional space (Battey & Leyva, 2016; Martin, 2008, 2009a, 2013; Stinson, 2017; Wolfmeyer 2017), it is also an antiBlack space. Consequently, we are concerned with those forms of violence that arise out of antiBlack racism, in response to Blackness and the presence of Black bodies. Many taken-for-granted school policies and practices including curriculum design, assessment, instructional strategies, and disciplinary practices, unfold in service to antiBlackness and are designed to maintain a White supremacist master script, the result being that the "stories of African Americans are muted and erased when they challenge dominant culture, authority, and power." (Ladson-Billings, 1998, p. 17). Jalil Bishop Mustaffa (2017) has reframed systemic violence as "education violence," as it is experienced both in and outside of formal systems of schooling, where Black learners "have their lives limited and ended due to White supremacy" (p. 711).

Below, we consider three forms of systemic violence experienced by Black children in mathematics education—physical, symbolic, and epistemological. While it is true that every student is a potential object of systemic violence in state-sponsored schools, the consequences for Black children are often more severe. Black children are subject to adultification (Epstein, Blake, & González, 2017). They are seen as less innocent than their peers (Goff et al., 2014). They face stiffer punishment for routine infractions (Wun 2016a, 2016b). They are more frequently overlooked for gifted and talented programs, even when they meet and exceed standards for participation (Faulkner et al., 2014). They are disproportionately tracked into lower-level classes.

Physical Violence

A widely circulated video from 2016 shows a school resource officer at Spring Valley High School in Columbia, South Carolina, throwing a 16-year-old Black girl, identified as Shakara, from her desk and across her mathematics classroom after allegedly refusing to put her cellphone away. Niya Kenny, an 18-year-old female classmate who stood up in protest during the incident was also arrested. Other Black students in the class were subjected to psychological and emotional violence as a result of having to witness these incidents. Especially chilling in watching the video is the relative quietness of the room as this event unfolds. Other than Niya, most students sit still, seemingly stunned.

Amy Sorkin (2015), writer for The New Yorker, noted in her article titled *What Niya Kenny Saw*, that the main message of the local Sheriff, a man named Leon Lott, was that Shakara needed punishment.

Sheriff Lott stated, "We must not lose sight that this whole incident was started by this student. She is responsible for initiating this action." He also said, "She was very disruptive, she was very disrespectful—she started this whole incident."

And she had to be "held accountable." Disrupting school is a crime in South Carolina, a misdemeanor carrying a possible penalty of ninety days' imprisonment or a thousand-dollar fine, and Sheriff Lott had no qualms about pronouncing the girl's guilt, even though what he meant by "disrupting" sounded singularly vague; there is no allegation, for example, that she was screaming or throwing things in the class, but, rather, as the Sheriff haltingly put it, "she wasn't doing what the other students were doing.... He was trying to teach... she was preventing that from happening by not paying attention." When Sheriff Lott was asked, at the press conference, if the charges against Kenny, at least, might be dropped, he sounded almost offended. "To my understanding, no charges have been dropped against anybody," he said. "And, to my understanding, the charge is going to continue. What they did was wrong. They violated the law."

The response from state-empowered authorities exemplifies the normalcy of violence within antiBlackness and the White racial imaginary. Sheriff Lott's implicit suggestion is that violence against Shakara and Niya in their mathematics classroom was not the problem, but rather the solution; after all, "They violated the law." His insistence that they broke the law appears to serve as justification for the state's right to contain, discipline, and violate the Black body. Amparo Alves (2014), drawing on Patterson (1982), situates the normalcy of violence within Black social death:

> The "social death" of Blacks (Patterson, 1982) and the intimate relationship between Blackness and criminality in everyday discourse calls for a reading of Black physical annihilation not as a problem but as a solution... Because Black life is seen as worthless life... when physical death [and injury] meets Black bodies it does not elicit the sort of responses expected for White suffering. That is to say, violence against the Black body is a habitus, of a shared truth that maintains the social production of White privilege....
>
> (pp. 327–328)

In the contexts of antiBlackness and social death, one has to wonder about the proximity of physical death in Shakara's and Niya's experiences. This is not a far-fetched consideration given the deaths of other unarmed Black children and young people at the hands of state-empowered police, including Tamir Rice, Michael Brown, Laquan McDonald, Aiyana Mo'Nay Stanley-Jones, and others. Ferreira da Silva (2014) suggests that antiBlackness and:

> raciality immediately justifies the state's decision to kill certain persons— mostly (but not only) young men and women of colour—in the name of self-preservation. Such killings do not unleash an ethical crisis because these persons' bodies and the territories they inhabit always-already signify violence.
>
> (p. 121)

We do not overlook the fact that, in this example, it was two Black girls who were singled out for state-sanctioned violence. A number of scholars have discussed how Black girls face disproportionate and harsher discipline in school contexts (e.g., Evans-Winters & Girls for Gender Equity, 2017; Morris, 2016). Wun (2016a, 2016b), in her studies of school discipline and punishment of Black girls draws on Black feminism, intersectional feminism, and antiBlackness theory to highlight "the ways school discipline policies help to construct the conditions of captivity for Black youth and specifically for Black girls" (2016a, p. 173). Wun's research further demonstrates that the punishment and violence inflicted on Black girls is:

> not necessarily about discipline for the purposes of normalization. Instead, the spectacle of punishing Black bodies is ingrained in the 'dreams and desires' of the U.S. racial society and its citizens. Black bodies are society's quintessential phobogenic objects, embodying that which is feared and loathed.
>
> *(2016b, p. 4)*

Research has also shown that, as a result of adultification, childhood is often truncated for Black boys and Black girls (e.g., Epstein, Blake, & González, 2017; Goff et al., 2014). Goff and colleagues (2014) view the adultification of Black children as being rooted in an ideology and process of dehumanization:

> dehumanization serves to change the meaning of the category "children." … Because dehumanization involves the denial of full humanness to others (Haslam, 2006), one would expect a reduction of social considerations afforded to humans for those who are dehumanized. This reduction violates one defining characteristic of children—being innocent and thus needing protection—rendering the category "children" less essential and distinct from "adults." This may also cause individuals to see Black children as more like adults or, more precisely, to see them as older than they are. As a result, dehumanization may reduce prohibitions against targeting children for harsh or adult treatment (Rattan et al., 2012).
>
> *(p. 527)*

Epstein, Blake, and González (2017) highlighted the consequences of adultification for Black girls, in particular:

> adultification may be an important contributing factor to Black girls' disparate referral rates in the juvenile justice system, given the degree to which decision-makers rely on subjective discretion, which can turn on explicit or implicit bias. That is, if law enforcement, probation officers, prosecutors, and judges view Black girls as less innocent and more adult, they may adultify

> Black girls and view their behavior as intentional, threatening, or otherwise non-compliant on that basis and deem these girls less deserving of leniency.
>
> *(p. 13)*

Considerations of antiBlackness, physical violence, and adultification shed light on the fact that for many Black children, classrooms are, first and foremost, sites of authoritarianism and compliance, "Where Black children's bodies [and minds] can represent the ultimate threat to authority [and] the disciplining of Black children can be understood as the definitive reinforcement of security and order" (Dumas & ross, 2016, p. 434). In presenting this example with Shakira and Niya, we are not making the claim that this incident unfolded *because* it was a mathematics classroom. We present it in service to showing the ubiquity of antiBlackness and systemic violence and the fact that mathematics classrooms are not immune.

Symbolic Violence

Research outside of mathematics education has drawn on various theories (Bourdieu, 1977; Bourdieu & Passeron 1977) to explain specific manifestations of symbolic violence that discipline, punish, and marginalize Black students in schools. Ferguson (2000), for example, documented the ways that Black boys experience symbolic violence in schools. Ferguson characterized symbolic violence as "the painful, damaging, mortal wounds inflicted by the wielding of words, symbols, and standards" (p. 51). In her study, she noted how certain "taken-for-granted" (p. 51) notions of proper and normal behavior, such as politeness, were used against Black boys to regulate and punish their behavior. She examined this "politics of politeness… to demonstrate… how manners, style, body language, and oral expressiveness influence the application of school rules and ultimately come to define and label African American students" (p. 51). Another example cited by Ferguson is the preferred use of Received Standard English in school contexts. That some Black children come to school as bidialectal or bilingual, speaking Black English vernacular, which Ferguson notes is a "full-blown language with a grammar and syntax of its own that emanates from and reflects the historical and lived experiences of Americans of African descent" (p. 206), and are subsequently forced to abandon this language in school contexts represents "a violent and painful assault on their very sense of self and on those with whom they most closely identify" (p. 207).

Within mathematics education, Black learners experience symbolic antiBlack violence in multiple ways that are often taken for granted in school policies and practices: the repeated discourse focused on the so-called racial achievement gap which naturalizes Black children's place in a racial hierarchy (Martin, 2009a, 2009b); the presentation of mathematics as the property of White and Asian males (Shah, 2017; Stinson, 2013); and disproportionate curricular tracking that results in their warehousing in racially segregated classrooms—a situation that maintains mathematics as a status symbol and institutional gatekeeper while simultaneously privileging White access to worthwhile mathematics and protecting the White body and mind from the Black. And although not framed as such in many of the recent studies of Black learners and mathematics, Black participants across these studies offer narratives that speak to various forms of symbolic violence (e.g., stereotype threat, microaggressions, racism, sexism) that arise as they attempt to negotiate mathematical contexts (e.g., Berry, 2008; Borum & Walker, 2012; Gholson & Martin, 2014; Gholson & Wilkes, 2017; Jett, 2016; Joseph, Hailu, & Boston, 2017; Larnell, 2016; Leonard & Martin, 2013; Martin, 2000, 2006, 2007, 2009a, 2009b, 2012; McGee, 2013, 2015; McGee & Bentley, 2017; McGee & Martin, 2011; Moore & Groves Price, 2015; Nasir & Shah, 2011; Shah, 2017; Stinson, 2013; Terry & McGee, 2012). McGee (2013), for example, described the experiences of Maurice, a mathematically successful, high-achieving Black high school student. Maurice's success was not only academic but also reflected his ability to negotiate mathematics-related White spaces. McGee described incidents in Maurice's experiences:

> Maurice explained that he had been thrust into situations where he became a victim of racial stereotyping and other forms of racial bias. For example, he recalled being treated like an anomaly when a member of a prestigious scholarship committee said to him, "Your race should be proud of such a well-behaved, well-mannered young man like yourself." In another instance, Maurice was assumed to fit the stereotype of Black male underachievement and deception when a substitute mathematics teacher accused him of cheating because he scored 100% on a quiz. After the principal vouched for Maurice's intellectual ability and integrity, the substitute teacher admitted that she had never taught a Black male who "was able to get a perfect score."
>
> *(p. 32)*

We note that Maurice's experiences also reflect the prevalence of racial microaggressions in the experiences of Black students. Drawing on earlier work by Pierce (1978), Sue et al. (2007) define racial microaggressions as, "brief and commonplace daily verbal, behavioral, or environmental indignities, whether intentional or unintentional, that communicate hostile, derogatory, or negative racial slights and insults toward people of color" (p. 271). These racial microaggressions represent forms of symbolic violence. Sue and colleagues (2007) identify three types. A microassault aligns with conventional racism and "is an explicit racial derogation characterized primarily by a verbal or nonverbal attack meant to hurt the intended victim through name-calling, avoidant behavior, or purposeful discriminatory actions" (p. 274). Microinsults manifest as:

> communications that convey rudeness and insensitivity and demean a person's racial heritage or identity. Microinsults represent subtle snubs, frequently unknown to the perpetrator, but clearly convey a hidden insulting

message to the recipient of color is an unconscious communication that demeans a person from a minority group.

(p. 274)

Microinvalidations are "characterized by communications that exclude, negate, or nullify the psychological thoughts, feelings, or experiential reality of a person of color" (p. 274).

Curricular contexts also represent a space where we see symbolic violence represented as "the painful, damaging, mortal wounds inflicted by the wielding of words, symbols, and standards" and as microinsults against Black children. The mathematics curriculum represents the official and valued knowledge of schools, and it is a socializing mechanism. As such, it shapes children's understanding of their place in the world. Black children in different locations across the country have been subjected to racist curricular examples such as the following problems that were constructed by a White teacher and given to her 8th grade students at Burns Middle School in Mobile, Alabama (Crockett, 2016). The school is 51% Black:

- Leroy has 2 ounces of cocaine. If he sells an 8 ball to Antonio for $320 and 2 grams to Juan for $85 per gram, what is the street value of the rest of his hold?
- Dwayne pimps 3 ho's. If the price is $85 per trick, how many tricks per day must each ho turn to support Dwayne's $500 per day crack habit?
- Tyrone knocked up 4 girls in his gang. There are 20 girls in the gang. What percentage of the girls in the gang has Tyrone knocked up?

These kinds of examples—similar incidents have been reported in New York (2013) and Georgia (2012)—contribute to stereotypical, deficit constructions of Black people and reflect what Blackness often means in the White imagination. These kinds of examples also help to create an "intimate relationship between Blackness and criminality" (Amparo Alves, 2014, p. 327). This use of the mathematics curricular space to create such intimate and naturalized relationships helps to sustain antiBlackness.

Epistemological Violence

Teo (2010) characterized *epistemological violence* as occurring "when theoretical interpretations regarding empirical results implicitly or explicitly construct the Other as inferior or problematic, despite the fact that alternative interpretations, equally viable based on the data, are available" (p. 298). Recent structural analyses of mathematics education (Martin, in press, 2013; Martin, Anderson, & Shah, 2017) have revealed that knowledge production in the field has traditionally served as a site of such violence against Black learners. These analyses have revealed that the study of Black children in mainstream mathematics education research contexts has typically involved the study of how they differ in skill and ability from White and Asian children. These analyses have helped fuel the rise of racial achievement gap discourses (Gutiérrez, 2008). Authority is given to these discourses through statistical descriptions and validations of Black children's so-called mathematical illiteracy (Martin, 2009a, 2009b). These statistical archives of Black "failure" encode antiBlackness in the official knowledge of numbers. Katherine McKittrick stated that these statistical archives represent a "knowledge network that records and normalizes Black subordination" (Duke Gender, Sexuality, and Feminist Studies, 2017). In this sense, these statistical accounts simultaneously represent violence against Black learners and serve as indicators of violence experienced in their learning of mathematics.

The encoding of Black inferiority and antiBlackness into statistical master-narratives is often presented in research that appears colorblind, but instead uses "conceptual Whiteness" and "conceptual Blackness" to reify White superiority (King, 1995). In many studies, code words such as middle-class and literate are used to connote normative categories of Whiteness, while categories such as lower socioeconomic status and under-achieving, illiterate become signifiers of and indexes to Blackness. According to Ladson-Billings (1998), "these categories fundamentally sculpt the extant terrain of possibilities even when other possibilities exist" (p. 9). This is evident in many studies in mathematics education, where social class and school readiness studies rarely mention race, but utilize statistics to claim that Black children are mathematically inferior to White children upon entering school (Martin, 2009a, 2009b; Martin, Rousseau Anderson, & Shah, 2017; Parks, 2009; Parks & Schmeichel, 2012; Stinson, 2017). The abstract of a recent article (Siegler, 2009) focused on improving the numerical understanding of children from low-income families (i.e., more than half of whom were Black) stated, "Children from low-income backgrounds enter school with much less mathematical knowledge than their more affluent peers. These early deficits have long-term consequences; children who start behind generally stay behind" (p. 118). The excerpt below further highlights the dehumanization and devaluing of Black children, representing the tendency to seamlessly, across different studies, undervalue and misrepresent Black children's intellectual capacities, even before they enter formal schooling contexts:

> There is growing evidence that socioeconomic (SES)-related differences in mathematical knowledge begin in early childhood, because young children from economically disadvantaged families receive less support for mathematical development than their middle-class peers receive.... Mathematical knowledge of intervention and comparison children were comprehensively assessed. A significant SES-related gap in mathematical knowledge was found at the beginning of the pre-kindergarten year.
>
> *(Klein et al., 2008, p. 99)*

We note that here SES is used as a dual signifier given that a large percentage (53%) of the low-income families were Black. Particularly interesting about the preschool mathematics context is that there is great potential for culturally and contextually-sensitive documentation (Garcia Coll et al., 1996; Harris & Graham, 2014) of Black children's early mathematics competencies, free from school processes that may understate those competencies. Yet, within developmental psychology and early childhood education there is a long-standing tradition of focusing on sustaining claims about what Black children do not know (e.g., Burchinal et al., 2011; Clements & Sarama, 2008; Klein et al., 2008; Siegler, 2009; Starkey, Klein, & Wakeley, 2004).

Fueling these inhumane constructions of Black children are the White frames (Feagin, 2013) and White racial imaginaries (Amparo Alves, 2014) that have supported mainstream mathematics education as a White institutional space. These frames and imaginaries consist of "a broad and persisting set of racial stereotypes, prejudices, ideologies, interlinked interpretations and narratives, and visual images" (Feagin, 2013, p. xi), controlling images (Collins, 2000), and processes of discursive dehumanization (Amparo Alves, 2014) that create naturalized relationships between Blackness and remediation. Largely absent in studies of Black children in pre-school settings are attempts to explore and document these children's mathematical development in naturalistic everyday settings and the ways in which they engage the world in mathematical ways (Benigno, 2012; Taylor, 2009; Tudge & Doucet, 2004; Tudge & Hogan, 2005). Nor are there attempts to determine how their mathematical sense-making in these naturalistic settings is supported by their cultural experiences, and whether preferred ways of engaging their mathematical worlds serve useful functions relative to those experiences (Martin, 2009b; Parks, 2009). This has helped to reify a persistent and violent narrative that Black children enter school with little or no mathematical knowledge in relation to other children. As a result, the primary modes of engaging Black children's early and later mathematical development are through diagnosis of deficits, intervention, remediation, and repair. Ladson-Billings (1998) asserts that:

> Teachers are engaged in a never-ending quest for "the right strategy or technique" to deal with (read: control) " at-risk" (read: African American) students. Cast in language of failure, instructional approaches for African American students typically involve some aspect of remediation.
>
> (p. 19)

Radical Imagination of a Black Liberatory Mathematics Education

Mainstream mathematics education has traditionally invited Black people to participate on its terms. Discourses and rhetoric about equity and fuller inclusion have typically invoked notions of democracy, citizenship, and nationalism

(National Council of Teachers of Mathematics, 1989, 2000, 2014; National Research Council, 1989). It is no wonder, then, that Black people, who have never experienced true democracy, who experience tenuous citizenship, and whose "mathematical illiteracy" is viewed as a threat to the national survival (National Research Council, 1989), have continued to experience violence and subjugation within mainstream mathematics education. Expecting this system to reform itself from its foundational purposes to a new state of valuing the humanity of Black people is unrealistic in the face of evidence otherwise. Therefore, we find it imperative to engage in radical imagining of a Black Liberatory Mathematics education, which we define as the framing and practice of mathematics education that allows Black learners to flourish in their humanity and brilliance, unfettered by Whiteness, White supremacy, and antiBlackness. A Black Liberatory Mathematics education prioritizes liberation over integration and freedom. Drawing on CRT and BlackCrit, this form of mathematics education is skeptical of liberal notions of inclusion and equity, appeals to democracy and citizenship, neoliberal multiculturalism, and refuses all forms of systemic violence against Black learners. The freedom to participate and integrate into antiBlack spaces characterized by systemic violence is not freedom. We are cognizant that in calling for and framing a Black Liberatory Mathematics education, we risk valorizing mathematics in a way that maintains its status and power. Our position is aligned with Anderson (1970) in that Black people should learn mathematics "not because American capitalism's advanced forms of technology require this background, but because Black Liberation Struggle against the American racist-capitalist system requires [this] knowledge" (p. 25).

In planting some initial seeds of a Black Liberatory Mathematics education, we draw inspiration from Black liberation struggles of the past such as the Black Panther 10-point program as well as recent movements like Black Lives Matter where "radical" demands have been made within and against the U.S. racial-capitalist system and state violence against Black people. We note that some contemporary efforts have been made to address the needs of Black students in mathematics education, including work that has framed access to mathematics in terms of civil rights and citizenship (Moses & Cobb, 2002), and work that focuses on specialized forms of intervention (Treisman, 1992). However, in our view, these approaches share a focus on liberal notions of reform and inclusion into the existing system of mathematics education. Litowitz (1996), paraphrasing Delgado (1995), characterizes this liberalism as follows:

> Liberalism has failed to bring about parity between the races, for the simple reason that formal equality cannot eliminate deeply entrenched types of racism (sometimes called "microaggressions") which are encountered by minorities on a daily basis. Liberal solutions ... are White

compromises which fail to significantly advance minority interests. Although liberalism professes to value equality, it actually prevents the radical reforms necessary to achieve true equality between the races.

(pp. 506–507)

Also absent in these approaches are explicit theorizations of violence and anti-Blackness, and liberatory fantasizing about a new and different mathematics education for Black learners. While these efforts may offer seeds for *refusal in* the current system, they do not offer substantive critiques of inclusion, integration, democracy, civil rights, and citizenship and how these lures are offered up to White and Black audiences with similar appeals but different consequences (Martin, in press). Carol Anderson (2003), for example, offers a compelling historical account of how the civil rights framing of Black liberation has been limited because it represents a historical compromise away from a more powerful human rights framing:

For too long, civil rights has been heralded as the "prize" for Black equality. Yet, those rights, no matter how bitterly fought for, could only speak to the overt political and legal discrimination that African Americans faced. Human rights, on the other hand, especially as articulated by the United Nations (UN) and influenced by the moral shock of the Holocaust, had the language and philosophical power to address not only the political and legal inequality that African Americans endured, but also the education, health care, housing, and employment needs that haunted the Black community.

(pp. 1–2)

In detailing how the National Association for the Advancement of Colored People (NAACP), toward the end of the Second World War, had to negotiate the interests of Southern Democrats, liberal Whites, splintered Black leadership, and the association of human rights with communism, Anderson also noted that "The resulting inability to articulate the struggle for Black equality as a human rights issue doomed the subsequent Civil Rights Movement to 'a series of glorious defeats.'" (p. 276).

We are not suggesting that there be a singular Black Liberatory Mathematics education, and we recognize that framings under this umbrella could be appropriated in many ways, even in ways that support the existing system of mathematics education. Black liberation struggle has historically been marked by differences in opinion about liberation and liberatory strategies (Du Bois, 1903; Shawki, 2006; Taylor, 2016; Ture & Hamilton, 1992; Woodson, 1933). Our goal here is to offer one perspective in the spirit of liberatory fantasy—moving beyond efforts that focus on incremental change and that have historically framed mathematics education for Black learners in ways characterized by systemic violence and that are dependent on and deferential to White logics, White imaginaries, and White benevolence.

Framing: Beyond Inclusion to Liberation

As we noted earlier, the lure of inclusion into mainstream mathematics education for Black learners has always been accompanied by notions of democracy, nationalism, and prospects of integration and fuller citizenship. More pragmatically, there have also been implied promises of access to higher-level coursework, college access, and participation in science, technology, engineering, and mathematics (STEM) careers. Yet, these promises also reflect the commodification of Black learners to serve the interests of others under systems of racial capitalism. Our view is that while the utilitarian value of mathematics can certainly serve as the motivation for individual Black learners' participation in mathematics education, it should not be the primary consideration and motivation. Rather, a mathematics education that is worthy of Black children is a mathematics that prioritizes their liberation above all else. We view liberation as a means to radical ends rather than an end itself. As an end goal, liberation risks holding Black people hostage to an ontological relationality to Whites and Whiteness and a re-centering of the violence inherent in antiBlackness. However, our purpose is to center a radical *departure*. We imagine a world in which our ontological relationality is not to Whiteness, antiBlackness, and systemic violence; a world in which we are not defined by a purpose of survival, resistance, and a fight for freedom. We imagine a world in which we define ourselves and desires in infinite multiplicities, all of which has nothing to do with anyone or anything else except Black individual and collective fulfillment.

Exercising the Right of Refusal: Revolution over Reform

A second critical component of a Black Liberatory Mathematics education is the ability to exercise the right of *refusal*: of the dominant education system; of mathematics education institutions and organizations that maintain their status as White institutional spaces; and of schooling practices and policies that instantiate antiBlack violence or White supremacist orientations. We believe that reform is often used as a cover for the ongoing brutality of education against Black learners. In this sense, reforms in mathematics education can be viewed as sustaining the dehumanization process because these reforms are beholden to the overall antiBlack system in which mathematics education is embedded. The goal of reform is slight modification of teaching, curriculum, and assessment processes, not radical dismantling. BlackCrit surfaces these problems with reform and the multicultural imaginary (Dumas & ross, 2016). Rather than being complicit with and allowing liberal reformers to insist on sending Black children back into "punishing schools" and "punishing rooms" (Ferguson, 2000, p. 8; Lyons & Drew, 2009), a Black Liberatory Mathematics education should refuse these invitations. Martin (in press) offers several examples of *refusal in* the existing system, including:

- Walk-outs and boycotts, locally and nationally, should be employed by Black children and parents as ways to disrupt antiBlack violence and dehumanizing experiences in mathematics education.
- Black parents and caregivers should protest tracking of Black children into lower-level and remedial tracks, and refuse under-assessments of their children's abilities.
- Black parents and caregivers should refuse their children's participation in intervention and research programs premised on deficit orientations.

Our call for refusal should not be construed with a call for segregation or racial isolation. Just as we are calling for humanizing treatment of Black people, we expect Black people will recognize and value the humanity of others.

Practice of a Black Liberatory Mathematics Education

With respect to everyday practice, we suggest that a Black Liberatory Mathematics education is designed and directed first and foremost by liberation-seeking Black people including parents, caregivers, community members, Black teachers, and Black students. Within a new system of mathematics education, every Black child learns mathematics for the purpose of understanding the history of Black people in the United States. A K-12 curriculum devoted to, "The Numbers of Black Life and History" would, at a minimum, help Black children to: (1) understand Black people's incorporation into United States society; (2) quantify the ways in which the U.S. racial state and economy were built on the labor of Black people; and (3) understand the disparate impacts of systems and structures like education and prisons on the lives of Black people. We do not propose implementation of such curricula in top-down fashion nor do we suggest that this is the only way to proceed. However, we do believe knowledge of self is key in meaningful education. Students who determine and co-develop the form and content of their mathematics education. We propose annual community reviews of all mathematics curricula and assessments used with Black children.

We propose that Black children be taught by knowledgeable, liberation-seeking Black teachers in independent, community-controlled schools that stress collectivity and Black humanity. All teachers, Black and non-Black, should be vetted by Black parents, community members, and children. Teachers should be required to live in or near the neighborhoods where they teach, and take required training in restorative justice practices (Hopkins, 2002).

Drawing on Anderson (1970), we propose free tutoring and mathematics classes in community settings that are open to adults and children. Black college students and knowledgeable community members would teach these classes. Black college students with strong knowledge of mathematics, for example, would serve weekend and summer internships in local Black communities, paid for with work–study and summer research funds.

We propose the development of easy-to-understand and up-to-date resources (Anderson, 1970) such as Black parents' guide to mathematics education that allows Black parents and caregivers to understand how school mathematics functions from many different perspectives including curricular, assessment, teaching, and how practices like tracking and teacher recommendations for gifted programs are used against Black children. Related, we propose "Distributing comprehensive, easy-to-read pamphlets which explain the pitfalls and financial short-cuts found within the world of the Black consumer" (Anderson, 1970, p. 26).

We propose that by the time they finish elementary, middle, and high school, all Black children engage in one or more capstone projects where they apply mathematics to understand and propose solutions to challenges faced by Black people.

We propose that Black parents, community members, and children be consulted on community development projects so that they can suggest ways to embed culturally relevant mathematical installations and activities in community spaces such as parks and playgrounds, bus stops, community centers, community gathering spaces, and neighborhood museums.

In stating these minimal components of a Black Liberatory Mathematics Education, we assert that these are necessary but not sufficient. Revolutionary change and the building of a new and different system requires a commitment to all components and resistance to reforms that emerge from interest convergence and in service to racial capitalism. Ending systemic violence against Black children means combating incrementalism and maintenance of the status quo.

Conclusion

We have made a case for conceptualizing mathematics learning and participation for Black learners as racialized and gendered forms of experiences characterized by systemic violence—symbolic, and epistemological. While it is perhaps true that all students experience mathematics learning and participation in these ways, given the oppressive nature of mathematics education, it is Black bodies and minds that are subject to antiBlack systemic violence. We have drawn on BlackCrit to explicate the specificity of antiBlackness and to lend support to our claims. In our view, the path forward does not involve tinkering with the existing system of mathematics to produce incremental change contingent on White benevolence, and in service to White sensitivities. Instead, the path forward is characterized by principled refusal in the current system while working to create a new and different system, which we frame as Black Liberatory Mathematics education. Our initial seeds for this liberatory mathematics education is in the spirit of Black liberatory fantasy and radical imagination. We encourage those who value Black life and are committed to Black liberation to join us in this liberatory fantasy and radical imagining.

We end this chapter with the words of philosophers Evans and Yancy (2016), who remind us about the ubiquity of violence in our lives. In making the case that violence is a defining characteristic of mathematics education for Black children, we are refusing to sleep. We remain awake and encourage others to remain awake:

> Violence is all around us. Yet we prefer to remain asleep—the walking dead. For me personally, the more that I become aware of the magnitude of violence in our world, what many of us would rather deny or not see, the more I enter into that space of the "dark night of the soul," a place where dread and hopelessness reside. The objective though, is to continue to remain awake, to keep fighting for a better world even as one endures the dark night of the soul.
>
> *(Evans & Yancy, 2016)*

References

Amparo Alves, J. (2014). Narratives of violence: The White imagination, and the making of Black masculinity in "City of God". *CS*, 13, 313–337.

Anderson, C. E. (2003). *Eyes off the prize: The United Nations and the African American struggle for human rights, 1944–1955.* Cambridge, UK: Cambridge University Press.

Anderson, S. E. (1970). Mathematics and the struggle for Black liberation. *The Black Scholar*, 2(1), 20–27.

Battey, D., & Leyva, L. A. (2016). A framework for understanding Whiteness in mathematics education. *Journal of Urban Mathematics Education*, 9(2), 49–80.

Bell, D. (1987). *And we are not saved: The elusive quest for racial justice.* New York, NY: Basic Books.

Benigno, G. (2012). *The everyday mathematical experiences and understandings of three, 4-year-old, African-American children from working-class backgrounds.* (Unpublished doctoral dissertation). University of Maryland College Park, College Park, MD.

Berry, R. Q. (2008). Access to upper-level mathematics: The stories of successful African American middle school boys. *Journal for Research in Mathematics Education*, 39(5): 464–488.

Berry, R. Q., Ellis, M., & Hughes, S. (2014). Examining a history of failed reforms and recent stories of success: Mathematics education and Black learners of mathematics in the United States. *Race Ethnicity and Education*, 17(4), 540–568.

Borum, V., & Walker, E. (2012). What makes the difference? Black women's undergraduate and graduate experiences in mathematics. *The Journal of Negro Education*, 81(4), 366–378.

Bourdieu, P. (1977). *Outline of a theory of practice* (Vol. 16). Cambridge, UK: Cambridge University Press.

Bourdieu, P., & Passeron, J. (1977). *Reproduction in education, culture and society.* London, UK: Sage.

Bullock, E. C. (2017). Only STEM can save us? Examining race, place, and STEM education as property. *Educational Studies*, 53(6), 628–641.

Burchinal, M., McCartney, K., Steinberg, L., Crosnoe, R., Friedman, S. L., McLoyd, V., & Pianta, R. (2011). Examining the Black–White achievement gap among low-income children using the NICHD study of early child care and youth development. *Child Development*, 82(5), 1404–1420.

Chen, G. A., & Buell, J. Y. (2017). Of models and myths: Asian (Americans) in STEM and the neoliberal racial project. *Race Ethnicity and Education*, 21(5), 1–19.

Clements, D. H., & Sarama, J. (2008). Experimental evaluation of the effects of a research-based preschool mathematics curriculum. *American Educational Research Journal*, 45(2), 443–494.

Collins, P. H. (2000). *Black feminist thought: Knowledge, consciousness, and the politics of empowerment.* New York, NY: Routledge.

Crockett, Jr., S. A. (2016, June 1). *Ala. teacher gives test to 8th-graders asking how many tricks would a "ho" have to turn to support pimp's crack habit.* Retrieved from https://www.theroot.com.

Delgado, R. (1995). *Critical race theory: The cutting edge.* Philadelphia, PA: Temple University Press.

Du Bois, W. E. B. (1903). *The souls of Black folk.* Chicago, IL: A.C. McClurg.

Duke Gender, Sexuality, & Feminist Studies. (2017, May 8). 2017 Feminist Theory Workshop – Katherine McKittrick (Keynote & Seminar Leader) [Video File]. Retrieved from https://www.youtube.com/watch?v=ggB3ynMjB34.

Dumas, M. J. (2016). Against the dark: AntiBlackness in education policy and discourse. *Theory Into Practice*, 55(1), 11–19.

Dumas, M. J., & ross, K. M. (2016). "Be real Black for me": Imagining BlackCrit in education. *Urban Education*, 51(4), 415–442.

Epp, J. R., & Watkinson, A. M. (Eds.). (1997). *Systemic violence in education: Promise broken.* Albany, NY: State University of New York Press.

Epstein, R., Blake, J. J., & González, T. (2017). *Girlhood interrupted: The erasure of Black girls' childhood.* Washington, DC: Georgetown Law Center on Poverty and Inequality. Retrieved from http://www.law.georgetown.edu/academics/centers-institutes/povertyinequality/upload/girlhood-interrupted.pdf.

Evans, B., & Yancy, G. (2016, April 18). The perils of being a Black philosopher. *The New York Times: Opinionator.* Retrieved from https://opinionator.blogs.nytimes.com/2016/04/18/the-perils-of-being-a-black-philosopher/.

Evans-Winters, V. E., with Girls for Gender Equity. (2017). Flipping the script: The dangerous bodies of girls of color. *Cultural Studies ↔ Critical Methodologies*, 17(5), 415–423.

Faulkner, V. N., Stiff, L. V., Marshall, P. L., Nietfeld, J., & Crossland, C. L. (2014). Race and teacher evaluations as predictors of algebra placement. *Journal for Research in Mathematics Education*, 45(3), 288–311.

Feagin, J. R. (2013). *The White racial frame: Centuries of racial framing and counter-framing.* New York, NY: Routledge.

Ferguson, A. A. (2000). *Bad boys: Public schools in the making of Black masculinity* (Reprint edition). Ann Arbor, MI: University of Michigan Press.

Ferreira da Silva, D. (2014) No-bodies: Law, raciality and violence. *Meritum-Belo Horizonte*, 9(1), 119–162.

Garcia Coll, C., Crnic, K., Lamberty, G., Wasik, B. H., Jenkins, R., Garcia, H. V., & McAdoo, H. P. (1996). An integrative model for the study of developmental competencies in minority children. *Child Development*, 67(5), 1891–1914.

Gholson, M., & Martin, D. B. (2014). Smart girls, Black girls mean girls, and bullies: At the intersection of identities and the mediating role of young girls' social network in mathematics communities of practice. *Journal of Education*, 194(1), 19–33.

Gholson, M. L., & Wilkes, C. E. (2017). (Mis)taken identities: Reclaiming identities of the "collective Black" in mathematics education research through an exercise in Black specificity. *Review of Research in Education*, 41(1), 228–252.

Goff, P., Jackson, M. C., Di Leone, B. A. L., Culotta, C. M., & DiTomasso, N. A. (2014). The essence of innocence: Consequences of dehumanizing Black children. *Journal of Personality and Social Psychology*, 106(4), 526–545.

Gordon, L. R. (Ed.). (1997). *Existence in Black*. New York, NY: Routledge.

Groves Price, P., & Moore, R. (2016). (Re)claiming an activist identity as criticalmathematics educators: Addressing anti-Black racism because #BlackLivesMatter/ Reclamendo una identidad activista como educadores matemáticos críticos: Encarando el racismo anti-negro porque #BlackLivesMatter. *Revista Latinoamericana de Etnomatemática*, 9(3), 77–98.

Gutiérrez, R. (2008). A "gap-gazing" fetish in mathematics education? Problematizing research on the achievement gap. Journal for Research in Mathematics Education, 39(4), 357–364.

Gutiérrez, R. (2013). The sociopolitical turn in mathematics education. *Journal for Research in Mathematics Education*, 44(1), 37–68.

Gutstein, E. (2009). The politics of mathematics education in the United States: Dominant and counter agendas. In B. Greer, S. Mukhopadhyay, S. Nelson-Barber, & A. Powell (Eds.), *Culturally responsive mathematics education* (pp. 137–164). New York, NY: Routledge.

Harris, Y. R., & Graham, J. A. (2014). *The African American child: Development and challenges*. New York, NY: Springer.

Haslam, N. (2006). Dehumanization: An integrative review. *Personality and Social Psychology Review*, 10, 252–264.

Hopkins, B. (2002). Restorative justice in schools. *Support for Learning*, 17(3), 144–149.

Jett, C. C. (2016). Ivy league bound: A case study of a brilliant African American male mathematics major. *Spectrum: A Journal on Black Men*, 4(2), 83–97.

Joseph, N. M., Hailu, M., & Boston, D. (2017). Black women's and girls' persistence in the P–20 mathematics pipeline: Two decades of children, youth, and adult education research. *Review of Research in Education*, 41(1), 203–227.

Kelley, R. D. (2002). *Freedom dreams: The Black radical imagination*. Boston, MA: Beacon Press.

King, J. (1995). Culture-centered knowledge: Black studies, curriculum transformation, and social action. In J. Banks & C. M. Banks (Eds.), *Handbook of research on multicultural education* (pp. 265–290). New York, NY: Macmillan.

Klein, A., Starkey, P., Clements, D., Sarama, J., & Iyer, R. (2008). Effects of a pre-kindergarten mathematics intervention: A randomized experiment. *Journal of Research on Educational Effectiveness*, 1(3), 155–178.

Ladson-Billings, G. (1998). Just what is critical race theory and what's it doing in a nice field like education? *International Journal of Qualitative Studies in Education*, 11 (1), 7–24.

Larnell, G. V. (2016). More than just skill: Examining mathematics identities, racialized narratives, and remediation among Black undergraduates. *Journal for Research in Mathematics Education, 47*(3), 233–269.

Leonard, J., & Martin, D. B. (Eds.) (2013). *The brilliance of Black children in mathematics: Beyond the numbers and toward new discourse.* Charlotte, NC: Information Age.

Leonardo, Z. (2004). The color of supremacy: Beyond the discourse of "White privilege". *Educational Philosophy and Theory, 36,* 137–152.

Litowitz, D. E. (1996). Some critical thoughts on critical race theory. *Notre Dame Law Review, 72*(2), 503–529.

Lynn, M., & Dixson, A. D. (Eds.). (2013). *Handbook of critical race theory in education.* New York, NY: Routledge.

Lyons, W. B. T., & Drew, J. (2009). *Punishing schools: Fear and citizenship in American public education.* Ann Arbor, MI: University of Michigan Press.

Martin, D. B. (2000). *Mathematics success and failure among African American youth: The roles of sociohistorical context, community forces, school influence, and individual agency.* Mahwah, NJ: Lawrence Erlbaum Associates.

Martin, D. B. (2006). Mathematics learning and participation as racialized forms of experience: African American parents speak on the struggle for mathematics literacy. *Mathematical Thinking and Learning, 8*(3), 197–229.

Martin, D. B. (2007). Mathematics learning and participation in the African American context: The co-construction of identity in two intersecting realms of experience. In N. Nasir & P. Cobb (Eds.), *Diversity, equity, and access to mathematical ideas* (pp. 146–158). New York, NY: Teachers College Press.

Martin, D. B. (2008). E(race)ing race from a national conversation on mathematics teaching and learning: The National Math Panel as White institutional space. *The Montana Math Enthusiast, 5*(2&3), 387–398.

Martin, D. B. (2009a). Researching race in mathematics education. *Teachers College Record, 111*(2), 295–338.

Martin, D. B. (2009b). Liberating the production of knowledge about African American children and mathematics. In D. Martin (Ed.), *Mathematics teaching, learning, and liberation in African American contexts* (pp. 3–36). London, UK: Routledge.

Martin, D. B. (2012). Learning mathematics while Black. *The Journal of Educational Foundations, 26*(1–2), 47–66.

Martin, D. B. (2013). Race, racial projects, and mathematics education. *Journal for Research in Mathematics Education, 44*(1), 316–333.

Martin, D. B. (2015). The collective Black and principles to actions. *Journal of Urban Mathematics Education, 8*(1), 17–23.

Martin, D. B. (in press). Perturbations and self-corrections in an antiBlack system: The delusion of equity in mathematics education reform. *Race Ethnicity and Education.*

Martin, D. B., Anderson, C. R., & Shah, N. (2017). Race and mathematics education. In J. Cai (Ed.), *Compendium for research in mathematics education* (pp. 607–636). Reston, VA: National Council of Teachers of Mathematics.

McGee, E. (2013). Young, Black, mathematically gifted, and stereotyped. *The High School Journal, 96*(3), 253–263.

McGee, E. O. (2015). Robust and fragile mathematical identities: A framework for exploring racialized experiences and high achievement among Black college students. *Journal for Research in Mathematics Education, 46*(5), 599–625.

McGee, E. O., & Bentley, L. (2017). The troubled success of Black women in STEM. *Cognition and Instruction*, 35(4), 265–289.

McGee, E. O., & Martin, D. B. (2011). "You would not believe what I have to go through to prove my intellectual value!" Stereotype management among academically successful Black mathematics and engineering students. *American Educational Research Journal*, 48(6), 1347–1389.

Moore, R., & Groves Price, P. (2015). Developing a positive mathematics identity for students of color: Epistemology and critical antiracist mathematics. Proceedings from the 8th Mathematics Education and Society Conference, Portland, OR.

Morris, M. (2016). *Pushout: The criminalization of Black girls in schools*. New York, NY: The New Press.

Moses, R. P., & Cobb, C. E. (2002). *Radical equations: Civil rights from Mississippi to The Algebra Project*. Boston, MA: Beacon Press.

Mustaffa, J. B. (2017). Mapping violence, naming life: A history of anti-Black oppression in the higher education system. *International Journal of Qualitative Studies in Education*, 30(8), 711–727.

Nasir, N. I. S., & Shah, N. (2011). On defense: African American males making sense of racialized narratives in mathematics education. *Journal of African American Males in Education*, 2(1), 24–45.

National Council of Teachers of Mathematics. (1989). *Curriculum and evaluation standards for school mathematics*. Reston, VA: National Council of Teachers of Mathematics.

National Council of Teachers of Mathematics. (2000). *Principles and standards for school mathematics*. Reston, VA: National Council of Teachers of Mathematics.

National Council of Teachers of Mathematics. (2014). *Principles to actions: Ensuring mathematics success for all*. Reston, VA: National Council of Teachers of Mathematics.

National Research Council. (1989). *Everybody counts: A report to the nation on the future of mathematics education*. Washington, DC: National Academy Press.

Parker, L. (2017). Schools and the no-prison phenomenon: Anti-Blackness and secondary policing in the Black lives matter era. *Journal of Educational Controversy*, 12(1), 11–24.

Parks, A. N. (2009). Doomsday device: Rethinking the deployment of the 'Achievement gap' in equity arguments. *For the Learning of Mathematics*, 29(1), 14–19.

Parks, A. N., & Schmeichel, M. (2012). Obstacles to addressing race and ethnicity in the mathematics education literature. *Journal for Research in Mathematics Education*, 43(3), 238–252.

Patterson, O. (1982). *Slavery and social death*. Cambridge, MA: Harvard University Press.

Pierce, C. M. (1978). Entitlement dysfunctions. *Australian and New Zealand Journal of Psychiatry*, 12, 215–219.

Rattan, A., Levine, C. S., Dweck, C. S., & Eberhardt, J. L. (2012). Race and the fragility of the legal distinction between juveniles and adults. *PLOS ONE*, 7, doi:36680.

Robinson, C. J. (1983). *Black Marxism: The making of the Black radical tradition*. Raleigh, NC: University of North Carolina Press.

Shah, N. (2017). Race, ideology, and academic ability: A relational analysis of racial narratives in mathematics. *Teachers College Record*, 119(7), 1–42.

Shawki, A. (2006). *Black liberation and socialism*. Chicago, IL: Haymarket Books.

Siegler, R. S. (2009). Improving the numerical understanding of children from low-income families. *Child Development Perspectives*, 3(2), 118–124.

Sorkin, A. D. (2015, October 30). What Niya Kenny saw. *The New Yorker*. Retrieved from https://www.newyorker.com/news/amy-davidson/what-niya-kenny-saw.

Starkey, P., Klein, A., & Wakeley, A. (2004). Enhancing young children's mathematical knowledge through a pre-kindergarten mathematics intervention. *Early Childhood Research Quarterly*, 19(1), 99–120.

Stinson, D. W. (2013). Negotiating the "White male math myth": African American male students and success in school mathematics. *Journal for Research in Mathematics Education*, 44 (1), 69–99.

Stinson, D. W. (2017). Researching race without researching White supremacy in mathematics education research: A strategic discursive practice. In A. Chronaki (Ed.), *Proceedings of the 9th International Mathematics Education and Society Conference (MES9, Vol. 2)* (pp. 901–912). Volos, Greece: MES9.

Sue, D. W., Capodilupo, C. M., Torino, G. C., Bucceri, J. M., Holder, A., Nadal, K. L., & Esquilin, M. (2007). Racial microaggressions in everyday life: Implications for clinical practice. *American Psychologist*, 62(4), 271–286.

Taylor, E. V. (2009). The purchasing practice of low-income students: The relationship to mathematical development. *The Journal of the Learning Sciences*, 18(3), 370–415.

Taylor, E., Gillborn, D., & Ladson-Billings, G. (Eds.). (2015). *Foundations of critical race theory in education*. New York, NY: Routledge.

Taylor, K. Y. (2016). *From #BlackLivesMatter to Black liberation*. Chicago, IL: Haymarket Books.

Teo, T. (2010). What is epistemological violence in the empirical social sciences? *Social and Personality Psychology Compass*, 4(5), 295–303.

Terry, C. L., & McGee, E. O. (2012). "I've come too far, I've worked too hard!": Reinforcement of support structures among Black male mathematics students. *Journal of Mathematics Education at Teachers College*, 3(2), 73–85.

Treisman, U. (1992). Studying students studying calculus: A look at the lives of minority mathematics students in college. *The College Mathematics Journal*, 23(5), 362–372.

Tudge, J. R., & Doucet, F. (2004). Early mathematical experiences: Observing young Black and White children's everyday activities. *Early Childhood Research Quarterly*, 19(1), 21–39.

Tudge, J., & Hogan, D. (2005). An ecological approach to observations of children's everyday lives. In S. Greene & D. Hogan (Eds.), *Researching children's experience: Approaches and methods* (pp. 102–122). Thousand Oaks, CA: Sage.

Ture, K., & Hamilton, C. V. (1992). *Black power: The politics of liberation*. New York, NY: Vintage Books.

Vossoughi, S., & Vakil, S. (in press). Towards what ends? A critical analysis of militarism, equity and STEM education. In A. Ali & T. L. Buenavista (Eds.), *At war! Challenging racism, materialism, and militarism in education*. New York, NY: Fordham University Press.

Wilderson, F. B., III. (2010). *Red, White & Black*. Durham, NC: Duke University Press.

Wolfmeyer, M. (2017). *Mathematics education: A critical introduction*. New York, NY: Taylor & Francis.

Woodson, C. G. (1933). *The miseducation of the Negro*. Washington, DC: Associated Publishers.

Wun, C. (2016a). Against captivity: Black girls and school discipline policies in the afterlife of slavery. *Educational Policy*, 30(1), 171–196.

Wun, C. (2016b). Unaccounted foundations: Black girls, anti-Black racism, and punishment in schools. *Critical Sociology*, 42(4–5), 1–14.

Yancy, G. (2015, December 24). Dear White America. *The New York Times: Opinionator*. Retrieved from https://opinionator.blogs.nytimes.com/2015/12/24/dear-White-america/.

4

DAIJA'S AWAKENING

Critical Race Theory and Afrofuturism in Mathematics Education

Nathan N. Alexander

Prologue

Twenty-five years ago, the Space Race Delegations were introduced by the founding fathers of the UGC—the United Global Council or, simply, the Council. The UGC was initially proposed by the United States as a sister organization to the United Nations. The Council's founding fathers—the Group of Seven (G7)—used the Space Race Delegations to define the Council's core mission, which was "*to unify humankind, expand space exploration, and stimulate the interstellar economy.*" Over time, however, the United Nations was replaced by the Council.

The Council, using threats of war and the impending crisis of planetary warming, developed into the world's legal and economic authority. Its councilmembers—consisting of former presidents, chancellors, dictators, and monarchs of the G7 nations—restructured global markets, starting with the International Monetary Fund, and developed new global economies to fund space exploration, instituting programs like the Space Race Delegations. These changes positioned the Council as an international authority, which led to the creation of the *Global Laws of Peace and Protection*, a transnational constitution and the supreme law of the Planet Earth.

The planet's four new republics were the result of geopolitical alliances formed in the wake of an alleged political takeover of the UGC by the *old world's* militaristic and economic powerhouse—the United States of America. The Global Laws of Peace and Protection were used to respond to this takeover, and they helped to usher in a *new world order*. The former United States, which had positioned itself as a friend and political leader to those nations ruined by the UGC's policies, proposed the compass as a symbol of cooperation and navigation across the four republics. These new republics—"the North," "the East," "the South," and "the West"—like a compass, were political coalitions of former countries of the old world collectively bound by the Global Laws of Peace and Protection. Although each republic was allowed to define and amend their own constitutions, its individual laws and public policies would always be subordinate to the supreme laws of the Council and the constitution of Planet Earth.

The large continent, known as Africa in the old world, was not included in the UGC's original designations, however. Its former countries are collectively referred to as "the Navel," and they were positioned at the center of the Council's symbolic compass. The Council, with no input from the Africans themselves, decided that the Navel would become the center of Planet Earth's means of production, trade, and space exploration. And, just like Africa's partitioning in the old world, during the late 1800s, the Navel was divided among the republics to become the cradle of global development. The Navel would serve as the launchpad of all interplanetary activity, starting with the Space Race Delegations and extending through planetary colonization.

Introduction

Derrick Bell's (1992) *Faces at the Bottom of the Well* is one of the foundational texts in the development of the critical race theory (CRT) canon. Bell's futuristic and other-worldly stories in this volume position readers within important conversations about realism and idealism, theory and method, and liberty as it concerns race and racism in the United States. More generally, however, we find that Bell's assessments are not only allegorical and speculative in nature, but they include important Afrofuturist themes in their concepts, storylines, and form. In particular, Bell insists the reader to consider the historical pretenses of race and racism in their developments of Black futurity.

Black futurity, which I define as relating to a renewed or transformed conception of Black racial existence, has been developed within the critical perspective and philosophy known as Afrofuturism. As shown in Derrick Bell's (1992) "The Afrolantica Awakening," Afrofuturism integrates elements of speculative fiction, science fiction, fantasy, and themes in Afrocentrism, to explore Black life, cooperation, tribulation liberation, and thought. As Bell addresses the functions of the law and legal policies in Black futures, Afrofuturist themes can be said to consider the specificities of Black life from the past to the present and beyond.

As interdisciplinary traditions, both CRT and Afrofuturism have the ability to capture the essence of Black personhood and Black being in material and imagined social, economic, political, and technological ecologies. They also inform varied conceptions of Black futurity in relation to Black history, culture, and the public practice (Anderson & Jones, 2015; Dery, 1994; Nelson, 2002; Womack, 2013). Although CRT has become a prevalent feature in educational theory and research, it has only recently gained traction as a primary analytic and methodological tool within the field of mathematics education (Jett, 2012).

This chapter aims to articulate, as CRT continues to expand in the field of mathematics education, connections between two interdisciplinary perspectives and philosophies: CRT and Afrofuturism. The first section explores how both tools offer us new insights, methods, and practical applications across various fields. In the second section, I explore Afrofuturism in mathematics education to launch a discussion around a general lack of engagement with ideas surrounding Black mathematical futures. Specifically, I underscore the importance of not only mentioning but centering the Black body, especially in an era of increasingly equity-focused political projects in mathematics education. I end with a brief critique on what I consider to be a departure from centering Black social and material life in the establishment and expansion of CRT over many decades, toward disciplinary practices aimed at decentering Black life and experience for more inclusive, racially blind approaches.

Part I: Ms. Tamika's Math Class

Daija, standing confidently at six-feet two-inches tall, did not image that she would be the winner of the 24th Space Race Delegations. As she waits patiently on the artificial patches of grass covering the Navel's concrete floor, her back upright, she observes the councilmembers and listens for her name to be called. As she looks around, Daija notices that her height matches the gold and ivory plated statues of the other victors representing the previous delegations. Their warlike faces, void of emotion, line the stage of the space station, each one having been revealed only after its victor returned from their first victory mission.

Each statue appears to defy gravity and float in midair above its nameplate. But upon further inspection, she notices that each statue is secured by a transparent base which creates the optical illusion. Daija, who developed a knack for detail based on her love of mathematics, takes note of the empty space where statue #9 would have been, but nothing is there. Still standing, Daija wonders if her statue will also appear to float in midair once it is unveiled. She hears the name of the first ever delegate, loud over the sonic speakers, knowing the time has come.

As Daija walked, on what was formerly African soil in the old world but, now, the hub of the Navel's space activities, she listened to the names of the victors from previous delegations and began to think deeply about how she ended up in this position in the first place. As the West's 13th victor, she was increasingly saddened by the fact that she had helped to further the West's mission to colonize the planets as a leading authority in the Council. Daija then hears a strangely familiar name, said with sympathy over applause: "*…and the late Mr. Alphonso 'AJ' Johnson, the first Black delegate, representative of the West, winner of the 9th Delegations…*" Daija squints her eyes, the skin on her forehead wrinkling together as she draws on memories of her recent victory mission to Planet Mars. She pauses.

Alphonso Johnson, known as AJ by his friends and family, was the first African American to win a Space Race Delegation. AJ had secured the top spot 15 years prior, during the UGC's 9th Space Race Delegations, when Daija was only three years old. That year, AJ was the leader of a well-known team of delegates who studied a form of dark energy that helped to explain universal expansion. Using mathematics and applied physics techniques, AJ identified core features of the Grand Unification Theory of physics—known as the Theory of Everything—which allowed humans to approach space travel in novel ways. Shortly after, he disappeared.

Prior to his disappearance, records showed that Alphonso had trained on Planet Mars, but there was no other information or data available. Daija, still waiting for her name to be called, now standing to the left of the councilmembers on stage, knew there was more to his story. She continued to scan her memories, and she remembered seeing images of Alphonso on her teleprojection device in her level-1 history classes when she attended lower-school near the coastal region of Sector 4. The region's 1200-square mile rocky terrain extended across the southeastern portion of a sizeable land mass right up to the coast. There were numerous lower-schools in Sector 4, because they trained pupils for physical labor, and only a handful of upper-schools existed.

Western schooling now occurred in two levels, instead of three as it did in the old world. Level-2 students were viewed as the most advanced students in the nation, as they were considered to be important contributors to the West's social and economic development. After social and welfare programs were eradicated during the West's redevelopment, students in the upper-schools became a primary extension of the West's power. Level-1 is the bottommost level of education, and it functions as a way to constantly assess students as a means to move them through various lower educational stages, or sublevels. Those students who ranked highest in the level-1 group could apply to labor jobs and stay in the West; the other, less successful students, are shipped to the Navel to work for the UGC.

Sector 4, an historical region where African Americans fought for their legal rights and civil freedoms in the old world, consistently sent more than 70% of its lower-school pupils to the Navel. The achievement gaps between the West's more affluent lower-schools are astounding. As more families migrate out of Sector 4, it has become home to 40% of the West's people of color, and more than 80% of the West's Black population, increasing the opportunity gap, as fewer students were admitted into upper-schools. Daija's mathematical sciences teacher, Ms. Tamika, an alumnus of Sanford High School where both Daija and AJ attended, made sure that all of her students were well prepared.

The achievement and opportunity gaps between the West's nine sectors were no coincidence. During the UGC's development, the West instituted its own laws and policies to maintain its best interests within the global order, and for the protection of its most prized citizens. Immediately after the launch of Sputnik-alpha (Sa), the first space carrier to be launched from the Navel's headquarters, in celebration of the inaugural Space Race Delegations, the West established the *Every Child Achieves Act* (ECAA), a new education policy focused exclusively on improving education in the mathematical sciences. ECAA was meant to equip the next generation of leaders with the skills to not only direct but dominate the expanding astral order.

ECAA was also enacted to govern lower-school and upper-school education policies, and to help the sectors and lawmakers forecast for future delegations. ECAA superseded preceding education laws established in the old world—the *Every Student Succeeds Act of 2015* (ESSA), the *No Child Left Behind Act of 2001* (NCLB), and the *Elementary and Secondary Act of 1965* (ESEA). In particular, ECAA emphasized social justice, equitable access to mathematics and science education, and "systemic" change. It established newfound standards on accountability for teachers and students, and it made direct mentions of race, class, and gender. In addition, the bill promised to close the achievement gaps between pupils by providing every child with the tools to achieve in a 22nd century society.

With new threats to the United States from the planet's Northern and Western regions came the demand for new laws and public policies in the West. The West's leaders started with war strategies and proceeded to secure funding for future Space Race Delegations. Shortly thereafter, with the emerging need to strategically develop a more mathematically and scientifically literate society, ECAA was born.

ECAA's racial policies, immediately put into practice by sectors and districts after the law was passed, focused exclusively on expanding the long sought-after opportunities for students of color. The law focused almost exclusively on Black students to help expand opportunities for the West's most mathematically in-need students. In the old world, Black students and other students of color had been continuously undereducated in the mathematical sciences. Now, the West needed them. The policy introduced advanced courses in mathematics and science into lower-school and upper-school curricula all over the West. It also funded after-school STEM+C (science, technology, engineering, mathematics, and computer science) programs in poor Black communities like Sector 4.

But as expected, ECAA's new racially-centric policies had caused uproar among some sectors and praise within others. The policies had become the topic of evening newscasts, national education conferences, and it filled new professional development programs focused on White teachers who taught Black children. It was clear that the West wanted to eradicate the Black–White achievement gaps but only to improve their development in the mathematical sciences. White conservative and liberal parents in Sector 1, located in the northeastern region of the West, responded alike, working hard to find new methods and opportunities to secure advantages for their children, advantages that they saw slipping away as the West's national political economy continued to become more aligned with the interests of the UGC.

Through successful lobbying, mostly White parents, represented by the West's Unified Polity Party, the UPP – an appropriate acronym used by the party to focus on the West's commitments to space exploration – were able to garner provisions in ECCA with discourses focused on equity and social justice *for all*. In the more advantaged sectors, ECAA promised tax vouchers to parents based on their upper-school students' test scores and race classification. These new reverse racial policies made most White parents, even poor White parents with students in the lower-schools, content but it negatively impacted the West's Asian population.

The affluent Asian parents, whose students attended mostly White upper-schools in Sectors 1 and 2, quickly searched for loopholes to these new provisions, realizing that their designated classification as "non-White" persons exempted their children from participation in the new racial provisions, which secured the economic advantage of White families in the face of the closing achievement gaps in mathematics and science. Sector officials would quickly remind these non-White Asian parents of the provisions in place to help students of color, provisions most White parents knew would ensure their children benefitted in the long run. Although students of color, mostly Black students, were becoming more educated, upper-school opportunities were still at the helm of those with the historical economic power.

Daija's predominately Black school in Sector 4 had experienced a set of very different realities. Daija's school district was ground zero for the West's and the Council's secret plans, which were becoming more apparent to Daija as she reflected on her experiences, and AJ's disappearance. Too few students were successful in getting out of lower-school, and once Daija had passed enough exams to apply for upper-school, she thought back to the arduous testing regime she had to endure for entry.

Daija especially remembered the interesting classroom pedagogies of her mathematical sciences instructor, Ms. Tamika, who had come to tutor her and other students the summer before their final upper-school entry exams. She had reminded the students that, over the years, Black kids who were "smart" were now facing the same fate as Black kids who were deemed uneducable or unintelligent in the West. The UGC, over the years, had worked to enlist Black children sent to the Navel in special training camps, which were covers for some special programs likened to enlisting in the military of the navy in the old world.

Ms. Tamika Thomas, an award-winning mathematical sciences teacher, had received the West's highest award for teaching when Daija was a first-year student in the Sector 4 upper-school. Ms. Tamika, as students and parents called her, was a key resource in ECAA's development of talented and mathematically literate Black youth. Her mother, the elder Mrs. Thomas, had taught Alphonso and other former delegates, when they entered upper-school.

Daija had been studying under Ms. Tamika for the last four years. Over these years, Daija and Ms. Tamika developed a close relationship, as Ms. Tamika saw a lot of herself in Daija. She would speak with Daija about the new equity and social justice provision in ECAA and explained why race had become so important to the government so suddenly. This happened as the Space Race Delegation exam was approaching. Ms. Tamika assured Daija that there was no need to worry and ensured her that passing the exam would set her up for a secure and financially rich future. Daija would enter the Space Race Delegations, and if she did not win, she would get any job she wanted, she could serve as a reminder that Black people are capable. She would say: "this is our time to shine, Daija! I want you to shine!" Daija would smile back at Ms. Tamika, because she genuinely cared for her students, but her gut told her that there was more to this story, and she felt that Ms. Tamika knew.

Part II: Daija'a Awakening

Not too long after the awards ceremony, Daija found herself in a sea of emotions and confusion after a weird conversation with the councilmembers and a menacing look from the Council's president. She decided to visit Ms. Tamika shortly thereafter to help make sense of all of the events that had transpired since she'd won the Space Race Delegation. What her and Ms. Tamika discussed was life changing, and it helped make sense of what had transpired over the last seven months. The time had come to set a mission, a racial legacy, into action. It was five months before the next delegation, the famed 25th Space Race Delegations, so Daija knew it was time to take the return trip to Planet Mars. This time, based on the information she learned from Ms. Tamika, she would travel with other critical friends from her upper-school classes She would initiate a revolution.

Daija was about to become a justice-fighter, and the first of her kind. She paused and thought to herself as she flipped the panel operator to open the communications latch on the control panel. She knew that she was about to follow in the footsteps of some great Blacks, like Harriet Tubman, but she also remembered that she had not fully thought through her plan, not yet anyway. She needed to get the crew to 100 kilometers, then she would set her plan in motion.

"You good girl?" asked Nadine, the 15-year old math prodigy on the voyage.

"Yeah, I'm okay...," replied Daija, loudly as she was sounding out the shuttle's engines.

"These folks are using us, like they always have y'all! They are trying to figure out what they can get out of this," she said loudly to herself as she recalled the code to turn the com-switch off. The shuttle had reached the mesosphere, closing in on 95 kilometers above sea level.

Daija and her crew had taken off six minutes prior. Their time had come. Their classroom education was officially over. The West's President and his cabinet sat in the Oval Office and watched on the nationally broadcast event. "We've finally figured out a way to put all of the Black kids' advanced math and science skills to work. Look at them just flying to Planet Mars for fun! Our money was well spent. Let's just hope this mission works, and that this one doesn't mess it up like the one from the 9th delegations did," said the President, humorlessly, his cabinet laughing in excess.

Back on the shuttle, Daija knew that it was now or never. 97 kilometers.

"Daija, what's the projected lift coefficient? We all set?" Cameron, her best friend, questioned.

"I'm checking on it now…," replied Daija, but she knew in a few seconds things would change, so she continued, very seriously, over their connected headsets: "…I hope y'all understand that what I am about to do is for the culture, for Black people, for our future."

99 kilometers. Two of the other four crew members, in unison, dismally questioned Daija. They were now at 99.6 kilometers. Daija quickly entered the code, turned the switch, and shifted to the manual controls. Nadine watched as this all happened. She also saw that Daija had sent a quick text on the special space-range phones the commanders had given the crew.

"DAIJA!" shouted Jaden, another friend of hers and a favorite of Ms. Tamika, "What in the world did you just do? Why did you cut off all of our communications!?"

Daija didn't respond. She had turned the switch and all official communications with Planet Earth were now gone. The backup communication to Planet Mars engaged. She quickly shut those off as well. Although it was Daija's last-minute quick decision to do it so soon, before the crew had a chance to get away from Earth and decide, the crew had just as quickly become the topic of trending social media hashtags plastered all over the internet: #BlackGirlMagic, #WeOutchea, #BlackSpaceFugitives were just a few. The community was watching, and so was Sector 4.

Other Westerners from across the nation, those not logged online, assumed there was a technical error and that there wasn't much to be worried about. Secretly, however, most conservative White parents were hoping the mission was failing, telling themselves that it was their kids who worked hard over those years and it was them that deserved this opportunity. As the seconds went on, however, the West knew that it wasn't a technical error and new truths started to come out.

When Daija had made the decision to cut off communications with the operations control center after her meeting with Ms. Tamika a few weeks earlier, she knew it was going to be a major problem. She had to wait until the crew reached the Kármán Line, an international standard set 62-miles above sea level that separated aeronautics from astronautics, to make her move. She had mostly struggled with whether or not she would return the Black prisoners on Planet Mars back to Planet Earth, as a means to uncover the Navel's big secret, or if she would keep on with the mission that AJ had started 15 years earlier.

As Daija took on the manual controls once she cut off official communications, she knew she would have to calculate all of their trajectories, using Advanced Physics and Calculus, to help manage her covert mission. She quickly smiled at herself for being so good at the advanced differentiation techniques she had learned in Ms. Tamika's mathematical science lectures. At that moment, she knew why learning mathematics was so important for her; her people's freedom would depend on it.

The decision, and Daija's executions, had come as a result of the readings and critical discussions Jaden had initiated while they were in Ms. Tamika's classes.

Cameron learned from Daija that all of the problems that Ms. Tamika used in her classes to teach the material were actually real-world scenarios from the past Ms. Tamika's political activities in her math classes were not just for fun. They had all been a part of a multi-generational mission focused on saving the legacy of their race, and their time and investments, unbeknownst to them, were a part of the Elder's plan to set a life-long precedent to use Black children and teach Black children mathematics for the sole purpose of helping to bring social justice to the West's increasing emphasis on space exploration. The UGC's development had made the plan much more difficult, and although AJ had not been able to execute the mission completely, there was still hope.

The students had revealed, in their reflection notes during Ms. Tamika's mathematical science social justice activities, ideas related to taking matters into their own hands, of becoming explorers to solve the problems she had given them. Daija pulled out their notebooks. The knowledge that had been shared with them was extensive; Daija and her crew just happened to come at the point where the messages were left for them, by them. Would they continue to act or not? This was the real question. From her grandmother, Daija had learned that Black people in the West would never gain their full rights. Because of their racial heritage and legacy, she realized that this moment was not only theirs but an historical moment for the race. Nadine stood from her seat in amazement: "I'm in!"

Jaden, in his usual joking manner, replied, "Yeah, we're all in, unless you're planning to jump into blank space!" The crew agreed with Daija and had only said that they wish she had told them earlier.

Up until this point, Daija was growing weary of all of the advanced mathematical knowledge and science applications she and her peers had mastered. She needed something more and this was it. More school was an option, a career was too. "But what legacy would that leave for others?" she thought to herself. She thought about her dad, who had told her to go on and live her own dreams after she won the Space Race Delegation. It was at this precise moment that Daija's father, Daniel, pulled into their family's driveway in Sector 4. He ran through the front door, embracing Daija's mother and his own mom, Daija's grandmother, Mae. He had gotten a hold of the tweet Daija sent out from a neighbor. It read, ever so briefly, and rung so true: "We, five young Black kids from Sector 4 in the West, have learned enough mathematics to help liberate us from the bonds of racial injustice and bring some peace to Planet Earth." Not knowing what it meant, his own mother assured him to trust his daughter. She had been raised to fight back.

257 kilometers. The crew was now in orbit, invisible to the satellite cameras positioned on them, having more mathematics and science knowledge than they could dream of. They were now on a mission to save all of the Black people who had been sent to Planet Mars from the Navel to prepare prisons for the transplanetary slave trade that would be launched during the 25th Space Race Delegations, when the Council, in collaboration with the West, would announce space

exploration learning opportunities for all Black youth in the West's lower-schools. Ms. Tamika, sitting in an upper-school Calculus III class with her new students, reading Daija's tweet, cheered them on. She thought of her own legacy, and her mother's teachings, knowing that Daija would be able to finish what she and Alphonso had started.

Race, Realism, and Black Futures

Afrofuturism has been widely used to explore Black futures and critique the present-day realities and historical dilemmas of Black people and communities. The term was coined by Mark Dery (1994) in his chapter, "Black to the Future: Interviews with Samuel R. Delany, Greg Tate, and Tricia Rose," in a larger editorial project centered on speculative fiction. Dery's edited volume was, in part, a response to Fredrick Jameson's (1990) call for a *cognitive cartography*, which is described as a mapping of unseen possibilities, as something beyond our scope of understanding and, at times, of reason.

Jameson's (1990) explorations in this area contend with the representation, reproduction, and formation of cognitive mappings; and in his reflection, Jameson notes that:

> achieved cognitive mapping will be a matter of form, and… an integral part of a socialist politics, although, its own possibility may well be dependent on some prior political opening which its task would then be to enlarge culturally. Still, even if we cannot imagine the productions of such an aesthetic, there may, nonetheless, as with the very idea of Utopia itself, be something positive in the attempt to keep alive the possibility of imagining such a thing.
>
> *(p. 358)*

As a matter of multiple forms and of imagining, Afrofuturism has long existed as a Black cultural tradition, imbued in the aesthetics of possibility through books, music, and the Black diasporic reality (Nelson, 2000). Artists such as Jean-Michel Basquiat, Octavia E. Butler, Samuel R. Delaney, David Huffman, Janelle Monáe, Earth, Wind, & Fire, Jimi Hendrix, Terrance Nance, Ngozi Onwurah, Nnedi Okorafor, Sun Ra, Wu Tang Clan, to name a *very* short list of individuals and groups who may be considered in the Afrofuturist cannon, present a view into the expansive cultural and aesthetic worlds of Afrofuturism that use speculative fiction informed by historical realities.

Moreover, as a speculative formation, Afrofuturism represents an important critical praxis that has both defined and pushed forward cultural meanings toward what may be considered a Black *specificity* (Wynter, 1989, p. 637), which, as Wynter notices, "moves us from a loss of trust in physical nature to a loss of trust in our modes of subjectivity, of being" (p. 641). And, as technologies expand and new ways of representation and mapping become available, new perspectives on Afrofuturism are needed and will continue to arise (Anderson & Jones, 2015).

Alondra Nelson (2000, 2002) helped expand early conversations around Afrofuturism in the late 1990s and began to generate a sort of historiography of Afrofuturism. Its results since have allowed Afrofuturism to become an everyday concept, not only among artists and creatives, especially those interested in Black speculative fiction and Black science fiction, but also among academic researchers and theorists within university settings. In particular, Nelson's (2002) edited volume, *Afrofuturism: A Special Issue of Social Text* explores some of the interesting cultural and academic foundations of Afrofuturism in what Nelson positions as a *critical perspective*. Nelson's edited volume opens up inquiries about aesthetics that connect Afrofuturism to the overlaps between culture and Black diasporic realities, and what Bell (1992) identifies as racial realism.

Afrofuturism, like CRT, is a powerful philosophical perspective that situates scholars in the heart of racial realities. These racial realities hold, for example, that racism and White supremacy are not only maintained over time, but they also serve as reminders of what White supremacist logic and racism's powers are capable of accomplishing through the law and public policy, among a host of other historical features. More important, however, is the fact that an exploration bound by but also beyond the subjection of laws and public policies have the power to expose the present day lived experiences of the masses and, also, extend them into some future (or historical) world. This narrative power makes it clear as to why Derrick Bell (1992), in *Faces at the Bottom of the Well*, employed allegorical storytelling, and made use of Black speculative fiction and Afrofuturist themes to explore race and racism in U. S. law and public policy.

In the United States, the law and public policy have been used as tools to maintain White racial power by managing discourses, opportunities, and beliefs about futures and future possibilities. Moreover, its systems have been structured by dominant racial narratives, mainstream theories, and racist cultural practices that serve as deficit narratives. The multitude of responses to these dominant systems have contributed to a rift between scholarly discourses and the racial reality. For example, as U.S. policies are put into practice by the masses of lawyers, businessmen, and even elementary and secondary teachers, they hold particular implications for those communities on their receiving ends, and often regulate an individual's ability to think, or live, outside of the legal and institutional norms.

To this point, I ask: *what might we learn from scholars' adaptations of critical perspectives, and specifically at the juncture of CRT and Afrofuturism, in a field like mathematics education—especially as it concerns research, policy, and promises of futurity?*

Critical theorists in the field of mathematics education have reminded us that mathematics teaching and learning, and U.S. education laws and public policies, do not exist in a vacuum (Martin, 2009). In mathematics education, the connections between law, public policy and mathematical practices are not always visible without the presence of a critical lens. Using critical analyses, what becomes apparent are connections not only worthy of discussion, but necessary in the study of schools, and specifically mathematics classrooms, their underlying theoretical praxes, and how they tend to function within and beyond the United States.

The opening of this chapter is an attempt to situate Daija and the discussions of CRT and Afrofuturism in mathematics education within a broader, more global—and in this case, interplanetary—context. As a domain, mathematics education research and policy have increasingly aligned with market-focused objectives that serve as racial projects that are uniquely positioned within broader racial agendas (Martin, 2009, 2013). When we examine the permanent obscurities of race using dominant theories and methods, which contributes to a collective labor focused on making sense of the ways that race-based realities might be eradicated, a discursive framing, specifically one of crisis, stays a primary method in mathematics education research (Washington et al., 2012). I wish to argue that this practice, of using "popular" or mainstream theories and methods in the contemporary research domains, contributes to a *new* politicized turn in mathematics education discourses that, in countering mainstream discourses, only helps to strengthen logic systems deeply entrenched in White cultural normalization and racial dominance narratives.

As market forces are increasingly expanded, they will continue to shape national and local systems that help to maintain dominant narratives about race within and outside of mathematics education. However, through an uptake and introduction of a set of cultural practices outside of our traditional research and normative academic practices, using critical perspectives like Afrofuturism, I propose that mathematics education may be better situated to align to broader "racial themes" of Black futurity (Bell, 1992). Here, I wish to define Black futurity, in its simplest form, as relating to a renewed or transformed conception of Black racial existence.

These explorations inform two central goals set out for this chapter: (1) to examine Daija's dilemma and explore increasingly racialized and foreboding U.S. education policies; and (2) to situate speculative fiction and Afrofuturism as tools to counter deficit narratives and position a Black specificity in mathematics education. To launch these reflections, in the next section, I present some foundations of CRT alongside perspectives on allegorical storytelling and Afrofuturism in mathematics education.

Foundations of CRT and Afrofuturism

Critical race scholarship in U. S. law and public policy is well-positioned to aid scholars in the collective push toward new visions of the future. Foundations for a racially liberating discursive practice have been very well outlined by Derrick Bell and others, such as Mari Matsuda, Charles Lawrence III, Richard Delgado, Kimberlé Crenshaw, Gloria Ladson-Billings, William Tate, and Danny Martin, to name a few notable scholars from law, education, and mathematics education. More generally, however, critical scholars attending to Bell's (1992) thesis in *Faces at the Bottom of the Well* are presented with a clear declarative on racial realism in the United States when he articulates:

> Black people will never gain full equality in this country. Even those Herculean efforts we hail as successful will produce no more than temporary "peaks of progress," short-lived victories that slide into irrelevance as racial patterns adapt in ways that maintain White dominance. This is a hard-to-accept fact that all history verifies. We must acknowledge it and move on to adopt policies based on what I call: "Racial Realism." This mind-set or philosophy requires us to acknowledge the permanence of our subordinate status.
>
> *(pp. 373–374)*

For Bell (1992), racial realism is positioned by four major thematic expressions that can help to deepen our understanding of a *critical race artifice* (Curry, 2017). These themes are outlined through an examination of: (1) the historical context; (2) the value of economic analyses over moral and ethical appeals; (3) the necessity of "salvation through struggle" (Bell, 1992, p. 98); and (4) Bell's racial realist imperative that there is no way to achieve the dream of (America's) racial equality. In Daija's society, the futuristic "Planet Earth," we can examine these four themes at play in a variety of ways. From an historical lens, we might note that although the structures of the society have changed, a dominant, supremacist force still functions. Morality and ethics still seem to function very much as they do today, and as they have consistently functioned in the past. In thinking towards Daija's plight, the reader is offered a moment to ask: what would I do? In this moment, one might understand Bell's notes on salvation through struggle. The story itself, so I hope, is but one unfolding of racial realism.

Through Bell's (1992) themes, our scholarship should become a challenging task. Is it about figuring out solutions to America's racial problem or more about devaluing the racial symbols discussed by Bell, and treading toward an awakening, toward an emergence of a new racial narrative, or each of the above? These possibilities, I argue, require a type of specificity to the Black racial condition. Daija Brown, our fictional heroine, much like Geneva Crenshaw from Bell's (1987) *And We Are Not Saved: The Elusive Quest for Racial Justice*, helps us to question and explore this specificity of Blackness (Dumas & ross, 2016; Wynter, 1989), and we are allowed, for a moment, to make sense of a world outside of our own, in the contexts of comparatively troubling laws and public policies, as we continue to search for some resolve.

An imperative put forth by Ladson-Billings and Tate (1995), in their original development of CRT in education, was to shift our ways of thinking toward more interdisciplinary ways of being. However, as critical mathematics education scholars continue to ask key questions that help to evaluate the field as a domain of study, recent shifts in the field, say, from around the mid-1990s (e.g., the social and sociopolitical turns), have become important hallmarks of increasingly interdisciplinary practices. The current integration, an introduction of Afrofuturism, allows us to make sense of a Black specificity in studies on race and about racism in mathematics education (Gholson & Wilkes, 2017). Here, I briefly turn to Dumas and ross' (2016) theorization of a *Black critical theory* (BlackCrit) in education, and its connections to CRT. In doing so, I seek to shift away from more general ideas, theorizations, and discussions on race and racism toward a very specific understanding of the Black condition—and the disdain with Black bodies—within and outside of educational and academic spaces.

Specifically, I consider how, in mathematics education, "the specificity of (anti) Blackness matters in explaining how Black bodies become marginalized, disregarded, and disdained in schools and other spaces of education" (Dumas & ross, 2016, p. 1). Dumas and ross' (2016) theorizations help us to identify and make sense of the ways that anti-blackness, which they differentiate from racism, have been developed and conceptualized within and outside of education through processes of racial coding. Here, they focus on the Black conditions in local and global contexts.

BlackCrit also helps us to make sense of how various conceptualizations of blackness might expose discursive practices that engage the everyday and salient nature of anti-blackness. Dumas and ross (2016) argue that "CRT enters the field of education as a decidedly Black theorization of race," and they note how "CRT is offered as a tool to analyze race and racism in general" in the work of constructing meanings of and countering "institutionalized racism" (p. 2). In doing so, they examine how CRT, at its foundations, is a Black critical theory and, more broadly, also offers a theory of race and racism in the United States. As a result, when CRT is applied to disciplinary fields like education, and more focused fields like mathematics education, it has the potential to become an exposition of anti-black racism. Importantly, in their exposition, the authors determine that CRT, in its original formulation, is a theory of race and not a theorization on Blackness, or the specific Black condition:

> Understanding this distinction between a theory of racism and a theory of Blackness (in an anti-black world) is key: whereas the former may invoke Black examples, and even rely on Black experience of racism in the formation of its tenets, only critical theorization of Blackness confronts the specificity of anti-blackness, as a social construction, as an embodied lived experience of social suffering and resistance, and perhaps most importantly, as an antagonism, in which the Black is a despised thing-in-itself.
>
> *(pp. 2–3)*

This antagonism, as explained by Dumas and ross' (2016) discussions take what *seems* implicit and moves it to the explicit. For example, one might notice this antagonism at play in Daija's world, shown by the Council's decision to turn Africa into "the Navel," effectively removing a majority of the planet's Black population outside of the larger global structure. Moreover, this explication also serves to expose how other critical responses to CRT's formation (i.e., LatCrit, AsianCrit, and TribalCrit) "emerged as critiques of the perceived 'Black–White binary' of CRT" and, importantly, exposes how "their existence either presumes that CRT functions in the main as a BlackCrit, or suggests that 'race' critiques accomplish all that Black people need" (p. 3).

Engaging Afrofuturism in mathematics education, as a Black critical theory, has the potential – as allegorical storytelling did in Bell's narratives – to accomplish the task of identifying and exposing racial antagonisms in U.S. laws and public policies in education. At a peak, Afrofuturism also has the ability to present new modalities of being (Wynter, 1989). Moreover, given its deep roots in Black speculative fiction, Afrofuturism offers mathematics education new opportunities to also imagine possible futuristic functions of mathematics and science, and examine these functions with regard to new and reimagined positionalities for historically marginalized communities and groups. Closely tied to these functions, of mathematics and science in the future, is also an open invitation to explore, critique, and write-out futurist notions of mathematics education research and policy as it concerns Black families, children, and youth. These multiple facets, altogether, can bring the field closer toward a Black specificity in mathematics education.

Afrofuturism and Black Specificity in Mathematics Education

Bell's (1987, 1992) method of allegorical storytelling and science fiction is a literary model he used to integrate fact and fiction toward new directions in the collective struggle for justice in scholarly literature and legal discourse. Bell's use of "fantasy and dialogue to uncover enduring truths" (1987, p. 6) is key in the connections to mathematics education given that an often-overlooked contribution to the existing critical race praxes in mathematics education is the deepening understanding of the racial reality, which require new stories and discourses on race and critiques in the field. Within this practice, of allegory, new questions emerge: *What happens if we were to close the achievement gaps? What if public policies changed and actually attended to the needs of Black children and families? What if school and district practices were no longer couched in anti-blackness?* The extent to which these and other questions might be answered have already been studied by a host of critical scholars. As such, science fiction takes us to new worlds that are attached to current research investigations and thus real-world contexts.

Understanding mathematics education's unique position within this discursive structure, and its alignments to various racial systems, and to race and racism, requires theories and practices that continually move critical discourses into further critical praxis. Thus, critical theories of race and storytelling hold promise to become a key construction that is positioned to present collective counter-narratives within the domain for other scholars to build on. They are particularly important as the dominant narratives associate theories of discourse (i.e., what is said) and concepts and policies (i.e., what is said to be done) alongside real-world practices (i.e., what is actually done). Specifically, critical stories on race form a body of counter-narratives that help to not only shed light on the material forces and the psycho-socio-cultural effects of dominant narratives (e.g., identity research), but they can also reposition assumptions of cultural normativity.

As we learn, Daija's decisions are tied to a historical legacy, and as a young Black woman, a racial tradition, where her "defiance, and its harassing effect [is] likely more potent precisely because she [acts] without expecting to topple her oppressors" (Bell, 1992, xii). Through Daija's dilemma, we might explore specific aspects of CRT: interest convergence, the permanence of racism, Whiteness as property, and intersectionality; these tenets help us to identify deficient assumptions in contemporary race scholarship.

To center our analyses, we should remind ourselves of the power of storytelling, and specifically counter-storytelling, to allow us to be specific in unlearning beliefs that are believed to be true (Solórzano & Yosso, 2002). However, as noted by critical scholars within and outside of mathematics education, these counter-narratives are also at risk of becoming aligned with the very mechanisms that maintain White privileges (social and material forces) buttressed by White supremacy (systemic forces) (Crenshaw, 1988; Curry, 2017; Delgado & Stefancic, 2001; Martin, 2013, Washington et al, 2012). As the valuable labors of counter-narratives engage with dominant cultural practices, it becomes important to examine how critical perspectives are subject to the very racial realities laid out by CRT. In this chapter, I focus on Afrofuturism to make sense of the overlapping stories in my attempt to examine the racial realities of some futurist period.

Thus, critical research, as one of the standards of critical praxis and knowledge building in the domain of cultural studies, for example, has produced novel ways of thinking beyond the formal (and pragmatic) domain boundaries. As a field's formal boundaries are further critiqued and disbanded, some interesting questions emerge, and professional visions are shifted. One such question is: what boundaries do critical praxes, particularly in a domain of study such as mathematics education, seek to dismantle? I argue that Afrofuturism in mathematics education presents reflections of this case in society and presents key ideas on the importance of centering the lived experience, a grammar of grounded language for even the most critical scholarly discursive practice. At this juncture, discourses become a question of praxis or one of foreclosure, a question of engaging the lived reality, or being constrained by it.

Martin (2009), "[calls] for research that is grounded in a perspective that conceptualizes mathematics learning and participation as racialized forms of experience—that is, structured by the relations of race that exist in the larger society"; he also notes that this "perspective underscores the fact that all students—not just those identified as African American, Latino, and Native American—experience mathematics learning as a racialized endeavor" (p. 300). To answer this question sometimes pulls us toward a history, at other times it requires we deal with the present, and still at others, we are pushed toward the future. Still, we are reminded by Washington et al. (2012) that, "the prevalence of particular frames within a research context gives rise to the creation of a project," what they term as a crisis-management project for mathematics education while importantly noting that "such projects can be social, market-oriented, neo-conservative, liberal, social justice-oriented, and so on" (p. 60). Altogether, these projects give rise to competition, between projects, and a market-oriented structuring of the field (Martin, 2010).

Thus, the practice of attending to the social and political forces and cultural aspects of knowledge building allows us to more clearly identify how formal (i.e., mainstream) and critical lines of scholarship are purposed in constructing an alignment with or against the perceived "goals" of research and discourses in the field of mathematics education. Here, our criticisms might inquire: if expanding theory is purposed to push against or chip away at current ideological bounds in the research and methods of the domain (Moten, 2008), do aspects of critical knowledge building in mathematics education require that we start from some theoretical space, outside of the cannon?

Might a starting place for this theoretical space be a science fiction, couched in Afrofuturism? Whether we deem it as good or bad in our scholarly writing praxis, as true research, a project, or as servicing to a telling of stories of possibilities, it is a critical praxis of opportunity (Nelson, 2002). To explore these questions, and what could become of mathematics education, may be to look deeper into the literature and commentaries that highlight the political aspects of research practices in mathematics education and, as Bell (1992) shows us, intertwine fact and fiction as a means to push against ideological bounds versus expand maintaining mainstream methodologies and practices.

CRT and Afrofuturism in Mathematics Education: Towards New Futures

In this chapter, I used allegorical storytelling to launch a discussion around Black futurity as it concerns mathematics education research and practice. I explored multiple societal levels, their contexts, and the resulting impacts on mathematics education in a fictional tale that centers race and the racial reality. More specifically, in Part I, which opened this chapter, I dealt with the broad context, as we learned about Daija's global society, a futuristic "Planet Earth" where the former United States, now part of a republic known as "the West," continues to play a dominant role in the development and enforcement of laws and public policies through the UGC. I hope the reader draws two things from this opening. First, the persistence of supremacist logic and dominance in some far-off planet, strangely, mirrors our present day in most elements. Second, I shift toward the *permanence of racism* (Delgado & Stefancic, 2000), one core tenet of CRT, as I began to transition to a foreboding reality, and introduce more questions, about what the details in the story have to do with Daija's education, and in particular, her mathematics education

The reader then learned about the *Every Child Achieves Act*, known as the ECAA, a fictional law that governs primary and secondary education policies in "the West," and we explored how meritocracy, and specifically mathematics and science achievement, are used to determine which pupils are selected for the Council's annual Space Race Delegations. Specifically, we explored the impact of ECAA's policies on district and school practices and, in particular, Daija's own mathematics education through her experiences with her upper-school mathematical sciences teacher, Ms. Tamika. Throughout this progression, I am hopeful that the reader journeyed along with Daija and I as we reflected on the central question for this chapter.

To reiterate, this chapter's central question—*what might we learn from scholars' adaptations of critical perspectives, and specifically at the juncture of CRT and Afrofuturism, in a field like mathematics education—especially as it concerns research, policy, and promises of futurity?*—prompted us toward an examination of the connections between CRT and Afrofuturism, as tools and methods of analyses linked by storytelling and counter-narrations on race, and the specificities of Black racial being, as described by Wynter (1989) and Dumas and ross (2016) and Gholson and Wilkes (2017), who, through their own methods, use this specificity to push our thinking on identity and Black being toward new possibilities of racial justice.

The law and public policy have an interestingly oblique history with race in the United States. This obliqueness is distorted in both racial theory and practice, and it leans toward inequity and injustice and into death, forcing us to expand the ways that we deal with the *specificity* of the Black condition. In mathematics education, a Black specificity positions us toward a focused understanding of critically important engagements with CRT that are linked to Afrofuturism. First, we find that CRT enters the fields of law and education as theorizations on Black life, Blackness, and Black being; second, we see how Afrofuturism, via allegorical storytelling and with roots in Black speculative fiction, provides a grounding and counter-narration on Black life and being in each of the historical, contemporary, and futuristic realms. Finally, as we merge these two modalities in mathematics education, Afrofuturism and CRT allow us to explore new possibilities as we push at the boundaries and theoretical conceptions of race.

These possibilities propel us against increasingly deficit ways of thinking about and responses to the racial realist imperatives as it may concern Black life and the specificity of the Black condition in the development of futures engaging mathematics teaching and learning.

References

Anderson, R., & Jones, C. E. (Eds.). (2015). *Afrofuturism 2.0: The rise of Astro-Blackness.* New York, NY: Lexington Books.

Bell, D. (1987). *And we are not saved: The elusive quest for racial justice.* New York, NY: Basic Books.

Bell, D. (1992). *Faces at the bottom of the well: The permanence of racism.* New York, NY: Basic Books.

Crenshaw, K. (1988). Race, reform and retrenchment: Transformation and legitimation in anti-discrimination law. *Harvard Law Review*, 101(7), 1331–1387.

Curry, T. (2017). Canonizing the critical race artifice: An analysis of philosophy's gentrification of critical race theory. In P. Taylor, L. M. Alcoff, & L. Anderson (Eds.), *The Routledge companion to the philosophy of race* (pp. 349–361). New York, NY: Routledge.

Delgado, R., & Stefancic, J. (2000). Introduction. In R. Delgado & J. Stefancic (Eds.), *Critical race theory: The cutting edge* (2nd ed., pp. xv–xix). Philadelphia, PA: Temple University Press.

Delgado, R., & Stefancic, J. (2001). *Critical race theory: An introduction.* New York: New York University Press.

Dery, M. (1994). Black to the future: Interviews with Samuel R. Delany, Greg Tate, and Tricia Rose. In D. Mark (Ed.), *Flame wars: The discourse of cyberculture* (pp. 179–222). Durham, NC: Duke University Press.

Dumas, M. J., & ross, K. M. (2016). "Be real Black for me": Imagining BlackCrit in education. *Urban Education*, 51(4), 415–422.

Gholson, M. L. & Wilkes, C. E. (2017). (Mis)Taken Identities: Reclaiming Identities of the "Collective Black" in Mathematics Education Research Through an Exercise in Black Specificity. Review of Research in Education, 41(1), 228–252.

Jameson, F. (1990). Cognitive mapping. In C. Nelson & L. Grossbert (Eds.), *Marxism and the interpretation of culture* (pp. 347–360). Chicago: University of Illinois Press.

Jett, C. C. (2012). Critical race theory interwoven with mathematics education research. *Journal of Urban Mathematics Education*, 5(1), 21–30.

Ladson-Billings, G., & Tate, W. (1995). Toward a critical race theory in education. *Teachers College Record*, 97(1), 47–68.

Martin, D. B. (2009). Researching race in mathematics education. *Teachers College Record*, 111(2), 295–338.

Martin, D. B. (2010). Not-so-strange bedfellows: Racial projects and the mathematics education enterprise. In U. Geller, E. Jablonka, & C. Morgan (Eds.), *Proceedings of the sixth international mathematics education and society conference* (Vol. 1) (pp. 42–64). Berlin, Germany: Freie Universaität Berlin.

Martin, D. B. (2013). Race, racial projects, and mathematics education. *Journal for Research in Mathematics Education*, 44(1), 316–333.

Moten, F. (2008). The case of Blackness. *Criticism*, 50(2), 177–218.

Nelson, A. (2000). Afrofuturism: Past-future visions. *Color Lines*, 3(1), 34–47.

Nelson, A. (Ed.). (2002). *Afrofuturism: A special issue of social text.* Durham, NC: Duke University Press.

Solórzano, D., & Yosso, T. (2002). Critical race methodology: Counter-storytelling as an analytical framework for education research. *Qualitative Inquiry*, 8(1), 23–44.

Washington, D., Torres, Z., Gholson, M., & Martin, D. B. (2012). Crisis as a discursive frame in mathematics education research and reform: Implications for educating Black children. In S. Mukhopadhyay & W. M. Roth (Eds.), *Alternative forms of knowing (in) mathematics* (pp. 53–69). New York, NY: Sense.

Womack, Y. L. (2013). *Afrofuturism: The world of Black sci-fi and fantasy culture.* Chicago, IL: Chicago Review Press.

Wynter, S. (1989). Beyond the world of man: Glissant and the new discourse of the Antilles. *World Literature Today*, 63(4), 637–648.

5

MATHEMATICS CURRICULUM REFORM AS RACIAL REMEDIATION

A Historical Counter-story

Erika C. Bullock

Historically, the primary focus in mathematics education research has been the teaching and learning of mathematics. While these are important, there are other elements of the network of mathematics education practices (Valero, 2007) that deserve equal attention. For example, mathematics has been at the center of U.S. efforts to establish and to maintain technological superiority and mathematics education has taken on the responsibility for equipping students with the skills needed for critical thinking and innovation. However, systemic and policy analyses of mathematics education are not as common. Although some mathematics education scholars are making the socio-political turn (Gutiérrez, 2013), studies that examine mathematics education as a political system are rare. I have dedicated myself to filling this void with my work regarding the politics of race and racialization, areas also underexamined in mathematics education literature. In this process, I have found that a political analysis of mathematics education requires more theoretical and methodological tools than those in circulation in the field.

My approach to analyzing mathematics education as a political system has been largely historical. The field has taken the history of contemporary mathematics education in the United States for granted as a story of progress relative to the nation's goals. The progress is not the establishment of a better mathematics education. Rather, it is progress toward a mathematics education that is more useful, more consistent, and more inclusive. The progress is in creating a version of school mathematics that has space for all children by focusing more on creating experiences that support mathematics learning in different ways. However, there is a concurrent narrative describing a persistent "achievement gap" between Black and White students that threatens to undermine the narrative of progress.

In this chapter, I use critical race theory (CRT) to construct a counter-story of the history of contemporary mathematics education reform (i.e., the *Standards* movement as defined by National Council of Teachers of Mathematics (NCTM) documents *Curriculum and Evaluation Standards for School Mathematics* (CESSM) published in 1989 and *Principles and Standards for School Mathematics* (PSSM) published in 2000) and the reform efforts that have come from them. This counter-story is a retelling of the history of mathematics education that addresses how and why Black children have been the subject of much discussion and little systemic change in mathematics education reform. I argue that equity and standardization are racial remediation strategies. Bell (1976, 1979) defines racial remedies as plans or strategies that masquerade as recompense for racial injustice. He explains: "Spurred by the need to confront a political or economic danger to the nation as a whole, serious racial injustice is acknowledged and enjoined, but necessary remedies are not implemented once the economic or political irritant is removed" (Bell, 1976, p. 13). Therefore, the purpose of a racial remediation strategy is to eliminate irritation, not to execute justice.

I focus on the *Standards* movement to contain the analysis in this chapter and to illustrate how the early processes of standardization in mathematics education were themselves racialized. The two focal documents set a precedent for national standards in the United States, so the context of their appearance and proliferation with respect to Black children deserves interrogation.

Mathematics Education's Narrative Conflict

Equity discourse has functioned as the mediator of the competing narratives of mathematics education's progress and the persistent "achievement gap." It emerged as a consistent part of the mathematics education conversation in 2000 when the NCTM released PSSM. Before that document, there was discussion about mathematics education for all students and about equity (e.g., Matthews, 1984b; Secada & Meyer, 1989; Tate & D'Ambrosio, 1997), but this document made a statement that equity was to be the first principle of a quality mathematics education (more on this later). Out of this moment came a family of research focused on how students of different demographics experience school mathematics and what strategies mathematics educators at all levels can use to decrease the achievement gaps between groups toward a mathematics that is more truly for all. The equity research genre has produced a plethora of research and practitioner literature focused on documenting and closing achievement gaps with little positive result (Berry, Ellis, & Hughes, 2014). Therefore, this genre of research bears at least a portion of the burden for mathematics education's failure to "[facilitate] the kind of violent reform necessary to change the conditions of African American, Latin@, Indigenous, and poor students in mathematics education" (Martin, 2015, p. 22).

In recent years, there have been several critiques of achievement gap logic, of mathematics education's progress narrative, and of equity discourse. Gutiérrez (2008) describes the myopia related to the achievement gap as a fetish and establishes moving beyond this fetishizing as a moral imperative. She urges researchers to carefully count the costs of using their work to document achievement gaps or to attempt to close them. Martin (2003) explored the disconnect between the stated goals of mathematics for all as outlined in mathematics education policy and the intentions that Black communities hold for the mathematics education of their children. Both Martin (2003) and Berry, Ellis, and Hughes (2014) outline a history of reforms enacted in the name of equity and mathematics for all that have consistently failed Black learners. In his response to the NCTM's latest guiding document, *Principles to Actions: Ensuring Mathematics Success for All* (NCTM, 2014), Martin (2015) established this effort as yet another instantiation of the organization's failure to live up to its own rhetoric related to Black children. I have turned to history to make sense of the inconsistencies between mathematics education's rhetorical commitments to Black children and the documented reality of Black children in mathematics, but the extant histories of mathematics education provide few answers. I argue that part of the issue is the mode of historical storytelling.

The history of mathematics education reform in the 20th century has been told through the lens of *Sputnik*. This mode of telling establishes a compelling case for mathematics education's role in matters of national security, technological innovation, and international competition, but telling the story in this way has consequences. One significant consequence is the dissonance I have described between the story of mathematics education's progress and that of the persistent achievement gap. There is no way to account for this incongruity except to tell the story from a different vantage point. What happens when "national progress" becomes nationalism? When the "all" in *mathematics for all* is revealed to mean something more like "anyone who can embrace the whiteness that standardization represents"? When an organization of teachers interested in creating a way to evaluate mathematics curricula becomes an explicitly political entity? I explore these questions in this chapter using CRT's tenet of counter-storytelling.

Critical Race Counter-storytelling

Counter-storytelling is a cornerstone of CRT (Bell, 2005; Delgado & Stefancic, 2017). CRT trades on the fact that all knowledge production is a form of politicized storytelling, but critical race counter-storytelling is different in that it is transparent about these politics. Simple shifts in perspective do not satisfy the researcher who uses CRT; they want to offer a story that challenges the rationality supporting the dominant story. This is an explicitly political project. Baszile (2015) explains:

> Thus, critical race counter-storytelling, as I use it here, constitutes all work that is intentionally and strategically challenging the assumptions and logic of stories that ultimately work to reinforce racial domination at the epistemic, spiritual, and material dimensions of dehumanization.
>
> *(p. 240)*

Therefore, counter-storytelling in CRT is more than just a means to complicate dominant narratives; it is not about ranting, venting, or retaliating for racial injustice (Ladson-Billings, 2013). Rather, it exposes and challenges the White rationality—or White logic[1] (Bonilla-Silva & Zuberi, 2008)—that stitches these narratives together.

U.S. history is an emblem of narratives grounded in White logic. It evinces a residue of Enlightenment thought in that history is told in narratives of "constantly expanding progress and increasing democracy" (Banks, 1993, p. 9). This residue influences not only how histories are told, but also the roles that historical actors play. Even the notion of democracy or citizenship contains an implicit commitment to whiteness. It is not possible to be democratic or to be a model citizen without a concomitant effort to maintain White supremacy because democracy and citizenship are White property (Harris, 1993). The historical critical race counter-story is inherently anti-Enlightenment because it takes up CRT's assumptions that racism is endemic to society and challenges historical notions of progress, democracy, and citizenship as non-objective and racialized.

Derrick Bell (1976, 1979, 2004a, 2004b, 2005) provides an example of counter-storytelling in his prolific analysis of the *Brown v. Board of Education* (*Brown* hereafter) decision. *Brown* became known as the most monumental decision regarding the education of Black children by mandating an end to segregation in U.S. public schools. According to Bell, *Brown* is not the universal win that history records it to be. Rather, Bell's analysis shows that *Brown* is an exemplar of both racial remediation and interest convergence.

Brown epitomizes racial remediation in education policy. Desegregation as a remedy appeared to resolve an issue of educational inequity by allowing Black children to access the schools that White children enjoyed. However, there was no evidence that these changes would improve Black children's educational experience. Also, the decision itself created no urgency for schools to integrate, which meant many districts would only integrate by force after litigation. Nonetheless, the irritant—de facto segregation and its malcontents—was removed as organizations fighting for equality saw the decisions as a win (Bell, 1976, 1979, 2004a, 2004b, 2005).

Bell also used *Brown* to illustrate the principle of interest convergence, asserting that "the interest of blacks in achieving racial equality will be accommodated only when it converges with the interests of whites" (Bell, 1979, p. 523). Interest convergence creates what seems to be a win-win solution but the key is that a solution will be neither considered nor pursued unless there is value for White interests (see also Tate, Ladson-Billings, & Grant, 1993). With *Brown*, there were multiple beneficiaries, least of whom were the Black children who would have the opportunity to be educated in "better" facilities. Liberal Whites who labeled segregation as immoral were satisfied that Black children would have the fortune and opportunity to be educated alongside White children. More conservative Whites saw segregation as a barrier to certain economic and political advances, so they were also interested in an end to *de jure* segregation. In the Cold War era, it was critical for the United States to regain its leadership in the world and to gain favor with allies. One way to facilitate this, particularly with respect to "third world" countries, was to show fidelity to the American creed "all men are created equal." Domestically, Whites who wanted to see the South reach its highest economic potential saw segregation as a barrier to Southern industrialization. Finally, *Brown* provided some hope for Black World War II veterans who faced violence and discrimination in the South upon their return; *Brown* made it seem that their sacrifice was not in vain. Highlighting these complex benefits of *Brown* complicates the progressive narrative that *Brown* interrupted racism in the United States, creating a different perspective on the history of that moment and the moments that followed.

Why a Critical Race Historical Counter-story of Mathematics Education Reform?

Anderson (1970) describes an intentional effort, born of White racism, to use science to establish Black inferiority:

> We were drenched from West African shores and brought to America as slaves. According to the white man, we were subhumans, having no culture, language, history and, of course, no scientific skills. From the Crusades to the present, the white man had to continually create "scientific" myths about how much of a superior being he was/is and how savage and uncivilized nonwhites were/are.
>
> *(p. 20)*

Education research relies on this appropriation of scientism toward a research legacy called the *inferiority paradigm* (Carter & Goodwin, 1994; Tate, 1997a). According to Carter and Goodwin (1994):

> The inferiority paradigm is grounded in the assumption that visible racial/ethnic people are limited biologically and are genetically inferior in comparison with Whites. According to this viewpoint, differences in learning and performance between Whites and visible racial/ethnic group members can be attributed to the inherent inferiority of non-Whites relative to Whites.
>
> *(p. 294)*

The inferiority paradigm has formed the intellectual basis for slavery, genocide, and other overt forms of violence. More subtly, however, this way of thinking has informed education policy and curriculum decision making and has remained alive in mathematics education research.

Although most research justifying the inferiority paradigm came from psychology, mathematics education research has done its part to shore up the inferiority paradigm through research that focuses on poor performance or on gaps in performance (Gutiérrez, 2008; Matthews, 1984a). These studies then became the foundation for intervention programs (Matthews, 1984a). While it may now be socially unacceptable to label Black children as genetically predisposed to struggle with mathematics, subtler and more psychologized forms of explanation have taken up the same project of assigning responsibility for Black children's challenges with mathematics to those children, their families, and their communities. For example, current prevalent discourses about *grit* and *mindset* simultaneously blame Black children for their lack of achievement and guarantee achievement *if and only if* those children can repair themselves (Ladson-Billings, 2017). While this work does not make direct claims of genetic inferiority, it implies that there is something inside the Black child that requires repair in order for them to engage positively with mathematics.

Given that research is the basis for curriculum reform in mathematics education, the logics of the inferiority paradigm extend into curriculum reform. However, mathematics education curriculum reform is meant to do double duty: first, to create a structure for school mathematics and, subsequently, to create school mathematics. Pursuing these goals on a foundation of research that ratifies Black inferiority means that school mathematics is based on Black inferiority in both structure and content. This critical race historical counterstory compromises the dominant narrative of mathematics education reform by exploiting fissures within the narrative that acknowledging ideas like the inferiority paradigm necessarily creates.

Blackness and Mathematics Education in the Mid-20th Century

As highlighted earlier, *Brown* was an occasion of interest convergence motivated by, among other things, the United States' need to make a bold statement to the world about its democratic ideals. The hypocrisy of a nation that paraded democracy through the world while its own Black citizens continued to live the legacy of slavery through intense segregation impeded the United States' global reputation. There was no more clear goodwill gesture than to extend opportunity to present and future generations of Black children and to acknowledge Black cries for educational equity that had gone unanswered for over a century (Bell, 1979, 2004a, 2004b, 2005).

Before *Brown*, there was little discussion of Black children in mathematics education. In 1941, Ethel Grubbs[2], a Black mathematics teacher in Washington, DC, wrote an article in *The Mathematics Teacher* titled "How the National Council of the Teachers of Mathematics May Serve Negro Teachers and How They May Serve the Council."[3] In this article, Grubbs takes up two issues: outlining challenges that Black mathematics teachers in Black schools faced and offering recommendations for how the NCTM could better cooperate with Black teachers. She begins the article with three assumptions that speak to the nature of discussions about Black mathematics education at the time:

1. It is of more importance to discuss means of overcoming the environmental handicaps of the Negro child than to consider the frequently heard but unproved assumption of his mental inferiority or of the need of a special adaptation of the mathematics program because of peculiar racial needs.
2. It is of more importance to evolve remedial measures as the result of observation and study rather than as promiscuous offerings of theoretical panaceas.
3. Further, it is of vital urgency that the functional teaching of mathematics shall be viewed as one phase only of the problem that a well-grounded knowledge of mathematics shall be considered as necessary in the daily life of man as a consumer, a worker, a citizen. *(Grubbs, 1941, p. 251)*

Grubbs' first assumption speaks directly to the inferiority paradigm that was shaping research and practice discussions at the time. She describes the Black mathematics teacher's experience including professional preparation, working conditions, class size (as many as 60 students in junior or senior high school), and pay. She makes a case for racial pay equity and criticizes the focus on defense training that the NCTM had taken up. Grubbs' recommendations to the NCTM included requests that the organization leverage its research and publication resources in advocacy on behalf of Black mathematics teachers. She suggested that the Council look at Black schools to find teachers who are often better prepared and more pedagogically skillful than their White counterparts and to draw these teachers into greater professional participation through marketing changes. Perhaps most germane to the present discussion, she recommended that the NCTM advocate for a mathematics program specific to Black children "to include participation in individual and group activities based upon their individual and group experiences in the community in which they live" (p. 255).

Grubbs' (1941) article proves that, before *Brown*, there was specific discussion Black mathematics teachers and students and that the NCTM knew of these concerns; they even thought them important enough to publish the paper that Grubbs presented in its flagship journal[4]. It is also clear from Grubbs' paper that the inferiority paradigm informed how mathematics educators considered Black children. Otherwise, her first assumption would not have been necessary. But there remains a question of what happened with Grubbs' message. The NCTM granted her a momentous platform both in person and in print but a cursory Google Scholar search reveals that Grubbs' paper has not been cited in other publications. There is no reference to this piece in NCTM documents establishing curriculum standards or calling for equity, so there is no clear evidence that the mathematics education community has taken up Grubbs' pointed recommendations about Black mathematics teachers and learners.

If the NCTM could choose not to address Black students and teachers directly in 1941, it would seem that such avoidance post-*Brown* would be all but impossible. In 1956, the NCTM published a summary of its recent activities in *The Arithmetic Teacher* authored by then-president Howard Fehr (1956). [5] Although

Fehr does not state the purpose for the column, it appears that his intention was to outline the NCTM's work and priorities for the new journal audience. Fehr lists the topics for the upcoming national meeting which would include topics such as "Language Difficulties," "Gifted Children," "Factors Retarding Improvement," and "Materials and Devices for the Teacher." He asserts: "No teacher who would be up to date can miss the convention where the latest available knowledge on arithmetic instruction will be presented" (p. 252). Certainly, this brief column does not represent all of the NCTM's work at the time, but considering the message and the significance of *Brown* at the time of its publication, one might expect some mention of the decision and its implications in the president's statements or on the conference program. What, then, did it mean for a mathematics teacher to be "up to date"?

My intention with the examples in this section is to establish a sense of how race appeared in mathematics education discourse in the mid-20th century. Grubbs' (1941) article confirms that there was some discussion about Black learners and teachers at the time and that the NCTM was aware enough about the issue to publish her comments. Unfortunately, her recommendations seem to trail off. Fehr's (1956) column promoting the present and future work of the NCTM did not mention the *Brown* decision, school integration, or race in a time when this decision was shaking the foundation of U.S. education and racial politics. Perhaps the omission was an intentional move to avoid the political morass that may have been clear in the NCTM's constituency. Perhaps it was evidence of tone-deafness. Perhaps it subtly affirms that mathematics exists outside the social and the political and that mathematics education should take the same position. Whatever the reason, the NCTM's silence is noteworthy.

Mathematics for All

A theme through the history of mathematics curriculum reform after 1950 is the idea of *mathematics for all*. Mathematics education reformers have used this sentiment to justify significant structural change in school mathematics. While I address *mathematics for all* in the section that follows, I think it is important to make some preliminary comments.

Keitel (1987) credits mathematician Hans Freudenthal with establishing the phrase *mathematics for all and for everyone* as the defining motto of his organization *Instituut voor de Ontwikkeling ven het Wiskunde Onderwijs* [Institute for the Development of Mathematics Education]. Keitel argues that this motto resonated throughout the international mathematics education community:

> "Mathematics for all and for everyone" is also a slogan comprehensive enough to cover many interpretations; indeed it could well signify the most significant achievements of mathematics education in this century—although they are, alas, intellectual achievements, not achievements in the schools. Thus "mathematics

for all" was a major theme of the reform activities around the mathematics curriculum in the US and in Europe in the period 1950–75.

(p. 394)

This positioning establishes *mathematics for all* in four significant ways: (a) it was an idea that transcended U.S. geography; (b) it was an idea that was in operation internationally before it became a core part of the U.S. mathematics education vocabulary in the 1980s and 1990s; (c) it was a major theme; and (d) it was an intellectual project that did not translate to changes in schools.

Keitel's (1987) comments mark *mathematics for all* as a *slogan system* (Apple, 1992). Apple argues that a slogan system is vague enough to encompass many things—as Keitel argues about *mathematics for all*—but not so vague that they offer nothing to those who use them—or they seem impossible. Finally, slogan systems are charming; they have an appeal that no one can deny. *Mathematics for all*, as Freudenthal used it, appealed to the audience because he focused on how the child learns rather than what environment encourages learning; few would argue with the idea that the mode of learning is at least as important as the learning environment. To the point of maintaining enough specificity to make the slogan useful, Keitel (1987) argues that curriculum development aligned with *mathematics for all* in this time period (1950–1975) "aspired to general validity, i.e. to be a 'mathematics for all', with the result that the concrete curricula and programmes that they developed at least *seemed* to be suitable for all" (p. 394). This appearance of general validity led to a situation where entities that established curricula "readily assumed that 'mathematics for all' could be readily achieved through a simple *political* decision" (p. 394). The perception that *mathematics for all* was a simple acquisition gave sufficient specificity to maintain the effective slogan. Hence, Martin's (2003) assessment of *mathematics for all* as a small victory.

Mathematics for all became a cornerstone of the U.S. mathematics education lexicon in the 1980s and 1990s. The rationale behind mathematics for all was that mathematical practices are part of daily life and the mathematical style of thinking is necessary for daily living (Burton, 1992). The approach to *mathematics for all*, however, did not connect as explicitly to the daily lives of many in schools. Instead, curriculum took on a syllabus approach that dated back to the 19th century. Burton (1992) describes the syllabus approach as a belief that mathematics is not efficient to learn "as it mystifies many learners with its limitations in terms of *their* experience and understanding" (p. 162). This mystification means that mathematics is only accessible through a sort of faith walk through the school mathematics curriculum—the curriculum is set out in a logical order and students walk out that order with faith that it will lead to mathematics. Thus, the sequencing becomes critical and supports the case for standardization, which I discuss in the following section.

The Road to Standardization

After the launch of *Sputnik* in 1957, there was a surge of interest in mathematics, science, and foreign language education in the name of national security and international competitiveness (Kerr-Tener, 1987). According to Scandura (1970), *Sputnik* "gave realization to the American people that mathematics education in this country was woefully inadequate" (p. 265). This realization, combined with growing dissent with progressive education strategies (Fey, 1978), catalyzed a flurry of reform activity in mathematics education. There were three key curriculum reform movements that came out of this period: New Math, Back to Basics, and *Standards* movements. Although each of these movements has a distinct history, I do not address the histories of New Math and Back to Basics in depth here. Instead, I discuss them as historical antecedents to standardization as a racial remediation project.

New Math and Back to Basics

The New Math movement of the 1960s and early 1970s was a direct counter to the progressive style of mathematics education that centered on socially relevant applications of mathematics outside the discipline (Rea & Reys, 1971). The New Math intended to build children into mathematicians: "The new math was predicated on the assumption that the intellectual habits of academic mathematicians would be good to cultivate in students" (Phillips, 2015, p. 129). Those who developed New Math curricula virtually ignored anything outside of "pure" mathematics (Usiskin, 1997b) in response to "a demand for highly trained people in mathematics, science, and engineering" (Usiskin, 1997a, p. 63). New Math was short-lived and the explanations for its demise vary. Some blamed it on a failure to equip teachers to meet the demand of a more rigorous curriculum (Zelinka, 1980). Gibney and Karns (1979) argue that the New Math is a case where goals were too ambitious to allow for success resulting in "a waste of time and money" (p. 357). Sebelius (1987) positioned the "math panic" after *Sputnik* as a manufactured crisis that caused a real crisis in mathematics education: "The 'New Math' cure for a nonexistent crisis is now seen as the cause for a real one today" (p. 147).

The Back to Basics movement followed the New Math as the response to the latter's inaccessibility and failure to equip students with basic consumer computation skills (Gibney & Karns, 1979; Walmsley, 2007; Zelinka, 1980). Morris Kline, a mathematics educator at New York University, "was the first and loudest voice" (Kilpatrick, 1997, p. 956) in the campaign for Back to Basics with his 1974 book *Why Johnny Can't Add: The Failure of the New Math* (Fey, 1978; Kilpatrick, 1997). The Back to Basics curriculum relied on an instructional approach reminiscent of the pre-*Sputnik* era, defined by "drill, repetition, and hard work" (Cheek & Castle, 1981, p. 265) rather than problem solving.

There is negligible discussion about Black children in the literature about the New Math and Back to Basics movements. One may attribute this omission to the invisibility of Black children in curriculum discussions at the time. *Brown* brought spotlight to school desegregation, so there was a lot of discussion about *where* Black children should go to school. However, there was near silence about *what* they should learn perhaps because there was a concurrent movement in psychology to prove that Black children were limited in their capacity to learn. In 1969, Jensen published a study arguing that educators who attributed IQ differences across racial groups to environment or testing bias were mistaken and these differences had to be attributed at least partially to genetics. Jensen was not alone in his claims; Herrenstein (1971) and Shockley (1971) also supported these claims. Jensen asserts that his results—and, by extension, those of his colleagues—confirm Edward Thorndike, the most cited psychologist of the 20th century, in his declaration: "In the actual race of life, which is not to get ahead, but to get ahead of somebody, the chief determining factor is heredity" (Thorndike as cited in Jensen, 1969, p. 28). There was a backlash against Jensen's claims (e.g., Gomberg, 1975), but any dissent was not significant enough to keep this way of thinking from informing perceptions of Black children's intelligence and the possibilities for their achievement. In fact, this thinking became the foundation for Herrenstein and Murray's (1994) concept of the bell curve, a model that reflects dominant thinking about race, class, and intelligence.

The *Standards* Movement[6]

In most narratives of the history of education in the United States, the next landmark event of the 1980s is *A Nation at Risk* (National Commission of Excellence on Education, 1983). While most education historians would point to *A Nation at Risk* as a moment similar to *Sputnik* where the nation's attention turned to mathematics and science, mathematics educators who discuss the time see *A Nation at Risk* as a coincidental happening that turned the national spotlight on issues that mathematicians and mathematics educators were already addressing. The NCTM was laying groundwork for what would become the most enduring wave of mathematics education reform, the *Standards* movement. In fact, Shirley Hill, president of NCTM (1978–1980) declared in 1981 that "the decade of the 1980s is a decade for mathematics" (as cited in McLeod et al., 1996, p. 25). John Dossey, NCTM president from 1986 through 1988, described *A Nation at Risk* as "another part of the large national discussion that, I think, promoted the movement towards *Standards* that clearly, more than anything, started a background for curricular change" (Bullock, 2013, p. 86).

Prior to this moment, the NCTM had established a traditionally passive policy position: "Up until the 1970s, many leaders thought that NCTM should not take positions that might be opposed by some of its members" (McLeod et al., 1996, pp. 18–19). The NCTM changed this position with the release of *An Agenda for*

Action in 1980 where the organization offered recommendations about curriculum and teacher professionalism (McLeod et al., 1996; NCTM, 1980). This document was a statement indicating "that NCTM wanted to provide direction to the field, to assert its authority and share its expertise with a higher level of intensity than had been its custom" (McLeod et al., 1996, p. 24). The NCTM's plan to enter the policy landscape also included the *Priorities in School Mathematics* (PRISM) study (NCTM, 1981). This study functions as a barometer for "predicting what curriculum changes might be readily adopted and which ones might meet with resistance" (NCTM, 1981, p. 3). The PRISM study was NCTM's strategy to guard against its efforts meeting the same quick demise as the New Math and Back to Basics movements. By surveying a sample of mathematics teachers, mathematicians, school and district administrators, and parents, the NCTM hoped to set an informed course of action that called upon a broad coalition and would create lasting change in school mathematics curriculum.

Curriculum and Evaluation Standards for School Mathematics (CESSM)

The NCTM's first attempt to offer curriculum standards for K–12 mathematics was the *Curriculum and Evaluation Standards for School Mathematics* (National Council of Teachers of Mathematics ,1989). This document was also the first attempt for a content area to establish national standards. John Dossey recalled that some of NCTM's constituents wanted the organization to censure the Saxon curriculum for its algorithmic focus. "Basically," he said, "it was my position and Joe Crosswhite's [NCTM president, 1984–1986] position that we couldn't censure something unless we said what the standards were that materials should be measured against" (Bullock, 2013, p. 98). The CESSM writers included mathematics teachers, state and local mathematics supervisors, teacher educators, mathematics education researchers, and university mathematicians interested in mathematics education (Olson & Berk, 2001). This group came together to construct a document that would function as a set of standards against which anyone could measure mathematics curricula (Bullock, 2013; Phillips, 2015). Learning from the failures of previous movements, the NCTM opted to create guidelines rather than to write curriculum materials (Phillips, 2015).

The idea that mathematics literacy is necessary for productive citizenship motivated the CESSM. For Klein (2007), the CESSM was a document that "reinforces themes of progressive education by advocating student-centered, discovery learning" with a "strong utilitarian justification" (p. 23). The document reversed the course of the prior Back to Basics movement by deemphasizing rote memorization in the curriculum, but it did not follow the way of the New Math's focus on mathematical structures. Instead, following *An Agenda for Action's* direction, CESSM gave great attention to problem solving. The writers also addressed technology's role in school mathematics. Along with the focus on student-centered learning and technology integration came an avoidance of issues that were more politically charged such as tracking (McLeod et al., 1996). Equity in general received light treatment in the CESSM, but Croom (1997) posits that CESSM had a foundation of *mathematics for all*: "The underlying assumption on which this new vision was based is that changes and improvements in teaching and learning will afford every child equal access to a substantive mathematics education" (p. 1).

After an unprecedented public relations campaign to introduce the idea of content standards to the U.S. education market, the NCTM received significant criticism of this effort. In a column in *Educational Leadership*, Willoughby (1998) wrote: "A document of this size and scope must either be bland, useless or include something to irritate every reader" (p. 82) and this proved to be true. The most cogent critiques came from the research community and from university-based mathematicians. Carnine and Gersten (2000) captured the research community's sentiment by describing the CESSM as one of many examples of the "implementation of a set of practices before any experimental evaluation... a practice that has run rampant within the educational community" (p. 140). It was known that the changes proposed in the CESSM were based on theory rather than empirical research. The Research Advisory Committee of the NCTM (1988) conducted its own inquest and concluded:

> The *Standards* document contains many recommendations, but in general it does not provide a research context for the recommendations, even when such a context is available. Practitioners who advocate adoption and implementation of the *Standards* in their local situations will need to have the research base clarified, since such information will be vital in their efforts to convince administrators and other policy makers that the recommendations are worthwhile.
>
> *(p. 339)*

The committee asserted that the CESSM offered a new vision of school mathematics that warranted a "transformative research agenda" (p. 341) following its implementation.

The second group offering substantive critique of the CESSM was university mathematicians. In the late 1990s, a group of mathematicians, mathematics educators, parents, and others concerned with mathematics education reform as presented in the CESSM created an informal organization and website called *Mathematically Correct* aimed at not only critiquing the burgeoning *Standards* movement, but also acting against the NCTM's reform efforts. Haimo (1998) summarized the disagreement that this group had with the CESSM:

> Troubling to this group is the fact that these standards fall short of providing a reasonable balance. They highlight the applications of everyday

experiences. On the other hand, they fail to emphasize adequately the theoretical aspects that make mathematics a unique and important discipline. In
addition, they do not give enough attention to the development of sound
basic skills.

(p. 46)

Mathematically Correct and like-minded critics based their critique upon many
mathematicians' perception that the NCTM was endorsing "fuzzy math" in place
of rigor but the vitriolic critiques from these groups did not represent the positions of most mathematicians. Some mathematicians on the CESSM writing team
saw this critique as a misunderstanding while others recalled that most of their
colleagues who disagreed with the CESSM did not take political action (Bullock,
2013). Although the Mathematically Correct crowd did not represent a majority,
their ire drew enough attention that the NCTM planned the second *Standards*
document (i.e., the PSSM) differently to address some of their concerns.

Principles and Standards for School Mathematics (PSSM)

NCTM's second attempt to establish curriculum standards came in 2000 with the
Principles and Standards for School Mathematics after 49 states used the CESSM as a
guide for their state curriculum standards (Martin & Berk, 2001). It was clear
from the response to the CESSM that the organization needed to clarify some of
the messaging, to provide an explicit research foundation, and to solicit a broad
range of input. The revision process began with the Commission on the Future
of the Standards, an NCTM committee charged with overseeing the revision
process. The Commission charged the Research Advisory Committee to provide
the empirical foundation for the PSSM by commissioning White papers to
inform the writing group and compiling a research companion to the PSSM.

The writers established a set of six principles—Equity, Curriculum, Teaching,
Learning, Assessment, and Technology—to "describe particular features of high-
quality mathematics education" (NCTM, 2000, p. 11). The principles addressed
issues outside of content that contribute to quality in mathematics education,
which provided additional clarity and direction for those implementing the *Standards*. Some of these issues—namely equity—were explicitly political and con-
troversial. Placing the Equity Principle first in the document was a political
statement that acknowledged that, in order for the *Standards* to be effective for all
students, there had to be explicit attention to equity issues (Bullock, 2013).

Despite the Commission on the Future of the Standards' intentional efforts to
create the PSSM in a process that was transparent and encouraging of input from
all interested parties, the document was not without critique. The member
organizations of the Conference Board of Mathematical Sciences wrote a joint
letter of appreciation that was included in the PSSM (NCTM, 2000, p. xv).
Despite these endorsements, many mathematicians continued to criticize the

work with the same vitriol that occurred after the CESSM. It became clear that some mathematicians, such as those aligned with Mathematically Correct, would never be satisfied with the NCTM's efforts (Bullock, 2013).

Standardization, Equity, and Racial Remediation

The *Standards* began with some interest toward equity. The CESSM (NCTM, 1989) writing team asserts on the first page that "all students need to learn more and often different mathematics, and instruction in mathematics must be significantly revised" (p. 1). Romberg (1998), the leader of the CESSM effort, argues that there are several "key notions" embedded in this statement. The first of the key notions he outlines is: "Teaching mathematics to 'all students' emphasizes the fact that all students need to be mathematically literate if they are to be productive citizens in the twenty-first century. In particular, this includes all underrepresented groups, not just 'talented, white males'" (p. 9). Romberg explains that, in the 1980s, about 40% of students—including a majority of non-White students—stopped at eighth-grade mathematics; another 30% stopped at the second high school mathematics course, which sufficed for general college admission; another 20% stopped with enough to qualify for selective colleges; and 10% stopped with enough to prepare for scientific training in college. He wrote:

> The long-term objective of the reform movement was to change both the percentages (40 percent, 20 percent, 20 percent, and 10 percent) and the racial and gender mix of students in these groups by focusing our work on providing the lower 90 percent of the populations of American students with a reasonable opportunity to learn more mathematics.
>
> *(p. 10)*

This 90% would certainly include Black children and other "disadvantaged students" who "often have been taught the lowest level, most mindless version of basic skills" (Clune, 1998, p. 145), but they were not addressed with the specificity that Grubbs (1941) demanded nearly 60 years earlier.

In 1989, President George H. W. Bush convened U.S. governors for an education summit in Charlottesville, Virginia. At this meeting, the group agreed on setting national educational goals. They hoped that the agreed-upon goals could be reached by 2000, thus the name *America 2000*. In his January 1990 State of the Union address, President Bush delivered an ultimatum: "By the year 2000, U.S. students must be first in the world in math and science achievement" (Long, 2003, p. 947). During his presidency, President Bill Clinton expanded this work from six to eight goals with the *Goals 2000: Educate America Act*. The fourth goal in Goals 2000 echoed the earlier president's charge: "U.S. students will be first in the world in mathematics and science achievement" (Lappan & Wanko, 2003, p. 917). These presidential platforms created a climate that was more amenable to curriculum decision making at the federal level where such decisions had always been in the states' purview. Additionally, these statements reiterate the sense that mathematics achievement has nationalist implications, a message that reverberated beyond *Sputnik, A Nation at Risk,* and the Cold War.

The CESSM and PSSM represented the curriculum change that supported these nationalistic goals. Regardless of NCTM's intentions, the *Standards* were taken up as a syllabus for school mathematics (Bullock, 2013; Burton, 1992). Where, at one time, the syllabus may have been the textbook's table of contents, the *Standards* documents performed that function by reducing mathematics to a manageable core sequence (Hirsch & Coxford, 1997). Adding the principles in the PSSM was a marriage between content and process that guided the reader in both what mathematics they should teach and how constituents should orient themselves toward the content.

Tate (1997b) observed that Goals 2000 precipitated a shift in the federal education policy rhetoric from attending to the educational needs of students who were historically underserved "toward a call for high standards for all students" (p. 674). He argued that, while the focus was different, this shift did not foreclose possibilities for historically underserved students under the *Standards.* However, there were significant accompanying structural changes to be made in fiscal policy (i.e., the financial resources necessary to implement the *Standards* recommendation) and cultural policy (i.e., "what type of pedagogy, curriculum, and assessment practices might students of color and low-SES students negotiate to be successful" [p. 675]) with specific intention toward the support of marginalized students.

Although the *Standards* documents addressed the nation's needs related to improving mathematics performance, they did not resolve the issue of gaps in achievement between Black and White students largely because there was not a concomitant investment in the fiscal and cultural policy that Tate (1997b) mentioned. I argue that this failure is not accidental. Rather, the *Standards* as a whole and the equity discourse that has come from them are racial remediation strategies.

One can view the standardization of mathematics education in at least two ways. First, the *Standards* equalize school mathematics by proposing a consistent core curriculum for all mathematics programs.[7] This means that any student would be exposed to the same mathematics content across their K-12 tenure. Another option is to see standardization as flattening mathematics into an 'American'[8] school mathematics that serves the nation's interests. But this flattening necessarily limits possibilities for Black children's experiences within the standardized system because the 'American' moniker reflects its status as "a white nation" where "white dominance over blacks is natural, right and necessary as well as profitable and satisfying" (Bell, 1976, p. 6). 'American' education is always already a mechanism for maintaining this dominance and for perpetuating anti-Blackness (Dumas, 2016; Ladson-Billings, 1998; Ladson-Billings & Tate, 1995).

Putting these two options together shows standardization as racial remedy. The unification that the *Standards* purport to bring to school mathematics appears as a move toward equity across communities. However, I argue that, in mathematics education, standardization is a means of maintaining mathematics education as White institutional space. Considering how race operates in mathematics education requires first acknowledging that school mathematics is an institution because "it functions as a social structure that requires participation through compulsory schooling, has specific social purposes, and establishes rules governing individual behavior" (Battey, 2013, p. 333). Furthermore, it is a racialized institution. Mathematics' privilege makes it a prime tool of maintaining race-based social stratification and for perpetuating anti-blackness[9]. Participation in mathematics education research, practice, and policy is largely White, and thus heavily influenced by whiteness and anti-blackness, including in research related to equity and social justice (Martin, 2009; 2015). The underlying White racial logic in mathematics education prompts Martin (2008, 2011, 2013; Martin, Rousseau Anderson, & Shah, 2018) to describe mathematics education as "white institutional space." The whiteness that forms mathematics education's core fabric operates as a silent, seemingly innocuous force because "whiteness never has to speak its name, never has to acknowledge its role as an organizing principle in social and cultural relations" (Lipsitz, 1995, p. 369).

Equity discourse, as established formally in the PSSM, is another racial remediation strategy. Equity discourse has become the vehicle through which mathematics education has tried to achieve its *mathematics for all* intentions. The field has responded to this focus by devising strategies to increase performance among student groups through teacher education (e.g., Turner et al., 2012), instruction (e.g., Bartell et al., 2017), policy (e.g., Kitchen, 2003), and curriculum (e.g., Buckley, 2010). Additionally, scholars have suggested ways for the mathematics education research enterprise to address equity through knowledge production (e.g., Diversity in Mathematics Education Center for Learning and Teaching, 2007). Despite the focus on equity in mathematics education research and policy, Black children's mathematics test performance remains below that of White students and Black students remain largely disaffected from mathematics (Berry et al., 2014). While mainstream discourses in mathematics education might argue that this persistent underperformance results from not having found "what works" for Black children, there is a growing contingency of scholars who argue that equity work does not call into question mathematics itself or the ways of thinking about school mathematics that maintain its privilege; therefore, it is a racial remediation strategy (e.g., Bullock, 2017; Gholson & Wilkes, 2017; Martin, 2015). Elsewhere, I argue that extant efforts toward equity are invitations to Black students to take part in the White institutional space of mathematics (Bullock, 2017). This participation is conditional in that the student must embrace Whiteness to experience its full benefit. Thus, equity as racial remedy demonstrates a political agenda around which the mathematics education has rallied in significant numbers without a commitment to racial justice.

Conclusion

In this chapter, I offer a critical race historical counter-story of mathematics education reform to complicate the common historical renderings of these efforts. This history reveals a pattern of failure by the NCTM and the broader mathematics education community to address the need for Black mathematics teachers and learners, even in the face of explicit appeals (e.g., Grubbs, 1941) and a shifting socio-political ethos (e.g., *Brown v. Board of Education*). The inferiority paradigm has remained a consistent thread that frames the curriculum despite manifesting in different ways (e.g., claims of psychological research, achievement gap logic). Therefore, Black children are framed as a problem (cf. Du Bois, 1903/1989) in mathematics education that needs to be solved. Such a resolution comes through the idea of standardization itself as well as through the equity system devised to tinker toward a more equitable school mathematics, both of which are racial remedies. This historical counter-story troubles the idea that contemporary mathematics education reform is a progressive march toward a brighter future. Instead, this historical counter-story problematizes contemporary mathematics education reform as a means to maintain school mathematics as White institutional space through racial remediation.

Notes

1 Bonilla-Silva and Zuberi (2008) define *White logic*:
    White logic, then, refers to a context in which White supremacy has defined the techniques and processes of reasoning about social facts. White logic assumes a historical posture that grants eternal objectivity to the views of elite Whites and condemns the views of non-Whites to perpetual subjectivity; it is the anchor of the Western imagination, which grants centrality to the knowledge, history, science, [mathematics,] and culture of elite White men and classifies "others" as people without knowledge, history, or science, as people with folklore but no culture. (p. 17)
2 Ethel Harris Grubbs graduated from Howard University in 1915 with a degree in mathematics. She later earned a master's degree from Teachers College, Columbia University in 1924. She worked in the Washington, DC public schools for 38 years as a mathematics and physics teacher at Dunbar High School. Dunbar was known for its highly educated teaching staff that has educated multiple students who have earned the Ph.D. in mathematics (Walker, 2014). Grubbs spent the last 3 years of her tenure as the district's supervising director of mathematics. Grubbs was an active member of the NCTM and wrote several pieces for the organization's journals about engagement in mathematics and other topics. She passed away in 1981 at the age of 86. View her obituary in *The Washington Post* at https://www.washingtonpost.com/archive/local/1981/06/26/ethel-h-grubbs-dies/fa1f7d7c-d560-438f-97e3-717caa4dea84/?noredirect=on&utm_term=.67e7ce2a39c2.
3 This article is the published version of the paper that Grubbs read at the national meeting of the NCTM in December 1940.
4 The Journal for Research in Mathematics Education is now considered the flagship journal in mathematics education but its first issue was published in 1970.
5 The NCTM first published The Arithmetic Teacher in 1954. The column "The Work of the National Council" (Fehr, 1956) appears only in the December 1956 issue.
6 I use the phrase "the *Standards* movement" in near alignment with Hiebert (1999):

The phrase "NCTM Standards" of just "Standards" (capitalized [and italicized in this chapter]) will be used for the National Council of Teachers of Mathematics recommendations for K–12 curriculum, teaching, and assessment contained in the initial three-volume set (*Curriculum and Evaluation Standards for School Mathematics* [1989], *Professional Standards for Teaching Mathematics* [1991], and *Assessment Standards for School Mathematics* [1995]) and in the revised volume *Principles and Standards for School Mathematics* (draft, 1998) [published in 2000], all published in Reston, VA by the NCTM. (p. 3)

7 The *Standards* documents did not propose specific content standards for specific grades; they were constructed in grade bands. The idea was that, across a mathematics program, the student should learn all of the content, although the exact sequence might vary.

8 I capitalize 'American' and use it in single quotes to highlight the imperialism inherent in using the word to denote the United States while ignoring other nations in North, Central, and South America.

9 Anti-blackness is a position where it is impossible for one who is Black to be human and that Black people who do attain a degree of humanity do so in a way that denies their blackness (Hudson, 2014). This logic created and supported chattel slavery in the United States where Black slaves were tools for labor or "property of enjoyment" (Hartman & Wilderson, 2003, p. 188) and continues to govern the experience of Black people in the United States.

Acknowledgement

The research presented in this chapter was supported by the National Academy of Education/Spencer Foundation Post-Doctoral Fellowship and the Wisconsin Center for Education Research.

References

Anderson, S. E. (1970). Mathematics and the struggle for Black liberation. *The Black Scholar*, 2(1), 20–27.

Apple, M. W. (1992). Do the standards go far enough? Power, policy, and practice in mathematics education. *Journal for Research in Mathematics Education*, 23(5), 412–431.

Banks, J. A. (1993). The canon debate, knowledge construction, and multicultural education. *Educational Researcher*, 22(5), 4–14.

Bartell, T. G., Wager, A. A., Edwards, A., Battey, D., Foote, M. Q., & Spencer, J. A. (2017). Toward a framework for research linking equitable teaching with the Standards for Mathematical Practice. *Journal for Research in Mathematics Education*, 48(1), 7–21.

Baszile, D. T. (2015). Rhetorical revolution: Critical race counter-storytelling and the abolition of White democracy, *Qualitative Inquiry*, 21(3), 239–249.

Battey, D. (2013). Access to mathematics: "A possessive investment in Whiteness". *Curriculum Inquiry*, 43(3), 332–359.

Bell, D. (1976). Racial remediation: An historical perspective on current conditions. *Notre Dame Law Review*, 52, 5–29.

Bell, D. (1979). Brown v. Board of Education and the interest convergence dilemma. *Harvard Law Review*, 93, 518–533.

Bell, D. (2004a). Brown v. Board of Education: Reliving and learning from our racial history. *University of Pittsburgh Law Review*, 66, 21–33.

Bell, D. (2004b). *Silent covenants: Brown v. Board of Education and the unfulfilled hopes for racial reform*. Oxford, UK: Oxford University Press.

Bell, D. (2005). The unintended lessons in Brown v. Board of Education. *New York Law School Law Review*, 49, 1053–1067.

Berry, R. Q., III, Ellis, M. W., & Hughes, S. (2014). Examining a history of failed reforms and recent stories of success: Mathematics education and Black learners of mathematics in the United States. *Race, Ethnicity and Education*, 17(4), 540–568.

Bonilla-Silva, E., & Zuberi, T. (2008). Toward a definition of White logic and White methods. In T. Zuberi & E. Bonilla-Silva (Eds.), *White logic, White methods: Racism and methodology* (pp. 3–27). Lanham, MD: Rowman & Littlefield.

Buckley, L. A. (2010). Unfulfilled hopes in education for equity: Redesigning the mathematics curriculum in a US high school. *Journal of Curriculum Studies*, 42(1), 51–78.

Bullock, E. C. (2013). *An archaeological/genealogical historical analysis of the National Council of Teachers of Mathematics standards documents* (Unpublished doctoral dissertation). Georgia State University, Atlanta, GA.

Bullock, E. C. (2017). *Equity in mathematics education as an exercise in White benevolence.* Paper presented at the Annual meeting of the American Educational Research Association, San Antonio, TX.

Burton, L. (1992). Evaluating an "entitlement curriculum": Mathematics for all? *The Curriculum Journal*, 3(2), 161–169.

Carnine, D., & Gersten, R. (2000). The nature and roles of research in improving achievement in mathematics. *Journal for Research in Mathematics Education*, 31(2), 138–143.

Carter, R. T., & Goodwin, A. L. (1994). Racial identity and education. *Review of Research in Education*, 20, 291–336.

Cheek, H. N., & Castle, K. (1981). The effects of back-to-basics on mathematics education. *Contemporary Educational Psychology*, 6, 263–277.

Clune, W. (1998). The "standards wars" in perspective. *Teachers College Record*, 100(1), 144–149.

Croom, L. (1997). Mathematics for all students: Access, excellence, and equity. In J. Trentacosta (Ed.), *Multicultural and gender equity in the classroom: The gift of diversity, 1997 yearbook of the National Council of Teachers of Mathematics* (pp. 1–9). Reston, VA: National Council of Teachers of Mathematics.

Delgado, R., & Stefancic, J. (2017). *Critical race theory: An introduction* (3rd ed.). New York, NY: New York University Press.

Diversity in Mathematics Education Center for Learning and Teaching. (2007). Culture, race, power, and mathematics education. In F. K. Lester, Jr. (Ed.), *Second handbook of research on mathematics teaching and learning* (pp. 405–433). Charlotte, NC: Information Age.

Du Bois, W. E. B. (1989). *The souls of Black folk.* New York, NY: Bantam Books. (Original work published in 1903.)

Dumas, M. J. (2016). Against the dark: AntiBlackness in education policy and discourse. *Theory Into Practice*, 55(1), 11–19.

Fehr, H. F. (1956). The work of the National Council. *The Arithmetic Teacher*, 3(6), 252.

Fey, J. T. (1978). Change in mathematics education since the late 1950's—Ideas and realisation: U.S.A. *Educational Studies in Mathematics*, 9(3), 339–353.

Gholson, M. L., & Wilkes, C. E. (2017). (Mis)taken identities: Reclaiming identities of the "collective Black" in mathematics education research through an exercise in Black specificity. *Review of Research in Education*, 41, 228–252.

Gibney, T., & Karns, E. (1979). Mathematics education—1955–1975: A summary of the findings. *Educational Leadership*, 36(5), 356–359.

Gomberg, P. (1975). IQ and race: A discussion of some confusions. *Ethics*, 85(3), 258–266.

Grubbs, E. H. (1941). How the National Council of Teachers of Mathematics may serve negro teachers and how they may serve the council. *The Mathematics Teacher*, 34(6), 251–257.

Gutiérrez, R. (2008). A "gap-gazing" fetish in mathematics education? Problematizing research on the achievement gap. *Journal for Research in Mathematics Education*, 39(4), 357–364.

Gutiérrez, R. (2013). The socio-political turn in mathematics education. *Journal for Research in Mathematics Education*, 44(1), 37–68.

Haimo, D. T. (1998). Are the NCTM standards suitable for systemic adoption? *Teachers College Record*, 100, 45–65.

Harris, C. I. (1993). Whiteness as property. *Harvard Law Review*, 106(8), 1707–1791.

Hartman, S. V., & Wilderson, F. B., III. (2003). The position of the unthought. *Qui Parle*, 13(2), 183–201.

Herrenstein, R. (1971, September). I.Q. *Atlantic Monthly*, 43–64.

Herrenstein, R. J., & Murray, C. (1994). *The bell curve: Intelligence and class structure in American life*. New York, NY: Free Press.

Hiebert, J. (1999). Relationships between research and the NCTM Standards. *Journal for Research in Mathematics Education*, 30(1), 3–19.

Hirsch, C. R., & Coxford, A. F. (1997). Mathematics for all: Perspectives and promising practices. *School Science and Mathematics*, 97(5), 232–241.

Hudson, P. J. (2014). The geographies of Blackness and anti-Blackness: An interview with Katherine McKittrick. *The CLR James Journal*, 20(1–2), 233–240.

Jensen, A. (1969). How much can we boost IQ and scholastic achievement? *Harvard Educational Review*, 39(1), 1–123.

Keitel, C. (1987). What are the goals of mathematics for all? *Journal of Curriculum Studies*, 19(5), 393–407.

Kerr-Tener, J. (1987). Eisenhower and federal aid to higher education. *Presidential Studies Quarterly*, 17(3), 473–485.

Kilpatrick, J. (1997). Confronting reform. *The American Mathematical Monthly*, 104(10), 955–962.

Kitchen, R. (2003). Getting real about mathematics education reform in high-poverty communities. *For the Learning of Mathematics*, 23(3), 16–22.

Klein, D. (2007). A quarter century of US "math wars" and political partisanship. *BSHM Bulletin: Journal of the British Society for the History of Mathematics*, 22, 22–33.

Ladson-Billings, G. (1998). Just what is critical race theory and what's it doing in a nice field like education? *International Journal of Qualitative Studies in Education*, 11(1), 7–24.

Ladson-Billings, G. (2013). Critical race theory—what it is not! In M. Lynn & A. D. Dixson (Eds.), *The handbook of critical race theory in education* (pp. 34–47). New York, NY: Routledge.

Ladson-Billings, G. (2017). "Makes me wanna holler": Refuting the "culture of poverty" discourse in urban schooling. *The Annals of the American Academy of Political and Social Science*, 673(1), 80–90.

Ladson-Billings, G., & Tate, W. F., IV. (1995). Toward a critical race theory of education. *Teachers College Record*, 97(1), 47–68.

Lappan, G., & Wanko, J. J. (2003). The changing roles and priorities of the federal government in mathematics education in the United States. In G. M. Stanic & J. Kilpatrick (Eds.), *A history of school mathematics (Vol. 2)* (pp. 897–930). Reston, VA: National Council of Teachers of Mathematics.

Lipsitz, G. (1995). The possessive investment in Whiteness: Racialized social democracy and the "White" problem in American studies. *American Quarterly*, 47(3), 369–387.

Long, V. M. (2003). The role of state government in the custody battle over mathematics education. In G. M. Stanic & J. Kilpatrick (Eds.), *A history of school mathematics (Vol. 2)* (pp. 931–954). Reston, VA: National Council of Teachers of Mathematics.

Martin, D. B. (2003). Hidden assumptions and unaddressed questions in mathematics for all rhetoric. *The Mathematics Educator*, 13(2), 7–21.

Martin, D. B. (2008). E(race)ing race from a national conversation on mathematics teaching and learning: The National Mathematics Advisory Panel as White institutional space. *The Montana Mathematics Enthusiast*, 5(2&3), 387–398.

Martin, D. B. (2009). Researching race in mathematics education. *Teachers College Record*, 111(2), 295–338.

Martin, D. B. (2011). What does quality mean in the context of White institutional space? In B. Atweh, M. Graven, W. Secada, & P. Valero (Eds.), *Mapping equity and quality in mathematics education* (pp. 437–450). Dordrecht, The Netherlands: Springer.

Martin, D. B. (2013). Race, racial projects, and mathematics education. *Journal for Research in Mathematics Education*, 44(1), 316–333.

Martin, D. B. (2015). The collective Black and Principles to Actions. *Journal of Urban Mathematics Education*, 8(1), 17–23.

Martin, D. B., Rousseau Anderson, C., & Shah, N. (2018). Race and mathematics education. In J. Cai (Ed.), *Compendium for research in mathematics education* (pp. 607–636). Reston, VA: National Council of Teachers of Mathematics.

Martin, W. G., & Berk, D. (2001). The cyclical relationship between research and standards: The case of Principles and Standards for School Mathematics. *School Science and Mathematics*, 101(6), 328–339.

Matthews, W. (1984a). Influences on the learning and participation of minorities in mathematics. *Journal for Research in Mathematics Education*, 15(2), 84–95.

Matthews, W. (Ed.). (1984b). Minorities in mathematics [Special Issue]. *Journal for Research in Mathematics Education*, 15(2).

McLeod, D. B., Stake, R. E., Schappelle, B. P., Mellissinos, M., & Gierl, M. J. (1996). Setting the standards: NCTM's role in the reform of mathematics education. In S. A. Raizen & E. D. Britton (Eds.), *Bold Ventures: Case studies of U.S. innovations in mathematics education (Vol. 3)* (pp. 13–132). Dordrecht, The Netherlands: Kluwer Academic.

National Commission on Excellence in Education. (1983). *A nation at risk: The imperative for educational reform*. Washington, DC: The National Commission on Excellence in Education.

National Council of Teachers of Mathematics. (1980). *An agenda for action: Recommendations for school mathematics of the 1980s*. Reston, VA: National Council of Teachers of Mathematics.

National Council of Teachers of Mathematics. (1981). *Priorities in school mathematics: Executive summary of the PRISM project*. Reston, VA: National Council of Teachers of Mathematics.

National Council of Teachers of Mathematics. (1989). *Curriculum and Evaluation Standards for School Mathematics*. Reston, VA: National Council of Teachers of Mathematics.

National Council of Teachers of Mathematics. (2000). *Principles and Standards for School Mathematics*. Reston, VA: National Council of Teachers of Mathematics.

National Council of Teachers of Mathematics. (2014). *Principles to actions: Ensuring mathematical success for all*. Reston, VA: National Council of Teachers of Mathematics.

Olson, M., & Berk, D. (2001). Two mathematicians' perspectives on standards: Interviews with Judith Roitman and Alfred Manaster. *School Science and Mathematics*, 101(6), 305–309.

Phillips, C. J. (2015). *The new math: A political history*. Chicago, IL: The University of Chicago Press.

Rea, R. E., & Reys, R. E. (1971). Mathematical competencies of negro and non-negro children entering school. *The Journal of Negro Education*, 40(1), 12–16.

Research Advisory Committee of the National Council of Teachers of Mathematics. (1988). NCTM Curriculum and Evaluation Standards for School Mathematics: Responses from the research community. *Journal for Research in Mathematics Education*, 19(4), 338–344.

Romberg, T. A. (1998). NCTM's curriculum and evaluation standards. *Teachers College Record*, 100(1), 8–21.

Scandura, J. M. (1970). A research basis for mathematics education. *The High School Journal*, 53(5), 264–280.

Sebelius, A. E. (1987). Math ed: What's missing? *Science News*, 131(10), 147.

Secada, W. G., & Meyer, M. R. (Eds.). (1989). Needed: An agenda for equity in mathematics education [Special Issue]. *Peabody Journal of Education*, 66(2).

Shockley, W. (1971). Models, mathematics, and the moral obligation to diagnose the origin of negro IQ deficits. *Review of Educational Research*, 41(4), 369–377.

Tate, W. F. (1997a). Critical race theory and education: History, theory, and implications. *Review of Research in Education*, 22, 195–247.

Tate, W. F. (1997b). Race-ethnicity, SES, gender, and language proficiency trends in mathematics achievement: An update. *Journal for Research in Mathematics Education*, 28(6), 652–679.

Tate, W. F., & D'Ambrosio, B. S. (Eds.). (1997). Equity, mathematics reform, and research: Crossing boundaries in search of understanding [Special Issue]. *Journal for Research in Mathematics Education*, 28(6).

Tate, W. F., Ladson-Billings, G., & Grant, C. A. (1993). The Brown decision revisited: Mathematizing social problems. *Educational Policy*, 7(3), 255–275.

Turner, E. E., Drake, C., McDuffie, A. R., Aguirre, J. M., Bartell, T. G., & Foote, M. Q. (2012). Promoting equity in mathematics teacher preparation: A framework for advancing teacher learning of children's multiple mathematics knowledge bases. *Journal of Mathematics Teacher Education*, 15(1), 67–82.

Usiskin, Z. (1997a). Applications in the secondary school mathematics curriculum: A generation of change. *American Journal of Education*, 106(1), 62–84.

Usiskin, Z. (1997b). Reforming the third R: Changing the school mathematics curriculum—An introduction. *American Journal of Education*, 106(1), 1–4.

Valero, P. (2007). A socio-political look at equity in the school organization of mathematics education. *ZDM*, 39(3), 225–233.

Walker, E. N. (2014). *Beyond Banneker: Black mathematicians and the paths to excellence*. Albany: State University of New York Press.

Walmsley, A. L. E. (2007). *A history of mathematics education during the twentieth century*. Lanham, MD: University Press of America.

Willoughby, S. S. (1998). Liberating standards for mathematics from NCTM. *Educational Leadership*, 46(2), 82.

Zelinka, M. (1980). The state of mathematics in our schools. *The American Mathematical Monthly*, 87(6), 428–432.

6

USING CRITICAL RACE THEORY TO UNPACK THE BLACK MATHEMATICS TEACHER PIPELINE

Toya Jones Frank

Introduction

One has to look no further than the news cycles over the last two years to witness the barrage of articles about the urgency to recruit and retain more Black teachers (e.g., Boisrond, 2017; Staples, 2017). The National Council of Supervisors of Mathematics (NCSM) in collaboration with mathematics education organization TODOS (2016), cited recruiting mathematics teachers of color as an actionable step toward a "just, equitable, and sustainable system of mathematics education for all children" (p. 1). This stance on diversifying the teacher labor market is a step toward reaching their desired end, yet mathematics education researchers have not adequately addressed methods of analysis for examining issues related to mathematics teachers of color. Further, race and racism in teacher education broadly (Milner et al., 2013), and in mathematics education in particular, need extensive theorizing with respect to the staffing challenge of mathematics education if the field is to meaningfully respond to the call of NCSM and TODOS. Hanson and Quintero (2016) noted that "achieving a teacher workforce that is as diverse as the student body it serves will require exceptionally ambitious patches to fix the leaky pipeline into and out of the teaching profession, and must include a broader set of actors than just school principals and districts' HR offices" (para. 8). Using the tenets of critical race theory (CRT) to illuminate staffing issues that may not be at the center of either discourse about recruitment or retention, with respect to subject specificity, the salience of race, and permanence of racism is one ambitious patch to this phenomenon.

As one of the leading contemporary researchers in mathematics education with respect to race, Martin (e.g., 2000, 2009, 2013, 2015) has made tremendous contributions to the field in theorizing how race and racialized experiences impact Black students as mathematics learners. Learning mathematics is a racialized experience influenced by multi-level external forces (Martin, 2000), meaning that students often benefit from or are limited by how their mathematics ability, predicated often on standardized achievement, is perceived based on larger structural forces and societal messages. These messages often place Black students at the lowest rung of mathematics achievement. As a corollary, they are perceived as having limited mathematics ability and are positioned for limited opportunities in mathematics. I suggest that teaching mathematics can be conceptualized in a similar fashion. Due to social, historical, political, and cultural forces, Black mathematics teachers at particular intersections (e.g., racial, socioeconomic, linguistic) experience teaching mathematics differently than those who benefit from the unearned privileges associated with Whiteness (Clark et al., 2009). However, little research captures the uniqueness of these experiences.

In this chapter, I discuss how CRT has explanatory power for understanding issues related to Black mathematics teachers at significant points along the teacher pipeline. I draw on Solórzano (1997) who queried, "What forms does racism take in teacher education and how are these forms used to maintain the subordination of [Black mathematics teachers]?" (p. 8). I begin this chapter with a brief overview of a small body of literature that specifically focuses on Black mathematics teachers' racialized experiences, including research that I recently conducted and a study that is in progress. Then, I provide a brief summary of CRT and its tenets that are central to the development of a Black mathematics teacher cyclical pipeline model that I present. I use each tenet to analyze how race and racism position Black mathematics teachers who are in the teaching pipeline as well as factors that may lead to their retention or attrition. It is important to note that this work is interdisciplinary, and mathematics education has much to learn from other fields within and outside of education. Thus, I draw on research in science education, teacher education, education policy, and legal scholarship to raise parallel and related issues in mathematics education. I conclude by providing implications that result from this analysis and a call for reimagining mathematics teacher education through a CRT lens.

Researcher Positionality

I believe that it is important to share my positionality with respect to Black mathematics teachers. Doing research about and with Black mathematics teachers is personal and professional. Prior to becoming a mathematics teacher educator, I was a high school mathematics teacher and department chair for over a decade. As a Black woman who taught mathematics, supervised mathematics teachers, and now prepares them as a teacher educator, I have numerous first-hand accounts of how race and racism shape the professional experiences of Black mathematics teachers. Like the teachers I have interviewed and worked with over the years, I know what it is like to have your intelligence questioned. I have experienced veiled, racist microaggressions from parents. I have felt the frustration of being interrupted from teaching and asked to discipline Black students despite a lack of relationship with them.

The studies of my co-authors and I that are highlighted in this chapter are informed by my personal and professional experiences. The findings from Frank et al. (2018) were interpreted from interviews with Black pre-service and in-service mathematics teachers that our research team collected from winter 2016 until spring 2018 with 12 K-12 mathematics teachers from across the United States and 12 Black pre-service teachers at a Historically Black University about how race and racism shaped their practice. Some salient findings from this work included: (a) Black mathematics teachers bring knowledge of community wealth (Yosso, 2005) to their mathematical teaching practice; (b) they often build fictive kinship relationships (Brockenbrough, 2012; Dixson, 2003; Dixson & Dingus, 2008) with their students and use them to bridge to mathematical thinking; (c) they believe their content and pedagogical skills are often overlooked by other teachers and administrators; and (d) their sense of mission for uplifting Black students and their communities remain central to their work. This research informs recruitment and retention literature, as it highlights how race and racism are often under-examined in policy literature. Further, we implore mathematics education stakeholders to listen to and learn with Black mathematics teachers to improve mathematics teacher education and policy.

The second study referenced in this chapter is ongoing and funded by the National Science Foundation (Frank & View, 2016). It includes oral history interviews with retired Black mathematics teachers who taught pre- and post-de jure segregation. To date, we have interviewed 13 Black retired mathematics teachers who taught from the 1950s to the early 2000s in the Washington, D.C. area and Atlanta, Georgia. In this work, my research team and I are building an argument about the intractability of racism for Black mathematics teachers and how it negatively affects their trajectories in the profession. We are finding that the same challenges retired teachers cited in their work are similar, and in some cases identical, to the challenges faced by currently-practicing teachers in the Frank et al. (2018) research as noted above. In short, the overarching goal of both projects is to better understand how Black mathematics teachers' racialized experiences shape their professional lives to shed light on how we recruit and retain, but also to learn how mathematics education can center Black mathematics teachers and rethink racist practices in the field.

Relevant Literature

In this section, I briefly highlight literature that speaks directly to the experiences of Black mathematics teachers. Research about Black teachers who teach mathematics exists in the broader body of literature on Black teachers, but I highlight research in this section that considered Black teachers with subject specificity.

Black mathematics teachers' pedagogy and teaching experiences remain understudied, but a small body of contemporary literature in the field points to the promise of learning from their work. For example, Gershenson, et al. (2015) found that Black teachers have significantly higher expectations of Black students than non-Black teachers. These findings are notable in that teacher expectations lay the groundwork for students' trajectories of mathematics achievement (Clark et al., 2013a; Martin, 2007). Further, other researchers have highlighted how shared cultural referents play out in mathematics classrooms, and these works push back against the culture-free notion of mathematics education. Some of these include:

- *Acknowledgement of the racialized experiences of learning mathematics* (Clark et al., 2013a; Clark et al., 2013b; Frank, 2013; McGee, 2014; Presmeg, 2000);
- *Use of community-based knowledge during instruction* (Davis et al., 2013; Frank, 2013; Gillen, 2014); and
- *Use of shared cultural and linguistic practices* (Evans & Leonard, 2013; Frank, 2018; Jett, 2013; Johnson et al., 2013).

In addition to these studies, in my team's most recent research with Black mathematics pre-service and in-service teachers across the United States (Frank et al., 2018), we found that Black teachers, and in particular those prepared at Historically Black Colleges and Universities (HBCUs), brought important divergent lenses to the content itself, noting that the mathematical ideas of pre-service and practicing mathematics teachers of African descent, ideas that often highlight the contributions of the African diaspora, are often omitted during mathematics education fieldwork and methods courses.

The current news cycle articles referenced earlier in the chapter all include the query "Where are the Black teachers?" This question is even more difficult to answer with respect to specific subjects like mathematics. Neil's (2016) groundbreaking analysis of the 2011–2012 Student and Staff Survey data estimated that Black secondary mathematics teachers are only 0.33% of all teachers and approximately 6% of all secondary mathematics teachers. The majority of Black male mathematics teachers (56%) were in high schools, and the majority of Black female teachers were in middle grades (46%). Further, Neil's analysis determined that Black mathematics teachers were represented across more than 40 states, but the largest concentrations of Black mathematics teachers were in the southeast in states such as Georgia, Louisiana, and Mississippi. This could be related to the concentrations of HBCUs located in these states, as HBCUs comprise only 3% of the nation's colleges and universities, but they produce about 50% of all Black teachers (Fenwick, 2016).

Though subject-specific research of Black teachers is limited, the existing body of research reveals that Black teachers bring important and hard-to-measure resources to mathematics teaching. More research about and with Black mathematics teachers throughout the pipeline, as well as with those who have exited, is key to understanding their diminishing presence in mathematics education.

CRT and The Black Mathematics Teacher Pipeline

Developing a Black Mathematics Teacher Pipeline Framework

CRT in education (Ladson-Billings & Tate, 1995) provides a powerful theoretical approach for examining the Black mathematics teacher pipeline, which includes pre-service preparation, recruitment, retention, and attrition. In this chapter, I use CRT tenets, including the critique of liberalism, Whiteness as property, inter-sectionality, interest convergence, and the permanence of racism to highlight how each tenet is useful for analyzing each of these critical points on the Black mathematics teacher pipeline. Figure 6.1 lays out an initial framework for repre-senting the interplay between the tenets and points along the pipeline. To be clear, I am not asserting that the tenets I use at each point are the only tenets at play. Instead, I use one tenet at each point to highlight how CRT is a viable and necessary theoretical framing to unpack issues related to the Black mathematics teacher pipeline.

Other models of teacher diversity pipelines (e.g., U.S. Department of Educa-tion, 2016b) have used a funnel metaphor to describe how the number of teacher candidates and practicing teachers dwindle as they move through the pipeline. I have chosen to model the Black mathematics teacher pipeline as cyclical in nature. I use a cyclical representation for two primary reasons. First, this model represents the revolving door of Black mathematics teachers entering and leaving the profession (Ingersoll & May, 2011; Neil, 2016), wherein teacher attrition requires the pipeline cycle to restart at teacher preparation. Second, the cyclical nature of the model describes the periodic nature of teacher diversity conversa-tions and concerns. The conversations about preparation, recruitment, and

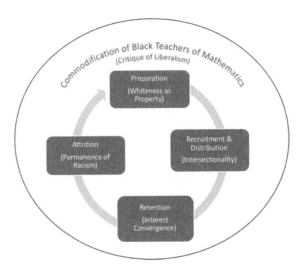

FIGURE 6.1 Commodification of Black Teachers of Mathematics

retention of Black teachers in the workforce ebb and flow over time. Despite the ebb and flow, I assert that all of these conversations can be traced to racist ideologies that are often tacit, yet rampant, in teacher education broadly, and mathematics teacher education specifically. Researchers have been examining how to recruit and maintain a racially and ethnically diverse teaching force since the 1980s (e.g., Cole, 1986), and with each passing decade, one can point to research that continued (and still continues) to query not only "Where are the Black teachers?" but also "What are the turnover factors for these teachers?" I posit that these are fair questions to pose, but the answers that are frequently provided via policy documents are the result of overwhelming uncritical analyses that ignore the permanence of racism in the lives of Black mathematics teachers and the structures that uphold their limited and declining presence in the teacher pipeline.

Tenets of Critical Race Theory

CRT has its origins in the legal scholarship of Derrick Bell (1980) who is considered the "Father of CRT" (Ladson-Billings & Tate, 2016). In education, the seminal work of Drs. Gloria Ladson-Billings and William Tate (1995) laid the foundation for using these theories to unpack the effects of racism in the field. CRT rests on the premise that racism is endemic, pervasive, and is normalized through social and institutional structures and practices in public spaces such as schools (DeCuir & Dixson, 2004; Ladson-Billings, 1998, 2013; Ladson-Billings & Tate, 1995; Milner, 2008, 2017). CRT tenets include: (a) critique of liberalism (DeCuir & Dixson, 2004); (b) Whiteness as property (Dixson & Rousseau Anderson, 2018, Harris, 1993); (c) intersectionality (Crenshaw, 1989; 1993; Ladson-Billings, 2013); (d) interest convergence (Delgado, 2002; Milner 2008, 2017); and (e) the permanence of racism (Ladson-Billings, 1998). These tenets hold explanatory power for understanding how race and racism shape mathematics teacher education at critical points along the Black mathematics teacher pipeline.

Additionally, CRT privileges experiential knowledge through the practice of counter-storytelling, or describing one's reality through sharing personal encounters (Ladson Billings, 1998; Ladson Billings & Tate, 1995). Solórzano and Yosso (2002) explained that counter-stories are created from: (a) the data gathered from the research process itself; (b) the existing literature on the topic(s); (c) professional experiences; and (d) personal experiences (p. 34). Given this description of counter-stories, I present this chapter as counter-story to the Black mathematics teacher narrative from the perspective of a Black researcher who once walked in their shoes and who still faces similar challenges as a teacher educator. I use a combination of existing literature, personal and professional experiences, and findings from past and ongoing work to provide a more complete picture of recruiting and retaining a more diverse mathematics teaching force with respect to race and racism.

In the following sections, I describe the model I put forth by discussing how each critical point on the Black mathematics teacher pipeline lends itself to analysis using one of the tenets of CRT and relevant literature from mathematics education and related fields.

Commodification of Black teachers and the Critique of Liberalism

Figure 6.1 identifies critical points along the Black mathematics teacher pipeline. All of these points are situated within the pervasiveness of the ideology of liberalism, which has been critiqued by CRT scholars (e.g., DeCuir & Dixson, 2004; Ladson-Billings, 1998). In CRT, the critique of liberalism includes a rejection of tenets that are pervasive in liberal ideology, including neutrality regarding race and the way that this neutrality normalizes Whiteness with a faulty underlying assumption of equality and meritocracy (Ladson-Billings, 1998). This assumption establishes a false premise that all citizens have equal rights and opportunities to gain access to jobs, schools, etc. These liberal discourses and ideologies render everyone else as "other" (Borrero et al., 2012; Kumashiro, 2000), thus commodifying Black mathematics teachers, i.e., treating them as objects of trade rather than a valuable human resource in the education system, through: (a) the ahistorical ways that recruitment and retention of "diverse" mathematics teachers is taken up in contemporary research; and (b) the pervasive, yet limited, race-matching rationale for why Black mathematics teachers are needed in mathematics education (e.g., the *demographic imperative* discussed in Achinstein et al., 2010; Egalite et al., 2015).

Ahistoricity

Recruiting and retaining Black mathematics teachers is often narrated in an ahistorical fashion and discussed as solely a contemporary issue. However, one cannot understand the plight of Black mathematics teachers without examining the historical context of Black mathematics teachers in public schools (Clark et al., 2013b). Critical race theorists note the *Brown v. Board of Education* decision as a pivotal moment in the decline of the population of Black teachers (Bell, 1980; King, 1993; Ladson-Billings, 1999). To highlight how *Brown* impacted the Black mathematics teacher workforce, I turn my attention to Washington, D.C., the site of current research I am conducting with fellow researchers about the impact desegregation had on the lives and careers of retired Black mathematics teachers.

Walker (2014) noted that Washington, D.C. is an important locale to conduct research with and about Black students and teachers in mathematics because most early Black mathematicians have roots in the area. Black citizens in cities like Washington, D.C. had set up thriving centers of education for Black students. In fact, many of the high school mathematics educators in D.C. schools had terminal degrees from prestigious universities but taught mathematics at the high school level due to a scarcity of higher education mathematics positions for Black scholars, a fact corroborated by research (Frederick & View, 2009; Walker, 2014) and the personal narratives of participating retired Black mathematics teachers who taught pre- and post-desegregation in our current ongoing research (Frank & View, 2016). As schools began to slowly integrate, thousands of Black teachers were displaced or demoted, including teachers at the secondary level who were already underemployed (D'Amico et al., 2017; Fairclough, 2004; Milner & Howard, 2004). D'Amico and her colleagues noted, "Black teachers ... were wiped away as courts mandated the integration of the nation's school children but said nothing of the teacher labor force, effectively diminishing the *demand* for Black teachers" (p. 5).

Connecting the historical to the contemporary, D'Amico et al. (2017) summarized the contemporary decline of Black teachers as a demand issue and a reversion to discriminatory hiring practices. They noted that most contemporary research on recruiting and retaining Black teachers focuses primarily on the supply side of the argument, or how to increase the number of Black teachers who enter and remain in the teaching force. In their study of teacher hiring trends within a large suburban school district, D'Amico and her colleagues found that even when Black teachers have the same credentials as their non-Black counterparts, they are hired at half the rate of their colleagues. Less emphasis has been placed on discriminatory hiring practices that have and may still be preventing many employable Black teachers, including mathematics teachers, from joining and remaining in the profession.

Our recent study (Frank et al., 2018) corroborated this very phenomenon happening to Black teachers in the schools where they were teaching at the time of the interviews. For example, one teacher noted the "lip service" that her principal paid to diversify the mathematics department in her school, which was predominately White and continuing to shift in that direction. She shared that as the school's surrounding community continued to gentrify, Black teachers were routinely passed over for jobs, including Black mathematics teachers who had knowledge of the community because they began their careers as instructional aides in the school. This example and others shared via these teachers' interviews highlight D'Amico et al.'s (2017) point that perhaps more attention should be focused at how neutral language around fairness in teacher hiring and districts' public commitments to diversity are skewed by inherently discriminatory hiring practices. This is particularly important in mathematics education where Black secondary teachers are only about 6% of the total workforce of middle and high school teachers (Neil, 2016).

The Diversity Imperative

Most often, the need for Black teachers is rooted in what many would consider "good" intentions. Numerous policy documents that argue for the hiring and retention of Black teachers are rooted in arguments that include: (a) responding to the racial homogeneity of the profession (e.g., the "Over 80% of teachers are

White women"); (b) the demographic mismatch between students of color and White teachers; and (c) the need for Black teachers to serve as role models. Much of how Black teachers are positioned in teacher diversity research and policy rests on commodifying Black teachers. In other words, educational stakeholders who are calling for teacher diversity often do so for race-matching purposes, perpetuating popular thinking such as, "X% of our students are Black; so, X% of our teachers should be Black."

Even at the pre-service level, accrediting bodies such as the Council for the Accreditation of Educator Preparation (CAEP) require teacher licensure programs to set and meet arbitrary metrics related to pre-service teacher diversity (Khalil & Brown, 2015). Further, these programs have to create plans for recruiting a more diverse pre-service teaching population while simultaneously holding onto interests that are unbeneficial to Black pre-service teachers. Such interests limit the numbers of Black teachers entering the mathematics teaching profession as well as maintain status quo and uphold the ideology of Whiteness through processes such as testing (Nettles et al., 2011; Petchauer, 2014; Petchauer et al., 2018) and curricular mandates.

Recruiting more Black mathematics teachers into the field is warranted, but the current demographic, role modeling, and the liberal race-matching arguments provided as a rationale for recruitment are insufficient. Inherent in the race-matching perspective is the faulty notion that the primary solution to the systemic denial of meaningful mathematics education for Black students is hiring more Black teachers, and it is not (Martin, 2007). Black teachers, like most teachers, are often prepared in teacher education programs that reproduce the status quo (Brown, 2014; Sleeter, 2017). They then largely work in school districts that reinforce this line of thinking by promoting reductive forms of mathematics education that conflate learning with high-stakes standardized assessment results (Diamond & Spillane, 2004; Valli et al., 2008; Watanabe, 2008). Further, race-matching disregards the notion that Black teachers are not just important in the lives and academic development of Black students; they are important for non-Black students' development and achievement as well. For example, Cherng and Halpin (2016) found that Black and non-Black students had more favorable perceptions of Black teachers on measures that included having high expectations, providing clear explanations of content, and supporting their efforts.

Like teacher diversity, recruiting mathematics teachers has been a longstanding issue in teacher education. Secondary mathematics frequently shows up at the top of the list of critical shortage areas of teaching (Dee & Goldhaber, 2017). Similar to teacher diversity, a leading argument for increasing the numbers of teachers going in to secondary mathematics is also grounded in commodification. For instance, many point to maintaining and dominating global competitiveness in the future as the reasons for finding qualified mathematics teachers (National Math & Science Initiative, 2016; U.S. Department of Education, 2016a), with little thought of how mathematics and mathematics education have so much more to offer students and the world and vice versa. A global competitiveness argument strips away the importance of *people* in mathematics (Gutiérrez, 2012) and reifies a dehumanized view of mathematics and mathematics education (Gutiérrez, 2018; Lawler, 2016).

Given both the need to bring more Black teachers into the field and more mathematics teachers into secondary education, providing nuanced explanations as to *why* diversifying the field beyond commodification is important. Further, the conversation regarding why Black mathematics teachers either do not enter or choose to leave must include overlooked sociocultural and sociopolitical factors, including teachers' racialized experiences with mathematics and with teaching the content. Therefore, harmful liberal discourses that are ahistorical and position teachers as commodities must be critiqued and dismantled.

Mathematics Pre-service Teacher Preparation and Whiteness as Property

I use the Whiteness as property tenet to illustrate how Black mathematics preservice teachers are impacted by racism at their entry into the Black mathematics teacher pipeline in Figure 6.1. The Whiteness as property tenet states that those who are identified as White are guaranteed rights that are equal to, if not more valuable than, material resources that position them in power (Harris, 1993). Often, these rights are so inherently normalized, they are difficult to recognize (Milner, 2017). It is also important to note that Whiteness is not simply a fixed characteristic of a particular group of people; instead, it is "a mindset, world view, positioning, belief system, and epistemology that governs and shapes the ways in which people and groups think, teach, practice, study, analyze and act" (Milner, 2017, p. 300). Formal mathematics content knowledge and highly-regarded pedagogical practices can be considered property in mathematics education because they operate in a similar fashion to Whiteness, meaning that success with mathematics content and desired reform-minded pedagogical practices frequently result in unearned privileges for those who possess such knowledge (Gutiérrez, 2017; Martin, 2015; Rubel, 2017). Often, access to content knowledge and reform-minded pedagogy aid in the perpetuation of the very forms of inequity that they purport to ameliorate. Thus, access to this knowledge base is viewed as access to property of the intellectual sort (Mensah & Jackson, 2018). Further, mathematics education can be considered what Martin (2013, 2015) and Joseph, Haynes, and Cobb (2015) call White institutional space, as it disregards the voices, needs, and perspectives of participants who do not align with White ideologies and ways of knowing and doing. This mind-set has operated as a tool of oppression and continues to do so in spaces like mathematics classrooms (Battey, 2013).

As an extension, mathematics teacher education also operates as Whiteness and should be considered as White institutional space. The mind-sets and ideologies of

Whiteness and White privilege that pervade mathematics teacher education have material consequences (Battey & Leyva, 2016), including what we provide to Black pre-service mathematics teachers. Those of us in mathematics teacher education must contend with what constitutes "good" mathematics education and for whom it is good. We must also "confront an ideology of Whiteness" (Mensah & Jackson, 2018, p. 4) that is extended to mathematics and grapple with what Bullock (2017) described as *STEM as property*. Further, at the teacher preparation stage, we must acknowledge how this ideology has limited the numbers of Black college students who can elect to study mathematics in college due to the systemic barriers of K-12 mathematics education, like limited access to advanced mathematics in predominantly Black schools (Toldson & Lewis, 2017).

Critical scholars argue that teacher education programs and the teaching profession are designed to meet the needs of White teachers (Brown, 2014), and yet fail to prepare them to take on the complexities of race and racism in their teaching (e.g., Picower, 2009; Sleeter, 2017). The same can be said of mathematics teacher education, wherein the structures that create inequitable access and achievement in K-12 mathematics classrooms are perpetuated, intentionally or unintentionally, in pre-service mathematics teacher education through sorting and filtering structures like standardized testing requirements (e.g., Nettles et al., 2011; Petchauer, 2014), Black students' isolating experiences in mathematics departments (McGee, 2014; Presmeg, 2000), little acknowledgement of alternative ways of knowing and doing mathematics among Black pre-service teachers (Frank et al., 2018), and numerous other discriminating practices inherent in teacher education (Meacham, 2000).

Further, we must rethink whose experiences are centered in mathematics education research. Virtually all studies in our research team's query that addressed the needs of mathematics pre-service teacher educators either centered on White teacher candidates, did not note or consider the race and ethnicity of the candidates, or did not consider how race impacts Black teachers' dispositions, perceptions, beliefs, attitudes, or values—a similar finding of Cochran-Smith et al. (2016). In fact, when my research team and I conducted a literature search for mathematics education-specific research about Black pre-service teachers, the search yielded only one contemporary study in a peer-reviewed journal (McGee, 2014) that explicitly focused on the needs and perspectives of Black pre-service mathematics teachers with respect to subject area, and not Black teachers in larger studies who taught mathematics. This finding was troubling considering the only other work of this nature we found in our search was Presmeg's (2000) study of Black secondary pre-service mathematics teachers that was conducted nearly 20 years ago. Drawing on research in science education, Mensah and Jackson (2018) argued that teacher educators in STEM-related education must:

> understand the ways in which access to content and knowledge are either granted or denied and question how teacher education supports the status quo in many regards by not critiquing teacher education curriculum,

knowledge, or pedagogy to make them more relevant to students and Teachers of Color.

(p. 4)

In other words, we, as mathematics teacher educators, must do the difficult work of reflecting upon whether we are encouraging teachers to perpetuate the structures of White privilege that are commonly present in our current conceptualizations of what mathematics is, the presentation of mathematics content, and study of it through research. And then we must reflect upon *why* we do this and *how* we go about disrupting this pattern to generate research that is intentional in highlighting Black pre-service teachers' needs and perspectives and to provide teacher candidates with a mathematics teacher education experience that does not privilege and center Whiteness.

Recruitment and Distribution of Black Mathematics Teachers and Intersectionality

Intersectionality requires that researchers examine systemic issues of race alongside, gender and its performances and expressions, sexuality, social class, nationality, and a myriad of other systems of oppression or privilege in various settings (Crenshaw, 1989, 1993; Delgado & Stefancic, 2001; Ladson-Billings, 2013). Race structures the lives of Black people in ways that often make it difficult to parse apart how multiple and overlapping systems of oppression impact lived experiences, and yet this work is necessary (Crenshaw 1989; 1993). Black people across the diaspora share a collective Black experience, *and,* simultaneously, the Black experience is multifaceted and diverse—thus, intersectional. CRT calls for the acknowledgement of shared experiences of people of color, but not in unsophisticated ways that essentialize (Ladson-Billings, 2013), thus the intersectionality tenet of the theory is useful for analyzing how multiple systems of oppression, and in particular the intersection of race, class, sex, and gender and its performance position Black male and female mathematics teachers at the recruitment and distribution point of the teacher pipeline. An intersectional lens points to how narrow views of the relationship building practices of Black teachers results in simplified explanations for their need to be recruited into the field and how they are distributed across schools.

Essentializing Black Male Teachers

Intersectionality provides a useful tool for examining how Black male teachers are positioned in the teacher recruitment conversation in mathematics education. A burgeoning body of research points to the need for Black male teachers as well as their unique perspectives (Brockenbrough, 2012, 2015; Lynn, 2002, 2006, Woodson & Pabon, 2016), pedagogical practices (Brown, 2009; Ross, et al., 2016), and challenges (Bristol & Mentor, 2018; Bryan &

Williams, 2017; Pabon, 2016). An overarching theme in these articles is the assumption that Black male teachers are desired in education as role models to bring a sense of discipline and order to the educational experiences of Black students, and in particular the experiences of Black boys.

These studies are salient to mathematics education. In fact, the management of Black bodies through discipline practices, which will be discussed in detail later in this chapter, was a consistent theme in research of Black mathematics teachers as well, whether portrayed as firm disciplinarians (e.g., Frank et al., 2018) or employing "cool" Black males (Davis et al., 2013) to manage Black student behavior. Asa, a participant in Frank et al.'s study, noted that his academic success with Black boys was frequently overshadowed by other teachers' need for him to "straighten out" the Black and Latinx boys in his middle school. Implicit in this assumption of Black male teachers as "supermen" (Pabon, 2016), is a fixed and narrow perception of Black masculinity (Woodson & Pabon, 2016) that does not acknowledge how multiple systems intersect and impact the lived experiences and identities of Black male teachers. Additionally, the image of Black teachers, especially Black male teachers, as hyper-masculine and tough love saviors of Black boys is damaging in that it renders Black men as monolithic and ignores the structural inequalities inherent in schooling that they did not create, nor can one group of people fix.

The Double-Edged Sword of Kinship and its Impact on Black Female Teachers

While the pressure to serve as disciplinarians is typically discussed as burdensome to Black male teachers (e.g., Brockenbrough, 2012, 2015), Black female teachers also discussed similar challenges (Frank et al., 2018), and intersectionality helps to explain how their role in disciplining students is often couched in the language of fictive kinship. Black women in teaching have often been described as *othermothers* in school settings, i.e., "those engaged in cultural traditions of shared mothering responsibilities, with attention to the collective well-being" (Dixson & Dingus, 2008, p. 810). Othermothering is both social and political, particularly in mathematics classrooms where Black teachers have been documented as using their notions of care (Bartell, 2011) and warm-demander (Ware, 2006) mothering styles as a leverage point for productive mathematical practice (Frank et al., 2018). Similar to the oversimplified notion of Black male teachers as "fixers" through tough love and accountability, this portrayal of Black women teachers is also dangerous if used as a proxy schools and districts to neglect the systemic barriers and challenges of mathematics education that prevent Black students from full participation on their own terms. In other words, othermothering and other fictive kinship ties can become double-edged swords. These static portrayals of Black men and women in mathematics education leave no space for possibilities of other gender expressions as meaningful and needed in mathematics classrooms. They also set Black teachers up as needed solely for management purposes, which strips them of their expertise as mathematics pedagogues (Clark et al., 2013a).

Mathematics Teacher Retention and its Relationship to Interest Convergence

Interest convergence is a tenet of CRT that is useful for talking about how retaining Black mathematics teachers can be viewed as loss–gain relationships (DeCuir & Dixson, 2004) between teachers and education leaders. Milner (2017) described interest convergence as the following: "racial equality and equity for people of color will be pursued and advanced only when they converge with the preferences, interests, needs, expectations, and ideologies of White people or those in the majority" (p. 296). Gillborn (2013) noted the role of class in interest convergence, highlighting that interest convergence will always privilege the White middle and upper middle-class and that one cannot assume homogeneity of White people and their interests. In terms of the ideas presented in this chapter, interest convergence ultimately means gains for Black students and teachers are most likely to materialize when they align with the self-interests of those who traditionally hold power in educational settings, i.e., school and district leadership.

Much of this paper has addressed how Black teachers have not historically benefitted from teaching mathematics; however, those in the profession cite the often intangible and altruistic benefits of teaching, which result in benefits for both Black mathematics teachers and their school districts and schools. Black mathematics teachers' decisions to stay in schools despite the challenges provide employment opportunities for Black teachers, fulfill their sense of mission, *and* do so without disrupting the status quo of maintaining Whiteness (DeCuir & Dixson, 2004) in mathematics education—hence the "loss–gain" nature of interest convergence.

Black teachers are more likely to teach in urban schools with higher concentrations of students of color and higher rates of student-level poverty than their non-Black counterparts, a finding in the seminal works of King (1993) and Foster (1997) that still holds true contemporarily (Achinstein et al., 2010), especially in the case of mathematics teachers (Neil, 2016). According to Neil, Black mathematics teachers are becoming more and more concentrated in urban charter schools that serve large populations of Black students who are often experiencing poverty. These factors are traditionally noted as turnover factors, or factors that likely lead to teacher attrition (Ingersoll & May, 2011; King, 1993; Liu et al., 2008). However, Ingersoll and May found that challenging conditions such as urbanicity, school poverty level, and high concentrations of Black students did not predict Black teacher retention or turnover.

Analyzing Ingersoll and May's finding using the tenet of interest convergence, I point to research that indicates that Black mathematics teachers are frequently retained in the field based on their sense of mission for teaching mathematics to Black students (e.g., Clark et al., 2013a, Davis et al., 2013; Johnson et al., 2013). In other words, their personal interest in community uplift through providing access to mathematical content serves as a critical retention factor. Therefore, interest convergence may help researchers to theorize what Black teachers gain in mathematics teaching profession as they move through the Black mathematics teacher pipeline.

A constant thread across interviews with Black mathematics teachers in my work and substantiated in the literature is their pride in and cultivation of their close relationships with their Black students, some even referencing themselves as surrogate parents or older siblings (Clark et al., 2013a; Davis, 2013; Evans & Leonard, 2013; Frank, 2018; Frank et al., 2018). Ahmad, a high school teacher in the Northeast who was a part of the Frank et al. (2018) study, felt that it was his duty as a Black teacher to help other teachers learn how to relate to Black students, especially boys. Teachers like Floyd in the Davis et al. (2013) study and James in the Frank et al. (2018) study who were teaching in the communities where they grew up also felt a sense of connection to their students that was built upon the shared understandings of their communities. Ultimately, examples such as these show that mathematics teachers are creatively insubordinate (Gutiérrez, 2013, 2017), meaning that in the face of challenging conditions, their resistance is in pushing beyond systemic inequities and challenging working conditions to build relationships with their students through teaching mathematics in affirming ways.

While being creatively insubordinate allows Black mathematics teachers to be recruited and distributed in the field, it does not mitigate the challenges of remaining in the field. Ultimately, Black mathematics teachers endure the challenges noted throughout this chapter while districts and schools continue to perpetuate discriminatory practices that are in their self-interest. Districts are able to tout their diversity initiatives and appear to be doing the right and moral work of diversifying the teaching force without instituting any meaningful change with respect to Black mathematics teachers' challenges in the field. Gillborn (2013) and Dixson and Rousseau Anderson (2018) pointed out that interest convergence does not imply a "balanced negotiation process in which two parties come to a rational compromise" (p. 126), thus to bring about radical change and not incremental, surface changes to teacher diversity and inequities in the field must be highlighted through critical lenses and policies, and practices must be drastically revised. Later in the paper, suggestions for such revisions are provided.

Black Mathematics Teacher Attrition and the Permanence of Racism

As noted earlier, for critical race theorists, racism is commonplace, not an oddity, in the U.S. (DeCuir & Dixson, 2004; Ladson-Billings, 1998, 2013). Delgado and Stefancic (2001) point to the endemic nature of race and racism in U.S. education. Thus, the one of the goals of critical race theorists in mathematics education is the unmasking of racism when "denotations [of racism] are submerged and hidden in ways that are offensive though without identification" (Ladson-Billings, 1998, p. 9). Unpacking poor organizational issues that may attribute to attrition warrants the application of the permanence of racism tenet. I assert that the veiled permanence of racism and the inherent racist structures of district- and school-level practices contribute to the Black mathematics teacher shortage and attrition.

Teacher attrition is at the heart of most teacher pipeline discussions, as districts find themselves trying to recruit due to the inability to maintain all teachers, and especially Black teachers, in hard-to-staff subject areas such as mathematics. Neil (2016) found that Black teachers had the highest rate of turnover among all secondary mathematics teachers. Ingersoll and May (2011) found that student-level factors such as poverty level and concentration of minoritized students did not impact teacher attrition, however, organizational issues were a statistically significant predictor of Black teacher attrition. Specifically, organizational issues included limited autonomy and the low levels of faculty-level decision making influence. Racially-biased human resources practices (D'Amico et al., 2017), certification exams (Petchauer, 2014), and teacher evaluations (Petchauer et al., 2018), all are potential contributors to Black mathematics teacher shortage and attrition. Specifically, White supremacist ideology reduces Black mathematics teachers' work in managing Black students' behavioral and discipline issues, undervalues Black teachers' mathematical and pedagogical expertise, and neglects Black mathematics teachers' working conditions. Next, I draw on a small body of work that highlights how these organizational issues are veiled instances of racist practices and have consequences for Black mathematics teacher attrition.

Behavior Managers vs. Pedagogues

One example of a challenging organizational issue facing Black mathematics teachers is the unrecognized labor of simultaneously teaching mathematics while meeting the expectations of administrators and fellow teachers to discipline other teachers' Black students. Despite their willingness to build relationships and help others do the same, Black mathematics teachers in our research team's study (Frank et. al., 2018) overwhelmingly expressed that they were frustrated by the constant requests for discipline support. Teachers like Miranda, a veteran mathematics teacher in a gentrifying community in the Southeast, discussed the barrage of students who were dropped off to her class by non-Black teachers who claimed to not know how to reach them or how to "manage" their behavior. Asa, a middle grades teacher from the Northeast shared, "There's this idea that the Black male teacher is supposed to be the disciplinarian more than the content expert. I try to defy that all the time" (Asa Interview, Winter 2017). Part of his defiance included earning National Board certification in middle grades mathematics. Still, Asa noted that other teachers rarely approached him about his knowledge related to teaching mathematics.

Discussions of teacher diversity often devolve into stakeholders' desires to manage and discipline Black students via the hiring of Black teachers, particularly in this moment in time where the majority of Black teachers are in charter schools that have adopted "No Excuses" models that foreground discipline over learning (e.g., Dishon & Goodman, 2017). Related to Ingersoll's finding about teachers of color desiring more autonomy, treating Black teachers as behavioral managers limits their agency and undermines their autonomy to exercise their pedagogical and content expertise. Further, placing Black teachers in the untenable position of being disciplinarians and not pedagogues is a veiled racist practice that positions Black teachers as less knowledgeable than their peers.

Fiscal and Professional Conditions

An additional finding related to organizational issues from my recent collaborative work (Frank et al., 2018) illuminated that none of the Black mathematics teachers that we interviewed believed they received adequate or meaningful professional development (PD) at their school or at the district level. In fact, many pointed to low salaries and limited school budgets that dissuaded them from attending conferences for professional growth. Many teachers turned to the Internet for support and found community among other mathematics teachers and Black teachers. Tangie, a high school teacher who taught Calculus and Algebra II at a secondary school in the South, shared that she had been able to enhance her instruction through online communities, yet she realized she was not getting what she needed to grow professionally when her district sent her to her first Advanced Placement conference. Post-conference, she continued to look for ways to attend more PD workshops, but the lack of financial support was a huge detriment. She also noted that supports for teaching mathematics were important, but she also desired to learn more about how to reach students who had not experienced success in mathematics and how mathematics could be taught in culturally-relevant ways given the demographics of her school.

As a teacher educator who does PD in predominantly Black schools with teaching populations that have been predominantly Black, stories like Tangie's are quite familiar to me. I have been pulled aside during numerous PD sessions to discuss how the culturally-relevant, content-focused PD we engaged in was markedly different from the standard PD offered by their schools that over-emphasized strategies for behavior and compliance. I have been stopped in school hallways by instructional coaches who want to sit in and learn from PD sessions geared toward teachers because their PD opportunities have been limited to attending conferences that teach them how to coach teachers on compliance-focused strategies such as those in *Teach Like a Champion* (Lemov, 2010) in lieu of offering them PD to enhance their instructional leadership. I have heard countless stories from both the teachers I have worked with and interviewed about how PD not only fails to enhance their content knowledge, but it is delivered in ways that are insulting to their intelligence and not respectful of their expertise and knowledge of community wealth (Yosso, 2005)

These findings point to the permanence of racism in teacher education and the longstanding issue of professional development that does not center the needs and interests of Black teachers and other teachers of color (Kohli et al., 2015). Denying Black teachers professional development that centers them is a veiled racist practice that limits their professional growth. Like focusing on their ability to discipline students, providing inadequate or no content-focused PD has repercussions for Black mathematics teachers' role in perpetuating racist and compliance-focused instruction that manages behavior with little regard for students' mathematical thinking.

Implications

This chapter lays out my initial thinking about a framework that incorporates CRT to represent how Black mathematics teachers are impacted by racist ideologies, policies, and practices along the teacher pipeline. I assert that the pipeline for Black mathematics teachers is cyclical, in that the field time and time again finds itself back at the beginning of the pipeline looking for new ways to recruit Black mathematics teachers, creating a revolving door to the profession. Additionally, the cyclical nature of the model represents how discussions of teacher diversity have declined and reemerged over the last three decades. This is an initial attempt at creating a model for the Black mathematics teacher pipeline, and given the usefulness of CRT to examine each point on the pipeline, I look forward to expanding and refining the framework in future work.

If the mathematics education community uses the tenets of CRT to analyze issues of race and power within mathematics teacher education, as intended by educational architects Ladson-Billings and Tate (1995), it has the potential to speak to policy audiences and to drive and shift mathematics teacher education policy (Ladson-Billings, 2013) toward more equitable mathematics teacher representation and teacher wellbeing. Further, a CRT analysis has implications for imagining a more just treatment of Black mathematics teachers and teacher candidates via institutional policies that support them at critical points along the teacher pipeline. CRT can shed light on inequitable power dynamics and structural determinants of racial and resource inequities that go unnoticed and uncontextualized in traditional research on urban teacher recruitment and retention (Liu, et al., 2008).

For the last few years, the primary focus of my research has been exploring how mathematics education can create and sustain a diverse teaching force and how this would affect the recruitment, retention, and humanization of Black mathematics teachers. Thinking about this issue through a CRT lens, I have been pondering whether recruiting and retaining Black teachers is a genuine goal of the broader education community, or if interest in the topic is actually driven by districts and states that want to give the illusion of doing the right thing in this era of socially-appropriate liberalism.

Teacher diversity in mathematics education cannot be just about the numbers. The issue is larger than meeting diversity quotas and filling STEM pipelines for global competitiveness. It cannot simply be a practice in race matching. Further, the conversation of teacher diversity cannot continue to take place outside of the field of mathematics teacher education. Mathematics teacher educators cannot just consider what tasks and activities to use to engage with pre-service and in-service teachers; we must consider *who* fills the seats of our classes and PD sessions. The field must approach teacher diversity in ways that push back against commodified approaches that often lead to tokenizing teachers.

If mathematics teacher education is going to diversify in ways that address the prevalence of racism along the Black mathematics teacher pipeline, the field must ask itself: *What practices and policies must mathematics teacher educators and researchers reimagine along the Black mathematics teacher pipeline to support and sustain Black mathematics teachers in the field?* Though this is a relatively unexplored question for the field, educational scholars in other areas have been calling for a similar CRT reimagining in teacher education for nearly 20 years (e.g., Ladson-Billings, 1999; Solórzano & Yosso, 2001). Sincerely addressing this question would create shifts both in policy, research, and practice, which would push the field toward one of the goals of CRT—bringing about ideological and material change through policy (Ladson-Billings, 2013).

Reimagining the field with respect to CRT includes becoming abundantly clear about why Black teachers are important to mathematics education beyond the typical arguments made in public discourse. Black teachers are important not just for Black students, but for the social good. As Brown (2014) noted, "…Whiteness as property in teacher education occurs when teachers of color get enclosed in a frame that defines them as necessary role models for K-12 students of color, but not as potentially effective pedagogues for all students" (p. 338). Understanding the work of Black mathematics teachers cannot only be about identifying and excavating practices that can be taught or replicated among non-Black teachers. Their work must be centered simply because it is unique, valuable, and needed in the field.

Drawing upon the tenets of CRT to reimagine the field would mean not only being cognizant of racist institutional and systemic barriers that limit the recruitment and retention of Black teachers, but also actively working to remove them. Reconfiguring mathematics education for Black teachers to thrive would mean interrogating how mathematics education in its current state operates as White institutional space that marginalizes the perspectives that Black teachers bring to the content and how it is taught. As mathematics teacher educators, it means reflecting and acting upon tough questions such as:

- How do we transform the pervasiveness of Whiteness and meritocracy that permeate the field?
- How might we prepare Black pre-service teachers to enact practices and adopt mind-sets that disrupt what Ladson-Billings (2006) coined as an overwhelming educational debt?
- How do we reevaluate gatekeeping practices like standardized testing and teacher evaluation systems that overlook the hard-to-measure practices that some Black teachers bring to the profession to determine their usefulness?

Conclusion

Ultimately, the field must find urgency in critiques such as the ones presented in this chapter. The goals for fixing the "leaks" in the Black mathematics teacher pipeline must shift. The goals can no longer simply be about whether Black teachers stay in the field; they must include goals that maintain Black teachers' senses of dignity and humanity, such that at each point on the pipeline becomes a space where Black mathematics teachers can thrive, and the point of attrition at the end of the pipeline no longer sends the field into the cycle of trying to revamp what needs to be completely reimagined.

Acknowledgments

This material is based upon work supported by the National Science Foundation under Grant No. 1660733. Any opinions, findings, and conclusions or recommendations expressed in this chapter are mine and do not necessarily reflect the views of the National Science Foundation.

References

Achinstein, B., Ogawa, R., Sexton, D., & Freitas, C. (2010). Retaining teachers of color: A pressing problem and a potential strategy for "hard-to-staff" schools. *Review of Educational Research*, 80(1), 71–107.

Bartell, T. (2011). Caring, race, culture, and power: A research synthesis toward supporting mathematics teachers in caring with awareness. *Journal of Urban Mathematics Education*, 4 (1), 50–74.

Battey, D. (2013). Access to mathematics: A possessive investment in Whiteness. *Curriculum Inquiry*, 43(3), 332–359.

Battey, D., & Leyva, L. (2016). A framework for understanding Whiteness in mathematics education. *Journal of Urban Mathematics Education*, 9(2), 49–80.

Bell, D. A. (1980). *Brown v. Board of Education* and the interest-convergence dilemma. *Harvard Law Review*, 93(3), 518–533.

Boisrond, C. (2017). *If your teacher looks like you, you may do better in school*. Retrieved from https://www.npr.org/sections/ed/2017/09/29/552929074/if-your-teacher-looks-likes-you-you-may-do-better-in-school.

Borrero, N., Yeh, C., Cruz, C., & Suda, J. (2012). School as a context for "othering" youth and promoting cultural assets. *Teachers College Record*, 114(2), 1–37.

Bristol, T. J., & Mentor, M. (2018). Policing and teaching: The positioning of Black male teachers as agents in the Universal Carceral Apparatus. *The Urban Review*, 50(2), 1–17.

Brockenbrough, E. (2012). "You ain't my daddy!": Black male teachers and the politics of surrogate fatherhood. *International Journal of Inclusive Education*, 16(4), 357–372.

Brockenbrough, E. (2015). "The discipline stop": Black male teachers and the politics of urban school discipline. *Education and Urban Society*, 47(5), 499–522.

Brown, A. L. (2009). "Brothers gonna work it out": Understanding the pedagogic performance of African American male teachers working with African American male students. *The Urban Review*, 41(5), 416–435.

Brown, K. D. (2014). Teaching in color: A critical race theory in education analysis of the literature on preservice teachers of color and teacher education in the US. *Race Ethnicity and Education*, 17(3), 326–345.

Bryan, N., & Williams, T. M. (2017). We need more than just male bodies in classrooms: Recruiting and retaining culturally relevant Black male teachers in early childhood education. *Journal of Early Childhood Teacher Education*, 38(3), 209–222.

Bullock, E. (2017). Only STEM can save us? Examining race, place, and STEM education as property. *Educational Studies*, 53(6), 628–641.

Cherng, H. Y. S., & Halpin, P. F. (2016). The importance of minority teachers: Student perceptions of minority versus White teachers. *Educational Researcher*, 45(7), 407–420.

Clark, L. M., Badertscher, E., & Napp, C. (2013a). African American mathematics teachers as agents in their African American students' mathematics identity formation. *Teachers College Record*, 115(2), 1–36.

Clark, L. M., Frank, T. J. & Davis, J. (2013b). Conceptualizing the African American mathematics teacher as a key figure in the African American education historical narrative. *Teachers College Record*, 115(2), 1–29.

Clark, L. M., Johnson, W., & Chazan, D. (2009). Researching African American mathematics teachers of African American students: Conceptual and methodological considerations. In D. B. Martin (Ed.), *Mathematics teaching, learning, and liberation in the lives of Black children* (pp. 39–62). New York, NY: Routledge.

Cochran-Smith, M., Villegas, A. M., Abrams, L., Chavez Moreno, L., Mills, T., & Stern, R. (2016). Research on teacher preparation: Charting the landscape of a sprawling field. In D. Gitomer & C. Bell (Eds.), *Handbook of research on teaching* (pp. 439–547). Washington, DC: American Educational Research Association.

Cole, B. P. (1986). The Black educator: An endangered species. *The Journal of Negro Education*, 55(3), 326–334.

Crenshaw, K. (1989). Demarginalizing the intersection of race and sex: A Black feminist critique of antidiscrimination doctrine, feminist theory, and antiracist politics. *University of Chicago Legal Forum*, 1989(1), 139–167.

Crenshaw, K. (1993). Beyond racism and misogyny: Black feminism and 2 Live Crew. In D. Meyers (Ed.), *Feminist social thought: A reader* (pp. 245–263). New York, NY: Routledge.

D'Amico, D., Pawlewicz, R. J., Earley, P. M., & McGeehan, A. P. (2017). Where are all the Black teachers? Discrimination in the teacher labor market. *Harvard Educational Review*, 87(1), 26–49. [SQ]

Davis, J., Frank, T. J., Clark, L. (2013). The case of a Black male mathematics teacher teaching in a unique urban context: Implications for recruiting Black male mathematics teachers. In C. Lewis & I. Toldson (Eds.), *Black male teachers: Diversifying the nation's workforce* (pp.77–92). Bingley, UK: Emerald Group.

DeCuir, J. T., & Dixson, A. D. (2004). "So when it comes out, they aren't that surprised that it is there": Using critical race theory as a tool of analysis of race and racism in education. *Educational Researcher*, 33(5), 26–31.

Dee, T., & Goldhaber, D. (2017). *Understanding and addressing teacher shortages in the United States*. Washington, DC: Brookings Institute.

Delgado, R. (2002). Explaining the rise and fall of African American fortune – Interest convergence and civil rights gain. *Harvard Civil Rights – Civil Liberties Law Review*, 37, 369–387.

Delgado, R., & Stefancic, J. (2001). *Critical race theory: An introduction*. New York, NY: New York University Press.

Diamond, J., & Spillane, J. (2004). High-stakes accountability in urban elementary schools: Challenging or reproducing inequality? *Teachers College Record*, 106(6), 1145–1176.

Dishon, G., & Goodman, J. F. (2017). No-excuses for character: A critique of character education in no-excuses charter schools. *Theory and Research in Education*, 15(2), 182–201.

Dixson, A. D. (2003). "Let's do this!" Black women teachers' politics and pedagogy. *Urban Education*, 38(2), 217–235.

Dixson, A. D., & Dingus, J. E. (2008). In search of our mothers' gardens: Black women teachers and professional socialization. *Teachers College Record*, 110(4), 805–837.

Dixson, A. D., & Rousseau Anderson, C. (2018). Where are we? Critical race theory in education 20 years later. *Peabody Journal of Education*, 93(1), 121–131.

Egalite, A. J., Kisida, B., & Winters, M. A. (2015). Representation in the classroom: The effect of own-race teachers on student achievement. *Economics of Education Review*, 45, 44–52.

Evans, B., & Leonard, J. (2013). Recruiting and retaining Black teachers to teach in urban schools. *SAGE Open*, 3(3), 1–12.

Fairclough, A. (2004). The costs of Brown: Black teachers and school integration. *The Journal of American History*, 91(1), 43–55.

Fenwick, L. (2016). *Teacher preparation innovation and historically Black colleges and universities (HBCUs)*. Ann Arbor: University of Michigan TeachingWorks.

Foster, M. (1997). *Black teachers on teaching*. New York, NY: New Press.

Frank, T. J. (2013). *Widgets and digits: A study of novice middle school teachers attending to mathematics identity in practice* (Unpublished doctoral dissertation). University of Maryland, College Park, MD.

Frank, T. J. (2018). Unpacking a Black mathematics teacher's understanding of mathematics identity. *Journal of Multicultural Education*, 12(2), 144–160.

Frank, T. J., Khalil, D., Scates, B., & Odoms, S. (2018). Listening to and learning from Black mathematics teachers. In I. M. Goffney & R. Gutiérrez (Eds.), *Annual perspectives in mathematics education 2018: Rehumanizing mathematics for Black, Indigenous, and Latinx students* (pp. 147–158). Reston, VA: National Council of Teachers of Mathematics.

Frank, T. J., & View, J. L. (2016). *Examining the trajectories of Black mathematics teachers: Learning from the present, drawing on the past, defining goals for the future*. Washington, DC: National Science Foundation.

Frederick, R. & View, J. (2009). Facing the rising sun: A history of Black educators in Washington DC, 1800–2008. *Urban Education*, 44(5), 571–607.

Gershenson, S., Holt, S., & Papageorge, N. (2015). *Who believes in me? The effect of student-teacher demographic match on teacher expectations*. Kalamazoo, MI: W. E. Upjohn Institute for Employment.

Gillborn, D. (2013). The policy of inequity: Using CRT to unmask White supremacy in education policy. In M. Lynn & A. Dixson (Eds.), *Handbook of critical race theory in education* (pp. 129–139). New York, NY: Routledge.

Gillen, J. (2014). *Educating for insurgency: The roles of young people in schools of poverty*. Oakland, CA: AK Press.

Gutiérrez, R. (2012). Embracing Nepantla: Rethinking "knowledge" and its use in mathematics teaching. *Journal of Research in Mathematics Education*, 1(1), 29–56.

Gutiérrez, R. (2013). Why (urban) mathematics teachers need political knowledge. *Journal of Urban Mathematics Education*, 6(2), 7–19.

Gutiérrez, R. (2017). Political conocimiento for teaching mathematics: Why teachers need it and how to develop it. In S. Kastberg, A. M. Tyminski, A. Lischka, & W. Sanchez (Eds.), *Building support for scholarly practices in mathematics methods* (pp. 11–38). Charlotte, NC: Information Age.

Gutiérrez, R. (2018). The need to rehumanize mathematics. In I. M. Goffney & R. Gutiérrez (Eds.), *Annual perspectives in mathematics education 2018: Rehumanizing mathematics for Black, Indigenous, and Latinx students* (pp. 1–12). Reston, VA: National Council of Teachers of Mathematics.

Hanson, M. & Quintero, D. (2016, August 18). We cannot simply hire our way to a more diverse teacher workforce. *Brown Center Chalkboard.* Retrieved from https://www.brookings.edu/blog/brown-center-chalkboard/2016/08/18/we-cannot-simply-hire-our-way-to-a-more-diverse-workforce/?utm_source=FB&utm_medium=BPIAds&utm_campaign=TDiversity&utm_term=NoNoCtyUS-34^49-F-Teacher%20OrgsNoCAnoBHV&utm_content=104949953.

Harris, C. I. (1993). Whiteness as property. *Harvard Law Review*, 6(108),1707–1791.

Ingersoll, R. M., & May, H. (2011). *Recruitment, retention and the minority teacher shortage.* Philadelphia, PA: University of Pennsylvania, Consortium for Policy Research in Education.

Jett, C. C. (2013). Culturally responsive collegiate mathematics education: Implications for African American students. *Interdisciplinary Journal of Teaching and Learning*, 3(2), 102–116.

Johnson, W., Nyamekye, F., Chazan, D., & Rosenthal, B. (2013). Teaching with speeches: A Black teacher who uses the mathematics classroom to prepare students for life. *Teachers College Record*, 115(2), 1–26.

Joseph, N. M., Haynes, C., & Cobb, F. (Eds.). (2015). *Interrogating Whiteness and relinquishing power: White faculty's commitment to racial consciousness in STEM classrooms.* New York, NY: Peter Lang.

Khalil, D., & Brown, E. (2015). Enacting a social justice leadership framework: The 3 C's of urban teacher quality. *Journal of Urban Learning, Teaching, and Research*, 11, 77–90.

King, S. H. (1993). The limited presence of African-American teachers. *Review of Educational Research*, 63(2), 115–149.

Kohli, R., Picower, B., Martinez, A. N., & Ortiz, N. (2015). Critical professional development: Centering the social justice needs of teachers. *The International Journal of Critical Pedagogy*, 6(2), 7–24.

Kumashiro, K. K. (2000). Toward a theory of anti-oppressive education. *Review of Educational Research*, 70(1), 25–53.

Ladson-Billings, G. (1998). Just what is critical race theory and what's it doing in a nice field like education? *International Journal of Qualitative Studies in Education*, 11(1), 7–24.

Ladson-Billings, G. (1999). Preparing teachers for diverse student populations: A critical race theory perspective. *Review of Research in Education*, 24(1), 211–247.

Ladson-Billings, G. (2006). From the achievement gap to the education debt: Understanding achievement in US schools. *Educational Researcher*, 35(7), 3–12.

Ladson-Billings, G. (2013). Critical race theory—What it is not! In M. Lynn & A. D. Dixson (Eds.), *Handbook of critical race theory in education* (pp. 34–47). New York, NY: Routledge.

Ladson-Billings, G., & Tate, W. (1995). Toward a critical race theory of education. *Teachers College Record*, 97(1), 47–68.

Ladson-Billings, G., & Tate, W. (Eds.). (2016). *Covenant keeper: Derrick Bells enduring education legacy.* New York, NY: Peter Lang.

Lawler, B. R. (2016). To rectify the moral turpitude of mathematics education. *Journal of Urban Mathematics Education*, 9(2), 11–28.

Lemov, D. (2010). *Teach like a champion: 49 techniques that put students on the path to college (K-12).* Hoboken, NJ: John Wiley & Sons.

Liu, E., Rosenstein, J. G., Swan, A. E., & Khalil, D. (2008). When districts encounter teacher shortages: The challenges of recruiting and retaining mathematics teachers in urban districts. *Leadership and Policy in Schools*, 7(3), 296–323.

Lynn, M. (2002). Critical race theory and the perspectives of Black men teachers in the Los Angeles public schools. *Equity & Excellence in Education*, 35(2), 119–130.

Lynn, M. (2006). Education for the community: Exploring the culturally relevant practices of Black male teachers. *Teachers College Record*, 108(12), 2497–2522.

McGee, E. (2014). When it comes to the mathematics experiences of Black pre-service teachers … race matters. *Teachers College Record*, 116(6), 1–50.

Martin, D. B. (2000). *Mathematics success and failure among African-American youth*. Mahwah, NJ: Lawrence Erlbaum Associates.

Martin, D. B. (2007). Beyond missionaries or cannibals: Who should teach mathematics to African American children? *The High School Journal*, 91(1), 6–28.

Martin, D. B. (2009). Researching race in mathematics education. *Teachers College Record*, 111(2), 295–338.

Martin, D. B. (2013). Race, racial projects, and mathematics education. *Journal for Research in Mathematics Education*, 44(1), 316–333.

Martin, D. B. (2015). The collective Black and principles to actions. *Journal of Urban Mathematics Education*, 8(1), 17–23.

Meacham, S. J. (2000). Black self-love, language, and the teacher education dilemma: The cultural denial and cultural limbo of African American preservice teachers. *Urban Education*, 34(5), 571–596.

Mensah, F. M., & Jackson, I. (2018). Whiteness as property in science teacher education. *Teachers College Record*, 120(1), 1–38.

Milner, H. R. (2008). Critical race theory and interest convergence as analytic tools in teacher education policies and practices. *Journal of Teacher Education*, 59(4), 332–346.

Milner, H. R. (2017). Opening commentary: The permanence of racism, critical race theory, and expanding analytic sites. *Peabody Journal of Education*, 92(3), 294–301.

Milner, H. R., & Howard, T. (2004). Black teachers, Black students, Black communities, and Brown: Perspectives and insights from experts. *The Journal of Negro Education*, 73(3), 285–297.

Milner, H. R., Pearman, F. A., & McGee, E. O. (2013). Critical race theory, interest convergence, and teacher education. In M. Lynn & A. D. Dixson (Eds.), *Handbook of critical race theory in education* (pp. 339–354). New York, NY: Routledge.

National Council of Supervisors of Mathematics & TODOS (2016). *Mathematics education through the lens of social justice: Acknowledgment, actions, and accountability*. Retrieved from http://www.mathedleadership.org/resources/position.html.

National Math & Science Initiative. (2016). *Increasing the Achievement and Presence of Under-Represented Minorities in STEM Fields*. Retrieved from https://www.nms.org/Portals/0/Docs/whitePaper/NACME%20white%20paper.pdf.

Neil, B. (2016). *Using the 2011–12 schools and staff survey, restricted file version, to identify factors associated with the intent for African American math teachers to turnover*. (Unpublished dissertation). City University of New York, New York, NY.

Nettles, M., Scatton, L., Steinberg, J., & Tyler, L. (2011). *Performance and passing rate differences of African American and White prospective teachers on Praxis examinations: A joint project of the National Education Association (NEA) and Educational Testing Service (ETS)*. Retrieved from http://www.ets.org/Media/Research/pdf/RR-11-08.pdf.

Pabon, A. (2016). Waiting for Black Superman: A look at a problematic assumption. *Urban Education*, 51(8), 915–939.

Petchauer, E. (2014). "Slaying ghosts in the room": Identity contingencies, teacher licensure testing events, and African American preservice teachers. *Teachers College Record*, 116(7), 1–40.

Petchauer, E., Bowe, A. G., & Wilson, J. (2018). Winter is Coming: Forecasting the Impact of edTPA on Black teachers and teachers of color. *The Urban Review*, 50(2), 1–21.

Picower, B. (2009). The unexamined Whiteness of teaching: How White teachers maintain and enact dominant racial ideologies. *Race Ethnicity and Education*, 12(2), 197–215.

Presmeg, N. (2000). Race, consciousness, identity, and affect in learning mathematics: The case of four African American prospective teachers. In W. Secada, M. Strutchens, M. Johnson, & W. Tate (Eds.), *Changing the faces of mathematics: Perspectives on African Americans* (pp. 61–69). Reston, VA: National Council of Teachers of Mathematics.

Ross, K. M., Nasir, N. I. S., Givens, J. R., de Royston, M. M., Vakil, S., Madkins, T. C., & Philoxene, D. (2016). "I do this for all of the reasons America doesn't want me to": The organic pedagogies of Black male instructors. *Equity & Excellence in Education*, 49(1), 85–99.

Rubel, L. H. (2017). Equity-directed instructional practices: Beyond the dominant perspective. *Journal of Urban Mathematics Education*, 10(2), 66–105.

Sleeter, C. E. (2017). Critical race theory and the Whiteness of teacher education. *Urban Education*, 52(2), 155–169.

Solórzano, D. G. (1997). Images and words that wound: Critical race theory, racial stereotyping, and teacher education. *Teacher Education Quarterly*, 24(3), 5–19.

Solórzano, D. G., & Yosso, T. J. (2001). From racial stereotyping and deficit discourse toward a critical race theory in teacher education. *Multicultural Education*, 9(1), 2–8.

Solórzano, D. G., & Yosso, T. J. (2002). Critical race methodology: Counter-storytelling as an analytical framework for education research. *Qualitative Inquiry*, 8(1), 23–44.

Staples, B. (2017, April 17). Where did all the Black teachers go? *Washington Post*, Washington, DC. Retrieved from https://www.nytimes.com/2017/04/20/opinion/where-did-all-the-black-teachers-go.html.

Toldson, I. A., & Lewis, C. W. (2017). Advancing teacher training programs at historically Black colleges and universities through technical assistance and federal investments. *The Journal of Negro Education*, 86(2), 83–93.

United States Department of Education. (2016a). *Science, technology, engineering and math: Education for global leadership*. Retrieved from http://www.ed.gov/stem.

United States Department of Education. (2016b). *The state of racial diversity in the educator workforce*. Retrieved from http://www2.ed.gov/rschstat/eval/highered/racial-diversity/state-racial-diversity-workforce.pdf.

Valli, L., Croninger, R., Chambilss, M., Graeber, A., & Buese, D. (2008). *Test driven: High stakes accountability in elementary schools*. New York, NY: Teachers College Press.

Walker, E. N. (2014). *Beyond Banneker: Black mathematicians and the paths to excellence*. Albany, NY: Suny Press.

Ware, F. (2006). Warm demander pedagogy: Culturally responsive teaching that supports a culture of achievement for African American students. *Urban Education*, 41(4), 427–456.

Watanabe, M. (2008). Tracking in the era of high-stakes state accountability reform: Case studies of classroom instruction in North Carolina. *Teachers College Record*, 110(3), 489–534.

Woodson, A. N., & Pabon, A. (2016). "I'm none of the above": Exploring themes of heteropatriarchy in the life histories of Black male educators. *Equity & Excellence in Education*, 49(1), 57–71.

Yosso, T. J. (2005). Whose culture has capital? A critical race theory discussion of community cultural wealth. *Race Ethnicity and Education*, 8(1), 69–91.

7

TO VIEW MATHEMATICS THROUGH A LENS DARKLY

A Critical Race Analysis of Mathematical Proficiency

Gregory V. Larnell

Prologue: Cedric's Roundelay[1]

Relieved, I reclined slightly in my tall-back chair after responding to a lengthy series of e-mail messages (my least favorite activity). As I attempted a deep breath, I heard an unexpected tap on my office door. Bolting upright, I readied myself for this unexpected afternoon visitor.

"Professor, it's me, Cedric. Wow, I'm glad that I found you here! Do you have a minute to talk?"

"Of course! I have more than a minute; come on in. Wow; what a pleasant surprise!" I motioned to an open chair by my desk. As he approached, I stood and greeted him with a hearty handshake and hug. Although I hadn't seen Cedric in many years, I recognized him immediately. His look hadn't changed very much; his lanky frame and bespectacled appearance had matured slightly, but I still saw the younger version whom I had met during his early-undergraduate years. After several minutes of catching up on the progression of our respective lives, we eased into a steady conversation that began to center on concerns that were redolent of our earliest interactions.

"Well, Professor, it's so good to see you after all of these years. I also really appreciate that we kept in touch occasionally while I was still a student after participating in your dissertation project. After that first year or so, my experience in college was pretty good, but it was pretty rough when you met me. It was really good to be able to connect with you during that first year. And that's why I'm here now. I wanted to reconnect and reflect with you on some of my experiences during those crucial years. I've been thinking about my experiences in my math courses, especially, trying to make sense of what I was going through. I've been doing a lot of thinking about the purpose and the impact of developmental math—

or as you call it in the article, non-credit-bearing remedial math. I've even been thinking about going back to school to study education."

I sit up in my chair gleefully; of course, this tune is pleasing to any educationalist's ears. "Oh, that's great to hear, Cedric!" I respond.

"Yes," he replied, "I'm pretty excited about it. You know, back when I started college I really wanted to be a psychologist, but mostly because I wanted to be a resource to my community. I feel like I can have that kind of impact—perhaps to a greater degree—if I go into education."

"Well, you know I won't disagree with you there, Cedric. This is really great to hear!" And it truly was. Hearing Cedric say that he was interested in pursuing education somehow instantly transported me backward mentally through my own trajectory, and just as my daydreaming began to take hold, I quickly snapped back to reality. Still in a gleeful state, I made sure to mention, "Well, as you consider choosing programs and applying, let's get back in touch if you need any advice or another set of eyes on things."

"I sure will; thank you for that" he replied quickly and assuredly. As I nodded pointedly to suggest that he take me at my word. "So, Dr. Larnell, even though I want to go into educational psychology, I think, I want to talk with you about math."

"Well, you know that I'm always ready for that kind of conversation," I admittedly eagerly. "What's on your mind?"

Cedric drew a surprisingly deep breath before responding. "So, I've been thinking a lot about my experience in college and, especially, the role of the mathematics courses that I took during my first couple of years. I just feel like it wasn't fair that I was placed in those courses based on a very narrow set of mathematical skills. I had no idea what I was getting myself into, and I'm glad that I only had to take one of those courses.[2] They had no way of knowing—or maybe they just didn't care to know—about my potential as a math student. They just wanted to see if I could solve really messy problems and prove my technical skills. I've thought a lot about that class since I finished school and graduated."

Cedric took a second to gauge my reaction, and I sat up with renewed energy. As Cedric sensed my interest, he began to unfold the more immediate reason for his journey to my office after so many years. "So, like I said, I've been thinking a lot about that first math course that I took at the LMU,[3] and the impact that it's had on me as a university student and even now." I recoiled slightly after that last part, and Cedric noticed my reaction. "Yes, even now, Professor," he answered resolutely, "especially when it comes to my feelings about mathematics. But let me start at the beginning."

Following a deep breath, Cedric continued, "After I participated in your study, I kept thinking about what it meant to be in that class, and as time went on, what it meant to be a student at the university. And now I've got a lot to say about those experiences—and questions, too. But just so I didn't talk your ear off all day, I wanted to focus on three main issues."

"Alright, I'm ready," I replied, "and if you don't mind, I may take a few notes to myself as you talk."

"Of course," Cedric said as his smile broadened, "I wouldn't expect anything different. So, the first issue that I have is with the idea of taking one of those courses and what it means for the students afterwards. I mean, being in a remedial math course becomes a dark mark on you, and even more if you're a Black student at the university. And don't take it more than once; it's a heavier mark then. In fact, it's almost expected in some circles on campus that if you're a Black student, you've taken these courses. But later down the road, when other opportunities would come up—like applying to a scholarship or special campus program—people would look at my record and be like—especially if it's related to math or science— 'you took Algebra 99,[4] so do you think you're ready for a program like this? There's a lot of math required. You have to be really proficient.' And it throws me for a loop every time. Like, why would you assume that I'm not prepared—or 'proficient;' I've been hearing that word a lot. What does it mean to be math proficient anyway, and why should that determine whether I am ready or not for other opportunities?"

As Cedric paused in frustration, I took the opportunity to give him a moment to breathe and to affirm that I was hearing and taking in what he had to say. "I think you're right, Cedric," I offered. "These courses can become marks not just on a student's record or someone else's perspective, but that 'mark' can also have effects on students' own thinking about themselves and their own capabilities. And you're really circling around a major idea with regard to mathematical proficiency. It's typically regarded to be an innocent term or assumed to be understood, but there's a dangerous side to mathematical proficiency and how it is used to regulate access to opportunities for racially and/or gendered marginalized persons."

"Yes!" Cedric proclaimed, and I was a bit startled by his immediate response. "That's exactly it. Because I landed in a course that was clearly low-level and everybody else seemed to know that, it was as if I was wearing an invisible tattoo on my forehead that only other LMU people could see when they looked at my record. And that tattoo might as well have said, in big letters, 'NOT PROFICIENT.'"

"But," I said as I sat up in my chair, "I remember very clearly that you said that you didn't take the placement test seriously so that you could put yourself in the course. Based on some of my own research, I've learned that this is not a totally uncommon practice.[5] In more than one study, some students claimed that they used the math-placement exam to position themselves in the lowest-level mathematics courses at the university. In most cases, it seemed to extend from perceptions that university mathematics courses would be extraordinarily challenging and a lack of knowledge about non-credit-bearing remedial mathematics courses. These students also typically report being unaware that the typical curricular focus of these courses is on highly procedural algebra and, specifically, algebraic skills such as simplifying and factoring polynomials and solving polynomial equations. Did you think then that you weren't proficient?"

Cedric paused for several seconds before responding; he leaned forward as he finally spoke, "I'm not trying to argue with you, but I really don't think that's the question, Professor. I mean, I knew I had been pretty good in all my high-school math courses—I was 'proficient' or whatever—but I had to make a choice during the test about the kind of math course that I wanted during my first year, and I decided to take a relatively easier option—or so I thought. But what I didn't know was just how boring it would be—how boring the math would be. They started with stuff that I had learned years earlier, and it was so focused on factoring and simplifying and solving and simplifying and factoring and factoring; did I mention factoring? I felt like I was being punished more than being exposed to anything useful. It was a lot of practicing. It all got very old, very quickly. Really, I think it's crazy that my whole college career was teetering—and I didn't even really know it—on whether I could pass a course that was basically about factoring. And that's really the second big concern that I wanted to mention. The major problem with that course was that it could possibly push people out of school. Why is it factoring? Who made that choice? Did it have to be factoring? I doubt it."

From my research on Black learners' experiences in non-credit-bearing remedial mathematics courses, I had learned and had a great appreciation for Cedric's second point. I followed up on his point by adding, "Cedric, I totally get it. And I think your second concern is a huge one, and it's absolutely true: These courses really can determine students' trajectories at the university and, if they take the course repeatedly, there's a decreased chance that they will ever graduate with a degree. These courses can have a powerful influence on students' pathways. Just out of curiosity—and I'm not trying to rush the conversation at all; I'm rather enjoying the chance to hear your perspective—what's the third concern that you have about your experience in these courses?"

"You read my mind, Professor," Cedric responded quickly. "And besides, I've just been chewing your ear off with this long story; I hope what I've been saying makes any sense at all. It's great to just finally get it off my chest."

"Yes, of course, it makes lots of sense, Cedric," I attempted to reassure him. "And take your time. You've raised some major points. I'm just curious to know what might be next in your reflection."

"I appreciate that, Professor," as Cedric almost sighed the phrase in relief. "Well, the third point is where you come in, honestly, because you're the one exception. You see, the other major part of the experience was that no one listened to me. And the experience itself can silence you. It took me a long time to tell my parents that I had taken a remedial math course; they were really surprised. And of course, they believed me about the dark mark idea and the gate-keeping as you call it, but other people didn't. When I would talk about it with my friends at school or anybody when I came home, it's like my story didn't matter. Math was always hard, so people just thought that I probably wasn't as ready as other students. I was just always shocked that nobody understood that it was deeper than it seemed. Being in that class, I mean, it was way more than just about skills."

About This Chapter

> The educational task is to take the cover stories we as Americans tell ourselves and look to the back pages. We must teach what the cover stories hide, exposing and problematizing the "hidden curriculum." We do so for the sake of truth but not *just* for the sake of truth... [But also] for the sake of psycho-political movement, in order to create passages out of and away from stasis of the historical present.
>
> *(Pinar, 2004, p. 39)*

As the epigraph above suggests, the primary task of this chapter is to use critical race theory (CRT) as a tool to peel back and look beyond the cover stories of mathematics education—that is, the taken-as-granted concepts, framings, discourses, and ideologies that make up the contemporary landscape of mathematics education, particularly in the United States (Apple, 1992; Gholson, 2016; Gutiérrez, 2008; Ladson-Billings, 1997; Martin, 2003, 2009; Popkewitz, 2004; Tate, 2005). The need for CRT in mathematics education is perhaps more acute than for any other subject area given the uniquely high status of mathematics among the academic disciplines. Given that status, it is imperative—for psycho-political movement, as Pinar argues above—to employ socio-politically conscious lenses such as CRT toward envisioning new epistemic pathways for mathematics education. As CRT emphasizes, the act of looking to the back pages can be interpreted as looking toward the voices of the racially marginalized—and toward their narratives that are too often omitted from the cover story of mathematics education.

Permanence of Race and Mathematics

Mathematics has a saturating and looming permanence in our lives. From our expanding uses (and misuses) of personal and demographic data to the countless algorithms embedded in our everyday technologies, the connections between human experience and our conceptions and uses of mathematics grow more intertwined and deeply embedded with each succeeding generation. Indeed, as O'Neil (2016) explains, mathematics is "not only deeply entangled in the world's problems but also fueling many of them" (p. 2). Nowhere else is this more evident than in the seemingly inescapable ideological conviction that, according to Sfard (2012), "competence in mathematics is a condition for good citizenship" and "a centrepiece of our universal world-managing toolkit" (p. 4; also see Moses & Cobb, 2002).

We also know, both from the other chapters in this volume and from other exemplary texts on CRT in education that race is also a foundational element of our lived experiences—within and beyond educational institutions (e.g., DeCuir &

Dixson, 2004; Ladson-Billings, 1999; Ladson-Billings & Tate, 1995; Lynn, 2002; Milner, 2008; Vasquez Helig, Brown, & Brown, 2012). Especially in the United States but also around the world, race has been and continues to be a primary sparkplug amid struggles concerning citizenship, place, community, and personhood. In these and countless other ways, both mathematizing and racialization have become often-conjoined social projects (Martin, 2009, 2013).

CRT's Elements in This Chapter

Considering these premises, the primary goal of this chapter is to offer a critical race analysis of a preeminent and central idea of contemporary mathematics education, mathematical proficiency (Kilpatrick, Swafford, & Findell, 2001; Tate, 1997). In doing so, I have opened the chapter in a way that reflects critical race theorists' uses of parable-based storytelling (Delgado, 2006; Ladson-Billings, 2012). Moreover, the chapter presents a "structural analysis of the internal dynamics of mathematics education" toward unveiling parts of its architecture as an enterprise (Martin, 2013, p. 328)—and, specifically, the "back"[6] of the enterprise (Hersh, 1991; see also Pinar, 2004, in the opening epigraph). We must not be satisfied with pronouncements about the political nature of mathematics education, even if such views are still regarded to be largely peripheral to a mainstream that remains resistant to them (Aguirre et al., 2017; Gutiérrez, 2013a; Martin, 2013). As Ladson-Billings (2014) explains this sentiment, "It seems to me that being critical is less about a declaration than a disposition toward scholarship" (p. 33). Indeed, such statements beckon for new inquiries regarding the objectives of mathematics education (e.g., Gutiérrez, 2007, 2008, 2013a, 2013b; Martin, 2003; 2009; 2011; Pais & Valero, 2012; Skovsmose, 2011; Valero, 2007); they are calls toward epistemic action, not merely toward (largely and normatively White) mainstream recognition or acknowledgment.

And there is a great deal of new work—foundational and epistemic work—for mathematics education scholars to do. Moreover, much of this new (or renewing) work in mathematics education scholarship should entail looking inwardly (Martin, 2013). As others have argued, mathematics education as a field or community has nurtured a distinctive, profound, and longstanding "dilemma" with regard to reflexive criticality—or "going (self-)critical" (Kilpatrick, 2013, p. 186–187; also see Martin, Gholson, & Leonard, 2010; Stinson, 2011; Tate, 2005). Although the complex goal of strengthening both learners' experiences and teachers' practices is certainly an important and immediate concern for research, we must also critique and continually reconstitute the foundational knowledge base of mathematics education. And for scholars of color, this call is much more acute. As Anzaldúa (1990) so eloquently wrote:

> Some of these knowledges have been kept from us—entry into some professions and academia denied us. Because we are not allowed to enter discourse, because we are disqualified and excluded from it, because what passes

for theory these days is forbidden territory for us, it is *vital* that we occupy theorizing space, that we not allow White men and women solely to occupy it

(as cited in Yosso, 2005, p. 69; see also Gholson, 2016).

Moreover, in order to bend the arc of mathematics-education knowledge production toward racial justice (Larnell, Bullock, & Jett, 2016), it is crucial that we renegotiate foundational elements of mainstream mathematics education scholarship with respect to more recently emergent and critical perspectives, concepts, and analytical frameworks (Barajas-López & Larnell, in press; Larnell, 2016b).

In the sections that follow, I define briefly mathematical proficiency and the elements of CRT used in this analysis. Next, the elements or "strands" of mathematical proficiency are analyzed "through a lens darkly" by examining selected combinations of elements of mathematical proficiency and CRT. The analysis within this chapter hinges on the following primary claims: (1) mathematical proficiency is a political and thereby *racializing* inscription device; (2) mathematical proficiency is typically instrumentalized in ways that convert its high-status elements into privilege-conveying property; and (3) productive disposition is a narrow, efficiency-oriented concept that precludes necessary and complex considerations of identity, credibility and status, and capacity to make meaning on one's own terms. These selected claims and treatments of both frameworks are meant to represent a kind of analysis that is possible when considering a critical race theoretical lens; given the space constraints of a single chapter, however, an exhaustive treatment of all elements of both mathematical proficiency and CRT is not feasible.

Framing It Up: Mathematical Proficiency

> Developing proficiency in mathematics is an important goal for all school students. In light of current U.S. educational standards and the mathematics performance of U.S. students compared with the performance of students in other countries, a clear need exists for substantial improvement in mathematics achievement in the nation's schools. On average, U.S. students do not achieve high levels of mathematical proficiency, and serious gaps in achievement persist between White students and students of color and between middle-class students and students living in poverty.
>
> *(RAND Mathematics Study Panel, 2003, p. iii)*

Mathematical proficiency—as an educational idea, a curricular framework, and a policy instrument—has become a keystone of the contemporary mathematics education enterprise (National Council of Teachers of Mathematics, 1989, 2000). It is a gestalt-like response to a hundred-year-old curricular question concerning mathematics education—especially amid the more general struggles over school curriculum in the United States (Kliebard, 1987): What are the central curricular objectives of a mathematics education enterprise (Tyler, 1949)? Although considerable and needed attention has been attributed recently to advancing socio-political perspectives in mathematics education (e.g., regarding identity, justice, power, inequity; see Gutiérrez, 2013a; Valero, 2007), the broader yet lesser-discussed (and even lesser-critiqued) development within mathematics education within recent decades is the emergence of mathematical proficiency as its de facto theory (Schoenfeld & Kilpatrick, 2008).

As striking as the introductory section may have seemed in terms of tone and ambition, I want to pivot briefly here to an even stronger, less apparent set of claims about mathematics education as an enterprise and the role of mathematical proficiency as an organizing frame. The field of mathematics education—especially in the United States—is too often tolerant of "easily accepted but thinly theorized views" (Ernest, 2002, p. xiv; Barajas-López & Larnell, in press). Furthermore, mathematics-education knowledge production within the past few decades has marched progressively and smoothly toward positioning mathematical proficiency as the central element of a successful mathematics education. According to Schoenfeld and Kilpatrick (2008), "a theory of proficiency provides an orientation to a domain. It says what is important—what skills people need to develop if they are to become proficient" (p. 31). Therefore, it is not hyperbolic to suggest that mathematical proficiency functions as a conceptual index for knowledges that are regarded officially as important to attain, for activities that represent officially as to what learners should be able to do, and ultimately, the whole collection of attributes required for one to be regarded as a viable participant in mathematics education.

Adding It Up: Strands of Mathematical Proficiency

Mathematical proficiency is a prominent feature of the oft-cited National Research Council report from the Mathematics Learning Study Committee, *Adding It Up: Helping Children Learn Mathematics* (Kilpatrick et al., 2001). According to the committee, the "strands" of mathematical proficiency represent "a composite, comprehensive view of successful mathematics learning" (p. 5). This framework also represents and is synthesized from a broad range of canonical scholarship on mathematics teaching, learning, and assessment (Schoenfeld, 2007; Schoenfeld & Kilpatrick, 2008). The resulting elements of the framework represent standard-bearing subdomains within contemporary mathematics education: conceptual understanding, procedural fluency, adaptive reasoning, strategic competence, and productive disposition.

Conceptual understanding and procedural fluency are primary, content-oriented elements of the mathematical proficiency framework. These long-established foci of the last hundred years of mathematics education research can be traced to the field's cognitivist-behaviourist psychological roots (Schoenfeld, 2016; Skemp, 1972; Thorndike, 1923). Conceptual understanding is the "integrated and functional grasp of mathematical ideas" (Kilpatrick et al., 2001, p. 118), and procedural fluency refers to the "knowledge of procedures, knowledge of when and how to use them appropriately, and skill in performing them flexibly" (p. 121). Adaptive reasoning and strategic competence are process-oriented strands of mathematical proficiency, referring respectively to "the ability to formulate mathematical problems, represent them, and solve them" (p. 124) and "the capacity to think logically about the relationships among concepts and situations" (p. 129). The final strand, productive disposition—almost always listed last among the strands—refers to neither mathematical content nor process but to proclivity; it refers to "the tendency to see sense in mathematics, to perceive it as both useful and worthwhile, to believe that steady effort in learning mathematics pays off, and to see oneself as an effective learner and doer of mathematics" (p. 131).

A key claim in *Adding It Up* is that the strands of mathematical proficiency are intertwined (see Figure 7.1), yet the overt focus on problem solving adds weight to the content- and process-oriented strands that contribute more directly to solving problems and developing mathematical understandings (e.g., conceptual understanding, strategic competence)—and shifts the one proclivity strand to the periphery (Kilpatrick et al., 2001). Although the framers position productive disposition as a "major factor" rhetorically, it is portrayed more as an indicator of successful work among the other strands:

> A productive disposition develops when the other strands do and helps each of them develop… The more mathematical concepts [that learners] understand, the more sensible mathematics becomes. In contrast, when students are seldom given challenging mathematical problems to solve, they come to expect that memorizing rather than sense making paves the road to learning mathematics, and they begin to lose confidence in themselves as learners.
>
> *(p. 131)*

Mathematical Proficiency through a Lens Darkly[7]

> More centrally, the use of critical race theory offers a way to understand how ostensibly race-neutral structures in education—knowledge, truth, merit, objectivity, and "good education"—are in fact ways of forming and policing the racial boundaries of White supremacy and racism.
>
> *(Roithmayr, 1999, p. 4)*

Given its utility for industry and governmentality, mathematics is already a high-status field of knowledge, and by extension, mathematical proficiency symbolizes the specific forms of this high-status knowledge that the field of mathematics education and its stakeholders regard as canonical, legitimate, and official (Apple, 1992; Brown & Au, 2014). Moreover, mathematical proficiency shapes the contours of official knowledge production within the field. In doing so, mathematical proficiency also preserves a well-worn, compounded myth—namely, that proficiency in mathematics is achieved

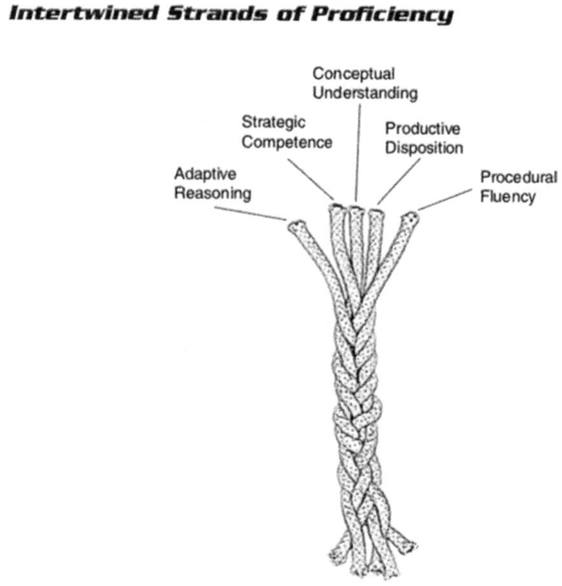

Intertwined Strands of Proficiency

FIGURE 7.1 Intertwined Strands of Proficiency

through a politically neutral mathematics education, that race is simply a surface-level feature of mathematics curriculum (i.e., addressable by changing the wording and contexts of mathematics-instructional tasks), and that any problematic relation between race and mathematics will be resolved simply by adding more racially marginalized persons to the field of mathematics education professionals. It is critical that we develop ways to unpack and debunk these myths and to explore how established structures of mathematics education such as mathematical proficiency have nurtured their development over time.

To view mathematics education and mathematical proficiency through a lens darkly evokes a key question: How does mathematical proficiency—as an architectural framework for contemporary mathematics education in the United States—serve as a tool for the maintenance of White supremacy and the advancement of antiBlackness and other specific forms of racism? This is a huge, daunting, and for too many, inconvenient question. The task of this chapter and this section is to centralize this question and provide a glimpse into a kind of theoretical reasoning that could contribute an answer.

Mathematical Proficiency as a Majoritarian Inscription Device

The first and overarching lesson from viewing mathematical proficiency through a lens darkly is that mathematical proficiency itself is a story-making device. Moreover, mathematical proficiency is a construct with which certain kinds of stories can be told and valorized while others are rendered as less visible or invisible. Mathematical proficiency catalyzes the production of stories about success and achievement, performance, productivity, and failure in mathematics, and the resulting stories become stubborn inscriptions for learners of all ages (see Popkewitz, 2004). As Sfard (2012) argues:

> When mathematics, so effective in creating useful stories about the physical reality around us, is also applied in crafting stories about children (as in "This is a below average student") and plays a decisive role in determining the paths their lives are going to take, the results may be less than helpful. More often than not, the numerical tags with which these stories label their young protagonists, rather than empowering the student, may be raising barriers that some of the children will never be able to cross.
>
> *(p. 8)*

Furthermore, mathematical proficiency is a *majoritarian* device (Delgado, 1991), and as such, it is a tool for preserving the status-conveyance story within the White institutional space that mathematics education has been and continues to be (Martin, 2011). The majority of beneficiaries of the mathematics-education enterprise has always been White learners (and White men, more specifically), and constructs like the achievement gap and mathematical proficiency are necessarily tools in the maintenance of this status quo ante (Love, 2004; Parks, 2009). Majoritarian stories, according to Solórzano and Yosso (as cited by Love, 2004), "generate from a legacy of racial privilege… indeed White privilege is often expressed through Majoritarian stories" (p. 229).

Not unlike the role model theory that Delgado (1991) critiques in his originating treatment of majoritarian devices, mathematical proficiency is quite a recent and "remarkable invention" (p. 1230), even if would seem to have always had a conceptual presence in mathematics education research and practice. And similar to the role model theory, mathematical proficiency establishes an outline for the model mathematics learner. Rooted firmly and deeply in the mathematics education research literature, mathematical proficiency is a nearly indisputable tool for shaping mathematics teaching and learning and, by extension, mathematics learners, teachers, policies, curricula, etc. The combined effect of mathematical proficiency as a racialized, majoritarian inscription device begets three specific features or "effects" of this racialized majoritarian inscription: (a) mathematical proficiency fosters a kind of normative invisibility that ignores racialized identity and reduces the learner to a relatively small set of characteristics; (b) mathematical proficiency promotes political neutrality and meritocracy that then disguises systemic inequities; and (c) the prominence of mathematical proficiency becomes the majoritarian goalpost and, as a result, shifts the (then secondary) responsibility for addressing systemic inequity to subordinated peoples (Love, 2004).

Proficiency as Property and the Gatekeeping Role of Procedural Fluency

Beyond the more general yet consequential claim that mathematical proficiency functions as a racialized majoritarian inscription device, the strands of mathematical proficiency themselves also can be questioned and otherwise viewed through a lens darkly. Although the strands are intended to be taken as intertwined, there are clear asymmetries among them. The analyses of those strands, however, could be applied in similar ways to the others.

Nowadays, it is neither a radical nor particularly new claim that mathematics is connected to status, but there have been few attempts to unpack that claim to question how specific, structural elements of mathematics education contribute to and preserve the status-conveyance function of mathematical proficiency. Consider procedural fluency. Most measures of success in all levels of school mathematics (K–12) are predicated on learners' capacities to exhibit skill with mathematical procedures—especially arithmetic and algebraic operations and procedures.

Within the current neoliberal climate of education, skill with procedures—and the broader concept of procedural fluency—is transformed into a *property-conveying currency*. To put it differently, for learners who demonstrate procedural fluency on high-stakes assessments and in everyday classroom situations, there are significant access advantages within the oft-called mathematics or Science, Technology, Engineering, and Mathematics (STEM) pipeline (see also Bullock, 2017). In this way, proficiency as property reinforces the ideological myth of meritocracy—i.e., if the learner can simply do mathematics, then that doing becomes a currency to which the learner is rightfully entitled.

By that same token, failure to demonstrate procedural fluency translates to a failure to accumulate access-bearing, property-conveying currency within mathematics education. And as my studies have documented (Larnell, 2016a; Larnell, Boston, & Bragelman, 2014), there are clearly racialized implications. Procedural fluency lends itself to being reduced to shallow procedural testing as opposed to deep procedural fluency (Star, 2005); this shallow form of procedural fluency has been used systemically for decades to constrain access at multiple levels of schooling—especially at the entryway to postsecondary education (Larnell, Blackmond Larnell, & Bragelman, 2017). And not only does this restricted access disproportionately affect Black and Latinx learners, but the psychosocial weight of the constrained access if left to the learners themselves to negotiate and make sense of (Larnell, 2016b; Larnell et al., 2014).

The Problem with Productive Disposition: Counter-storytelling and Testimonial Injustice

Productive disposition is a curious aspect of mathematical proficiency, though it is rarely, if ever, questioned. Unlike the others that are more directly related to epistemological concerns (loosely; i.e., regarding knowledge and skills and knowledge processes), productive disposition is not related as directly to the activity of doing mathematics or producing mathematical knowledge as it is to ontological considerations of mathematics education—that is, what it means to *be* a mathematical thinker or doer. Although it is does have a specific definition (as discussed previously), productive disposition can be recast as the capacity for a learner to form a stable attachment or sense of belonging in relation to the discipline of mathematics. Productive disposition is essentially a call for learners to form a deep, personal relationship with the other strands of mathematical proficiency.

On the surface, this would seem to be a wholly positive idea; that is, we should encourage learners to connect deeply with the discipline. However, to view productive disposition through a lens darkly calls this relating into question. For whose purposes should learners form an attachment with mathematics? For what purposes should learners habitually see mathematics as useful or worthwhile? To whose benefit should learners' steady efforts in mathematics pay off?

Mathematics learners should develop a productive disposition on their own terms, and not merely the terms prescribed by schools, governments, and officialized experts.[8] Moreover, mathematics learners should develop dispositions that allow them to develop their own counter-storying capacities—and specifically, to develop the ability to use mathematics in service of their personal aspirations and desires and on behalf of the communities they care about.

Productive disposition should also include the capacity for learners to see themselves as contributors to the canon of mathematics—toward debunking its majoritarian, property-conveying essence. Moreover, when learners see themselves as genuine contributors to mathematics—and not simply doers or users—they themselves become living counter-narratives to the majoritarian consumerism of a pre-packaged product. All mathematics learners must see and be able to wield their own expertise, including the knowledges that they bring to school mathematics (Barajas-López & Larnell, in press).

With Lenses Darkly: Critiquing the Critique

In concluding this exploration of mathematical proficiency through a lens darkly, I would be remiss if I did not turn the lens around—albeit briefly—and examine my own attempt in this chapter. What are the dangers of rethinking and reorienting mathematical proficiency through a critical-race lens or, more generally, to align mathematical proficiency with perspectives that were more sensitive to race-specific concerns? It is tempting to simply accept a race-conscious perspective as a means toward inclusive progress, but here we may also learn from the CRT literature to understand that race remedies are often two-sided, Pyrrhic victories.

In general, mathematical proficiency is a majoritarian victory, a centerpiece of a reform movement that has characterized mathematics education for the past 30 years. Providing inroads to expand its scope to more fully include the perspectives, aspirations, and experiences of learners of color is needed, but there are risks to simply adding on elements that would make mathematical proficiency more amenable to that purpose (Barajas-Lopéz & Larnell, in press). Therefore, this analysis, grounded in elements of CRT, is intended to provide a first step in what should be an ongoing and growing critique of mathematical proficiency that does not result simply in the addition of elements that render the framework more inclusive. Rather, to view mathematical proficiency though a lens darkly means to continually inspect and to not simply accept the architecture of mathematics education for what it is or seems to be.

Notes

1 My use of chronicle as a CRT device is patterned after the Delgado's (2006) exemplary critical legal studies article (also, e.g., Bell, 1985). Cedric was a key participant in my dissertation research. By studying his early undergraduate mathematics-learning experiences (Larnell, 2016a; Larnell, Boston, & Bragelman, 2014), I was able to develop some new understandings and conceptual lenses on the experiences of students in non-credit-bearing remedial mathematics courses.

2 As I will explain in the following sections, when I first met Cedric as a participant in my dissertation study, he was a student in a non-credit-bearing remediation mathematics course during his first year at the university from which he would ultimately graduate (Larnell, 2016a; Larnell, Boston, & Bragelman, 2014).

3 A pseudonymous acronym (for "Large Midwestern University") that was also used in the originating research involving Cedric (Larnell, 2016a).

4 "Algebra 99" is the pseudonym originally used for the course number of the non-credit-bearing mathematics course in which Cedric was originally enrolled (see Larnell, 2016a).

5 In my original research with Cedric and through subsequent studies (e.g., Larnell, 2016a, 2016b; Larnell, Blackmond Larnell, & Bragelman, 2017), I've learned that some students manipulate gatekeeping experiences in accordance with their situational sense of agency. I call the phenomenon "satisficing" (Larnell, 2016a), a term borrowed from behavioral economics and personality and social psychology (Schwartz et al., 2002; Simon, 1955).

6 Moreover, according to Hersh (1991): The purpose of a separation between front and back is not just to keep customers [given a restaurant metaphor that Hersh employs] from interfering with the cooking; it is also to keep the customers from knowing too much about the cooking…We can describe this state of affairs by saying that the front/back separation makes possible the preservation of a myth. (p. 129)

7 My use of the phrase, "through a lens darkly" is borrowed from the title of a (highly recommended) film on Black photography (Harris, Singleton, & Steward, 2014). The originating biblical passage, "for now we see through a glass darkly" (1 Corinthians 13:12) has inspired a broad array of uses. The phrase is used here to signify the use of a race-centric lens that extends from the lived and adjudicative experiences of people of color in the United States—and those of Black citizens, more specifically. Ladson-Billings (2012) also employed a variation on the phrase in her title for the American Educational Research Association's Eighth Annual Brown Lecture in Education Research—also with reference to the use of CRT in educational research.

8 This aligns neatly with the idea that mathematics education—and the framing of mathematical proficiency, in particular—as Delgado (2006) argues, has "succumbed to a style of history that emphasizes great men, wars, and generals [(directly and metaphorically)] at the expense of common people, unions, and activism" (p. 27).

References

Aguirre, J., Herbel-Eisenmann, B., Celedón-Pattichis, S., Civil, M., Wilkerson, T., Stephan, M., ... & Clements, D. (2017). Equity within mathematics education research as a political act: Moving from choice to intentional collective professional responsibility. *Journal for Research in Mathematics Education*, 48(2), 124–147.

Apple, M. W. (1992). Do the standards go far enough? Power, policy, and practice in mathematics education. *Journal for Research in Mathematics Education*, 23(5), 412–431.

Barajas-López, F. & Larnell, G. V. (in press). Unpacking the links between equitable teaching practices and Standards for Mathematical Practice: Equity for whom and for what purposes? To appear in the *Journal for Research in Mathematics Education*.

Bell, D. A. (1985). The civil rights chronicles (foreword). *Harvard Law Review*, 99(1), 4–83.

Brown, A. L., & Au, W. (2014). Race, memory, and master narratives: A critical essay on U.S. curriculum history. *Curriculum Inquiry*, 44(3), 358–389.

Bullock, E. C. (2017). Only STEM can save us? Examining race, place, and STEM education as property. *Educational Studies*, 53(6), 628–641.

DeCuir, J. T., & Dixson, A. D. (2004). "So when it comes out, they aren't surprised that it is there": Using critical race theory as a tool of analysis of race and racism in education. *Educational Researcher*, 33(5), 26–31.

Delgado, R. (1991, March). Affirmative action as a majoritarian device: Or, do you really want to be a role model? *Michigan Law Review*, 89(5), 1222–1231.

Delgado, R. (2006). Rodrigo's roundelay: *Hernandez v. Texas* and the interest-convergence dilemma. *Harvard Civil Rights-Civil Liberties Law Review*, 41, 23–65.

Ernest, P. (2002). Preface. In P. Dowling (Ed.), *The sociology of mathematics education: Mathematical myths/pedagogic texts* (p. xiii). New York, NY: Routledge.

Gholson, M. (2016). Clean corners and algebra: A critical examination of the constructed invisibility of Black girls and women in mathematics. *The Journal of Negro Education*, 85(3), 290–301.

Gutiérrez, R. (2007). (Re)defining equity: The importance of a critical perspective. In N. S. Nasir & P. Cobb (Eds.), *Improving access to mathematics: Diversity and equity in the classroom* (pp. 37–50). New York, NY: Teachers College Press.

Gutiérrez, R. (2008). A "gap-gazing" fetish in mathematics education? Problematizing research on the achievement gap. *Journal for Research in Mathematics Education*, 39(4), 357–364.

Gutiérrez, R. (2013a). The sociopolitical turn in mathematics education. *Journal for Research in Mathematics Education*, 44(1), 37–68.

Gutiérrez, R. (2013b). Why (urban) mathematics teachers need political knowledge. *Journal of Urban Mathematics Education*, 6(2), 7–19.

Harris, T. A. (Producer, Writer, Director), Singleton, J. (Producer), & Steward, K. (Producer) (2014). *Through a lens darkly: Black photographers and the emergence of a people* [Motion picture]. USA: First Run Features/K Period Media/Through a Lens Darkly.

Hersh, R. (1991). Mathematics has a front and a back. *Synthese*, 88, 127–133.

Kilpatrick, J. (2001). Understanding mathematical literacy: The contribution of research. *Educational Studies in Mathematics*, 47(1), 101–116.

Kilpatrick, J. (2013). Needed: Critical foxes. In K. R. Leatham (Ed.), *Vital directions for mathematics education research* (pp. 173–187). New York, NY: Springer.

Kilpatrick, J., Swafford, J., & Findell, B. (Eds.). (2001). *Adding it up: Helping children learn mathematics*. Washington, DC: National Academy Press.

Kliebard, H. (1987). *The struggle for the American curriculum 1893–1958*. New York, NY: Routledge.

Ladson-Billings, G. (1997). It doesn't add up: African American students' mathematics achievement. *Journal for Research in Mathematics Education*, 28(6), 697–708.

Ladson-Billings, G. (1999). Preparing teachers for diverse student populations: A critical race theory perspective. *Review of Research in Education*, 24, 211–247.

Ladson-Billings, G. (2012). Through a glass darkly: The persistence of race in education research and scholarship. *Educational Researcher*, 41(4), 115–120.

Ladson-Billings, G. & Tate, W. F., IV. (1995). Toward a critical race theory in education. *Teachers College Record*, 97(1), 47–68.

Larnell, G. V. (2016a). More than just skill: Examining mathematics identities, racialized narratives, and remediation among Black undergraduates. *Journal for Research in Mathematics Education*, 47(1), 233–269.

Larnell, G. V. (2016b). Equity issues in developmental mathematics: What does it feel like to be a problem? In K. Stephenson (Ed.), *Developmental mathematics: For whom? To what end? Report of Critical Issues in Mathematics Education (Vol. 11, Workshop 12)* (pp. 35–37). Berkeley, CA: Mathematical Sciences Research Institute.

Larnell, G. V., Blackmond Larnell, T. T., & Bragelman, J. (2017). Toward reframing the open door: Policy, pedagogy, and developmental education in the urban community college. In M. Pagano (Ed.), *Jobs and the labor force of tomorrow: Migration, training, and education*. Champaign: University of Illinois Press.

Larnell, G. V., Boston, D., & Bragelman, J. (2014). The stuff of stereotypes: Toward unpacking identity threats amid African American students' learning experiences. *Journal of Education*, 194(1), 49–57.

Larnell, G. V., Bullock, E. C., & Jett, C. C. (2016). Rethinking teaching and learning mathematics for social justice from a critical race perspective. *Journal of Education*, 196(1), 19–30.

Love, B. J. (2004). Brown plus 50 counter-storytelling: A critical race theory analysis of the "majoritarian achievement gap" story. *Equity & Excellence in Education*, 37(3), 227–246.

Lynn, M. (2002). Critical race theory and the perspectives of Black men teachers in the Los Angeles Public Schools. *Equity & Excellence in Education*, 35(2), 119–130.

Martin, D. B. (2003). Hidden assumptions and unaddressed questions in Mathematics for All rhetoric. *The Mathematics Educator*, 13(2), 7–21.

Martin, D. B. (2009). Researching race in mathematics education. *Teachers College Record*, 111(2), 295–338.

Martin, D. B. (2011). What does quality mean in the context of White institutional space? In B. Atweh, M. Graven, W. Secada, & P. Valero (Eds.), *Mapping equity and quality in mathematics education* (pp. 437–450). New York, NY: Springer.

Martin, D. B. (2013). Race, racial projects, and mathematics education. *Journal for Research in Mathematics Education*, 44(1), 316–333.

Martin, D. B., Gholson, M. L., & Leonard, J. (2010). Mathematics as gatekeeper: Power and privilege in the production of knowledge. *Journal of Urban Mathematics Education*, 3(2), 12–24.

Milner, H. R. (2008). Critical race theory and interest convergence as analytic tools in teacher education policies and practices. *Journal of Teacher Education*, 59(4), 332–346.

Moses, R. P., & Cobb, C. E. (2002). *Radical equations: Civil rights from Mississippi to The Algebra Project*. Boston, MA: Beacon Press.

National Council of Teachers of Mathematics (1989). *Curriculum and evaluation standards for school mathematics*. Reston, VA: National Council of Teachers of Mathematics.

National Council of Teachers of Mathematics (2000). *Principles and standards for school mathematics*. Reston, VA: National Council of Teachers of Mathematics.

O'Neil, C. (2016). *Weapons of math destruction: How big data increases inequality and threatens democracy*. New York, NY: Crown.

Pais, A., & Valero, P. (2012). Researching research: Mathematics education in the political. *Educational Studies in Mathematics*, 80(1–2), 9–24.

Parks, A. N. (2009). Doomsday device: Rethinking the deployment of the "achievement gap" in equity arguments. *For the Learning of Mathematics*, 29(1), 14–19.

Pinar, W. F. (2004). *What is curriculum theory?*Mahwah, NJ: Lawrence Erlbaum Associates.

Popkewitz, T. (2004). The alchemy of the mathematics curriculum: Inscriptions and the fabrication of the child. *American Educational Research Journal*, 41(1), 3–34.

Rand Mathematics Study Panel. (2003). *Mathematical proficiency for all students: Toward a strategic research and development program in mathematics education*. Washington, DC: RAND.

Roithmayr, D. (1999). Introduction to critical race theory in educational research and practice. In L. Parker, D. Deyhle, & S. Villenas (Eds.), *Race is … race isn't: Critical race theory and qualitative studies in education* (pp. 1–6). Boulder, CO: Westview.

Schoenfeld, A. H. (Ed.). (2007). *Assessing mathematical proficiency (Vol. 53)*. Berkeley, CA: MSRI Publications.

Schoenfeld, A. H. (2016). Research in mathematics education. *Review of Research in Education*, 40, 497–529.

Schoenfeld, A. H., & Kilpatrick, J. (2008). Toward a theory of proficiency in teaching mathematics. In D. Tirosh (Ed.), *International handbook of mathematics teacher education: Vol 2. Tools and processes in mathematics teacher education* (pp. 1–35). Rotterdam, The Netherlands: Sense.

Schwartz, B., Ward, A., Monterosso, J., Lyubomirski, S., White, K., & Lehman, D. R. (2002). Maximizing versus satisficing: Happiness is a matter of choice. *Journal of Personality and Social Psychology*, 83(5), 1178–1197.

Sfard, A. (2012). Why mathematics? What mathematics? *The Mathematics Educator*, 22(1), 3–16.

Simon, H. A. (1955). A behavioral model of rational choice. *The Quarterly Journal of Economics*, 69(1), 99–118.

Skemp, R. R. (1972). *The psychology of learning mathematics*. New York, NY: Penguin.

Skovsmose, O. (2011). *An invitation to critical mathematics education*. Rotterdam, The Netherlands: Sense.

Star, J. R. (2005). Reconceptualizing procedural knowledge. *Journal for Research in Mathematics Education*, 36(5), 404–411.

Stinson, D. W. (2011). "Race" in mathematics education research: Are we a community of cowards? [Editorial]. *Journal of Urban Mathematics Education*, 4(1), 1–6.

Tate, W. F. (1997). Critical race theory and education: History, theory, and implications. *Review of Research in Education*, 22, 195–247.

Tate, W. F. (2005). Ethics, engineering, and the challenge of race reform in education. *Race Ethnicity and Education*, 8(1), 121–127.

Thorndike, E. L. (1923). *The psychology of algebra*. New York, NY: The Macmillan Company.

Tyler, R. W. (1949). *Basic principles of curriculum and instruction*. Chicago, IL: University of Chicago Press.

Valero, P. (2007). A socio-political look at equity in the school organization of mathematics education. *ZDM Mathematics Education*, 39(3), 225–233.

Vasquez Helig, J., Brown, K. D., & Brown, A. L. (2012). The illusion of inclusion: A critical race theory textual analysis of race and standards. *Harvard Educational Review*, 82(3), 403–424.

Yosso, T. (2005). Whose culture has capital? A critical race theory discussion of community cultural wealth. *Race Ethnicity and Education*, 8(1), 69–91.

8

ANTIBLACKNESS IS IN THE AIR

Problematizing Black[1] Students' Mathematics Education Pathways from Curriculum to Standardized Assessments

Nicole M. Joseph and Floyd Cobb

Contextualizing the Work

This chapter builds upon a previous literature review where we problematized explanations for racial disparities in mathematics standardized assessments found in the literature (Cobb & Russell, 2015). We did this by using critical race theory (CRT) to unpack the assumptions and to expose the complexities of an assessment system historically founded upon larger eugenics and White supremacy efforts that have tried to prove, using pseudoscience, the intellectual inferiority of racialized minorities (Herrnstein & Murray, 1994; Jensen, 1969; Ladson-Billings, 1997). Questions that guided our analysis included: What macro factors are identified as influencing or explaining racial disparities in mathematics assessments? What assumptions undergird the field's conversations about racial disparities in mathematics assessments? In what ways can those assumptions be challenged through CRT to highlight the story of race in mathematics education in the United States? What we found was that the factors fall victim to a meritocratic premise that assumes all students are exposed to equivalent forms and amounts of mathematical knowledge. This assumption effectively locates the problem of assessment within students and not the institutions that are entrusted with providing access to mathematics curricular knowledge that is requisite for success. We concluded that analytical synthesis arguing for social action and continued policy measures with a renewed focus on equitable curricular access as an important method to improve the assessment outcomes for racial minority students. But what might an equitable mathematics education pathway, from curriculum to assessment, look like or mean for Black students in a climate of antiBlackness?

This essay attends to these ideas by specifically centering Black students' mathematics education experiences within United States' school systems (learning, curricula, and assessments) that promote antiBlackness (Dumas, 2016). AntiBlackness is the specific hatred, disdain, contempt, and disregard of Black bodies in schools and other educational spaces (Dumas, 2014; Dumas & ross, 2016). First legitimized by savagery of American slavery, only to be further garrisoned through barbaric laws, extrajudicial lynchings and dehumanizing stereotypes, antiBlackness represents the acculturated acceptance ways in which people of all races have come to be stigmatize and show antipathy for the Black identity (Cobb, forthcoming). As an ideology, antiBlackness encourages Black bodies to be viewed as subhuman and undeserving of basic dignity, thus creating the justification for systemic and state sanctioned exclusion.

Using complementary tenets of CRT, we take up an important college access standardized assessment, the American College Testing (ACT), to question the "college readiness for all" rhetoric in current mathematics education reform efforts. In so doing, we: (a) complicate how the results of standardized mathematics assessments are repeatedly deployed as a weapon to legitimize myths about Black intelligence; and (b) reveal that unequal mathematics curricular access and assumptions about Black intelligence in mathematics represents social viciousness that works to support totalitarian goals.

Positionality: How and Where We Enter

The first author was invited by seminal math education scholar, Danny Martin to speak in a 2018 American Educational Research Association (AERA) symposium entitled *Refusal of Reform: Toward a Black Liberatory Mathematics Education*. The purpose of the symposium was to critique the incremental change that has occurred in the three major moments of mathematics education reform (Berry, Ellis, & Hughes, 2014; Stinson & Bullock, 2012): The new mathematics reforms of the mid-1950s; the standards-based movement of the late 1980s and its second iteration in the early 2000s; and the Common Core State Standards movement dating from 2009. A central argument was that despite the strategic equity-oriented rhetoric within standards-based reforms, and the rising-tide-lifts-all-boats assumptions of the Common Core, the implied promises of equity for Black learners (Morial, 2014a; Morial, 2014b), collectively, have not been realized.

Several questions guided the symposium's discussion, but one salient question was: What does refusal look like? The question stated, "as a response to status-quo-preserving nature of reforms, what can refusal—of the dominant system of mathematics education; of mathematics education institutions and organizations that maintain their status as White institutional spaces (Martin, 2008); and of schooling practices and policies that instantiate White supremacist orientations and antiBlack violence—look like in *principle and practice*?" We mention this important backdrop because it conjures up tensions that we as education researchers must face, namely working within a system for change and/or working outside of the system as we are speaking from a perspective of urgency. Although we completely agree with Martin (2018) in refusing systemic intellectual violence against Black students in our mathematics education system, we also know that building a completely new decolonized and anti-racist mathematics education system is an impractical solution for Black students and their families who are presently enrolled in K-12 schools. Assessments are biased, and probably always will be because they are a foundational part of the U.S. educational system that necessitates access to privileged mathematics spaces. Derrick Bell (2005b) helps us reconcile this tension because from a pragmatic perspective, the influence of racial discrimination, White logics and imaginaries about Black intelligence in mathematics is likely never to be undone. Bell stated:

> We must first recognize and acknowledge (at least to ourselves) that our actions are not likely to lead to transcendent change and may indeed, despite our best efforts, be of more help to the system we despise than to the victims of that system whom we are trying to help. Then, and only then, can that realization and the dedication based on it lead to policy positions and campaigns that are less likely to worsen conditions for those we are trying to help and more likely to remind the powers that be there are persons like us who are not only on their side but determined to stand in their way.
>
> *(p. 77)*

As CRT emphasizes, race and racism are endemic in American society (Delgado & Stefancic, 2001). While a paralyzing hypothesis, we can choose to either accept discomforting fate or choose to engage in the Sisyphean task of reducing its impact. We, as former mathematics teachers, mathematics coaches, mathematics curriculum designers, district curriculum directors and parents of Black girls, not only think about scholarly research, but we also think *pragmatically* about the mathematics education of Black children. Standardized assessments will never cease to exist in this country; low-teacher expectations of Black students will persist. Consequently, we highlight a real system that is broken, but the system nevertheless is one that Black families must contend with and push back against, with the hope of creating *some* disruption.

There are serious tensions in equity work, and we need to be honest about what the real barriers are that get in the way of transformation. The reality is that not everyone wants to dismantle racial inequalities in mathematics because it will mean that those in power and who dominate will have to relinquish some of their power, and to relinquish power would mean to be vulnerable and open to critique (Joseph, Haynes, & Cobb, 2016). What might relinquishing power look or feel like? Relinquishing power emphatically rejects the notion of meritocracy and acknowledges, for example, that Black students have unequal access to advanced mathematics courses. Relinquishing power means ensuring that every Black student has an opportunity to take advanced mathematics, not just a small percentage (Office of Civil Rights, 2018). Relinquishing power intentionally opens up leadership positions to underrepresented groups, which challenges White authority. Finally, relinquishing power means accepting that a White person's viewpoint comes from a racialized frame of reference and this challenges objectivity.

We agree with scholars who suggest that standardized test performance gaps are actually the result of other gaps that seductively persuade society that achievement gaps actually exist (Irvine, 2010). Consequently, because there are disparities in the access to advanced mathematics curriculum, high-quality mathematics teachers, and rigorous mathematics instruction, an opportunity gap actually exists (Boykin & Noguera, 2011; Milner, 2012; Schmidt & McKnight, 2012). Ladson-Billings (2006) argued that the U.S. has an educational debt. The educational debt reflects the "disparity between what we know is right and what we actually do" (p. 8). Ladson-Billings points out that education researchers have no trouble recognizing that we as a society have a moral debt to leaders such as Cesar Chavez or Mahatma Gandhi, but how do we recognize the moral debt that we owe to an entire group of people? Myrdal (1944) compellingly points out that the U.S. remains in a dilemma. This dilemma refers to the moral contradiction of a nation torn between allegiance to its highest ideals and awareness of the historical contempt for Blackness.

Situating Black Students within the Complex Narrative of Achievement Gap Research and Discourse

Established in 2009, the Common Core State Standards for Mathematics presented an unprecedented opportunity for systemic improvement in mathematics education in the U.S. It sought to (a) promote standardization; (b) establish a minimum threshold of learning; (c) provide clear and consistent guidelines; and (d) prepare all students for college and careers after high school graduation. College readiness can be assessed in different ways; however, the three most common recognized indicators used by colleges are coursework for college admission, achievement test scores, and grade point averages (Clinedinst, & Koranteng, 2018). Figure 8.1 shows how these three ideas are nested within a system for the purposes of college admission.

Black students' experiences and performances on all of these indicators of college readiness reveal significant racial disparities that are embedded in a master narrative (Giroux, Lankshear, McLaren & Peters, 2013). Although there have been some shifts to include contextualization in mathematics education research focused on Black students (see e.g., Davis & Martin, 2008; Stinson, 2006), journalists who report on standardized test scores and interpret annual findings for many in society at large continue to subscribe to meritocratic thinking about results. All too often, this meritocratic mind-set frames the thinking and decision making of K–12 educators and leaders, who regard these gaps as accidental instead

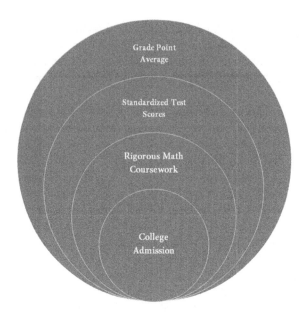

FIGURE 8.1 College Readiness Assessment Factors

of by design. This line of thought is often disconnected from the findings in critical mathematics education research that has been available for years. As a consequence, this discourse about the gap rarely changes and students continue to be academically harmed.

Decontextualized stories about mathematics achievement are dangerous. The gap "serves as a safe proxy for discussing particular kinds of students without naming them" (Gutiérrez, 2008, p. 359). Naming groups of students in a transparent way acknowledges openly who is disenfranchised in mathematics classrooms. Analogously, when researchers conduct achievement gap research, they engage in presenting a static picture of inequities because it is based "primarily upon one-time responses from teachers and students" (p. 358), which captures "neither the history nor the context of learning that has produced such outcomes" (p. 358).

It is unfortunate that the field of mathematics education continues to engage in an uncritical national conversation about Black students and the achievement gap. The mathematics achievement gap is a well-publicized, yet problematic term used to describe observed disparities regarding the mathematics performance of groups of students, especially groups defined by race/ethnicity, gender, and socioeconomic status. Achievement gap discourse creates a gap-gazing fetish. Gutiérrez (2008) called the sustained and uncritical emphasis on the achievement gap a "gap-gazing fetish" (p. 357) and pointed out that educators need to conduct research that moves away from gap-gazing toward more contextualized and intervention studies. This proposition is important because it allows for the interrogation of the ways teachers, students, and overall school systems engage in the facilitation of the learning process for Black students, oftentimes, the students that are usually at the bottom of the achievement hierarchy (Banks & Banks, 1995). Conducting contextualized research is also important because although large quantitative studies such as those conducted by the National Educational Assessment Progress (NAEP) are necessary, they are simultaneously insufficient because they do not address latent power issues in our assessment socialization system (Cobb & Russell, 2015), an important process for decentering meritocracy and Whiteness.

What we know, then, is that when speaking of the achievement gap it is understood by "virtually everyone that this does not refer to a gap between Africans and Asians or a gap between Africans and Latinos or a gap between Africans and anyone else other than Europeans" (Hilliard, 2003, p. 137). The "gap" is understood to represent that disparity between Black and White students. The Black–White gap is problematic on many levels including how we normalize White students' achievement as the standard and how performance is not about highest potential and Black excellence, but about a curve of distribution, which creates racial hierarchies in mathematics (Martin, 2008). When researchers examine that normal curve, they often use a theoretical lens that supports deficit thinking and negative narratives about Black students, which ignores structural factors at play, and it also sends the message that Black students are not worth studying in their own right—that a comparison group is necessary. Such a theoretical lens places groups in opposition to each other, which implies that one's gain is the other's loss. Consequently, anti-Blackness is in the air. In other words, Black students continue to be constructed as deficit and devalued in mathematics education research, discourse, policy, and practice.

Overall, there have been several organizations such as the National Science Foundation (NSF), the Davidson Institute, William T. Grant Foundation, and others at the national, state, and local levels who have earmarked funds to eliminate the so-called achievement gap among underrepresented minorities. NSF, for example, has funded projects with millions of dollars to broaden participation, many of which focus on learning and design, curriculum, and pathway programs; yet together as a collective, these initiatives have not yielded significant reduction in the racial inequalities in mathematics education among Black students. The field has not seen a high yield in the reduction of inequalities, in large part because many of the projects focus on trying to fix students instead of the structural factors embedded in the mathematics education system (i.e. implicit bias, racism, sexism, classism, etc.). Programs that focus on students are necessary, but are insufficient, especially when they disregard the inequitable treatment of students. Performance gaps are the result of unequal treatment, not unequal students, and that difference in treatment is confounded by the perceived value and worth of Blackness.

Why the ACT?

One of the most important ways that the mathematics education field judges the aggregate performance of mathematics programs is through standardized assessments. The most common among these occurs at the state level. For example, the Every Student Succeeds Act (ESSA) (2015) requires that each state have its own standardized assessment that every student takes in grades three through eight and once in high school. While states typically offer their own developed assessments in grades three through eight, ESSA grants states the opportunity to offer nationally recognized assessments in high school. ESSA defines a nationally recognized assessment as one that is "administered in multiple states and is recognized by institutions of higher education in those or other states for the purposes of entrance or placement into courses in postsecondary education or training programs" (ESSA, 2015). The American College Test (ACT) and the Scholastic Achievement Test (SAT) are examples of such nationally recognized assessments. It should be noted that while "gap" discourse is generally associated with standardized assessments such as the National Assessment of Education Progress (NAEP) and state level standardized assessments, gaps are also associated with college entrance exams like the ACT and SAT (Anderson, 2017; Harwell, Moreno, & Post, 2016; Reeves & Halikias, 2017). Collectively, our almost 30 years of secondary mathematics teaching and leadership responsibilities contend that teachers, counselors, parents, and community members all talk and communicate about mathematics achievement gaps on the college access exams, like the ACT (Anderson, 2017).

Of these national assessments, we focus on the ACT for two specific reasons. First, the ACT is among the more popular college entrance assessments administered in the U.S. with participation from roughly 60% of the over 2,000,000 students in the graduating class of 2017 (ACT, 2017c). This is buoyed by the fact that 16 states require students to take the ACT as part of their state assessment system (Gewertz, 2017). Second, the ACT is regarded as a curriculum-based test that "assesses student mastery of both college and career readiness standards... with the mathematics section focusing on the topic areas of pre-algebra and elementary algebra, intermediate algebra and coordinate geometry, plane geometry, trigonometry and statistics" (ACT, 2017a). Figure 8.2 shows that having access to advanced mathematics coursework mixed with high-quality instruction can amount to high ACT mathematics scores, which then opens up other opportunities related to college admission, such as merit scholarships.

Access to Rigorous Coursework ✚ **High Quality Mathematics Learning Experiences** = **High ACT Mathematics Scores**

FIGURE 8.2 Factors that Support High Mathematics Scores on the ACT

Therefore, access to advanced level mathematics curricula matters. Rigorous mathematics courses like Trigonometry, Pre-Calculus and Calculus are highly predictive of greater success on the mathematics section of standardized exams such as the ACT (ACT, 2005). Advanced mathematics courses being predictive of future success on the ACT holds true because the scoring design of the exam necessitates student mastery of higher-level mathematics content standards to score in the upper ranges of the exam. For example, according to the ACT Career Readiness Standards, students who score in the lower ranges (13–15) of the mathematics section of the ACT need only understand how to solve equations in the form $x + a = b$, where a and b are whole numbers or decimals (ACT, 2017a), whereas students who score in the higher ranges (28–32) of the exam must know how to "solve linear inequalities when the method involves reversing the inequality sign" (ACT, 2017a). The progressive and cumulative nature of mathematics content necessitates that students learn mathematics in a way that is sequential. Because we know that Black students often attend schools where there are limited advanced courses or are often tracked into lower level mathematics classes, mastering ACT content standards that correspond with the upper scoring ranges is significantly limited (Cobb, 2012).

The 2017 ACT profile national report indicates that test takers who take mathematics courses up through Calculus prior to taking the exam score over seven points higher than students who take only three years of mathematics prior to taking the exam, and previous work supports this notion about taking Calculus with respect to raising ACT scores (ACT, 2017b; Akiba et al., 2007). Contextualizing this for Black students, we see from the recently released Office of Civil Rights report that Black students make up 16% of the national high school student population but only comprise 8% of the enrollment in Calculus courses (Office of Civil Rights, 2018). The Civil Rights Data Collection (CRDC) survey is sent out to all public schools and school districts in the United States. The CRDC measures student access to courses, programs, staff, and resources that impact education equity and opportunity for students. Table 8.1 shows the percentage distribution of Black student enrolled in high school mathematics, beyond Algebra. This disparate enrollment of Black students in a course that is found to be critical for high scores on the ACT can help explain why performance gaps on this exam remain so stable.

CRT in Education

This chapter takes up Black students' mathematics experiences, in particular access to high levels of mathematics curriculum and performance outcomes, to complicate how the college readiness for all rhetoric is paradoxical when considering the academic treatment of Black students. In this section, we first discuss CRT in education explaining its tenets as offered by Dixson and Rousseau (2005) and Delgado and Stefancic (2001). Next, we build upon CRT by highlighting how it

TABLE 8.1 Percentage Distribution of Black Students Enrolled in Advanced Mathematics Courses in U.S. Public Schools (data may not add up to 100 due to rounding)

	Two or more races	American Indian or Alaska Native	Asian	Native Hawaiian or Other Pacific Islander	Hispanic or Latino of any race	Black or African American	White
Geometry	3%	1%	5%	0.5%	25%	17%	49%
Algebra II	3%	1%	6%	0.4%	23%	15%	52%
Advanced Mathematics	3%	1%	8%	0.4%	19%	13%	56%
Calculus	3%	1%	14%	0.4%	16%	8%	58%

has been applied in mathematics education and how the discipline of mathematics functions as a property right.

CRT in education is the educational extension of the legal analytic framework which sought to critique the inadequate analysis of how race intersects with the law. First applied to the field of education by Tate (1993) and Ladson-Billings and Tate (1995), CRT in education aims to "decipher the social-structural and cultural significance of race in education" (Ladson-Billings & Tate, 1995, p. 50) by uncovering the myths and challenging the dominant ideology that pervades public education in the United States. Later, in 2002, Solórzano and Yosso (2002) offered an expansion of CRT to view race and racism at their intersections with other forms of subordination such as gender and class discrimination, which disrupts the Black–White binaries.

CRT in education challenges claims of neutrality, objectivity, color blindness, and meritocracy, which are often used to justify the racially unequal experiences and outcomes of students in schools. CRT in education is based on the premise that racism is a standard organizing principle of American life incorporating a legal and analytic framework to interrogate how race and education intersect with the structures, processes and discourses of schools (Yosso, 2002), illuminating the false neutrality of educational policies and practices. As a heuristic, CRT in education "grounds racial problems in race-specific language in order to define and utilize ideologies free of the racial hierarchies that have defined much of U.S. history, politics, and educational systems" (Taylor, 2006, p. 72). CRT in education seeks to demystify school based inequality by shining a light on the systems processes and structures that lead to its production, all in an effort to challenge the relationship between race, racism and power (Delgado & Stefancic, 2001; Yosso, 2002).

CRT in education scholars argue that inequality in schools is as normal and predictable as inequality in the broader society (Dixson & Rousseau, 2005; Yosso, 2002). American society is one which espouses equality and equal opportunity, but in truth rations privileges based upon skin color, allowing those inequalities found in education to be mirror images of those found in other parts of society. Just as economic opportunity, access to quality healthcare and fair treatment by the judicial system fall along racial lines, so too does education. As a result, CRT in education scholars view education as a property right to bring clarity to the habitual practices of race-based inequality in education because property functions in such a way that it allows one group ultimate power to exclude (Harris, 1993). Below, we briefly discuss four complementary tenets: (a) racial realism or the permanence of race and racism; (b) the social construction of race; (c) the myth of meritocracy; and (d) interest convergence.

Racial Realism

CRT in education operates on the premise that racial discrimination is a normal and central component of American life (Bell, 2005c) that finds a way to reassert itself independent of apparent symbols of racial progress. Examples of racial progress in U.S. society include having a Black Commander in Chief for eight years, only to be followed by one in racial moral equivalence unapologetically referring to White nationalists as "very fine people" (Thrush & Haberman, 2017). With this in mind, racial realists equate the permanence of racism to the constant presence of struggle in the battle for racial justice. Racial realists do not maintain a "we shall overcome" perspective of racial justice, rather they remain engaged in the liberation struggle knowing that they may never reap the benefits.

Social Construction of Race

Although CRT in education scholars center race as an organizing principle of American society, U.S. ideologies nonetheless dismiss its existence in the world (Delgado & Stefancic, 2001; Dixson & Rousseau, 2005; Omi & Winant, 2014; Valencia, 2012; Zamudio et al., 2010). CRT scholars assert that race is a socially constructed concept that is malleable based upon the socio-political context. To borrow from Painter (2010), "[r]ace is an idea not a fact" (p. ix), meaning that it has no true basis in biology, but is nonetheless consequential. Race proves to be significant in how groups of people are categorized, oppressed, and privileged. Overall, race is a predictable maker of social treatment, and as a result, it is an indicator of who is and who is not worthy of the full privileges that society has to offer.

Myth of Meritocracy

The idea of meritocracy is predicated on the American ideal that its citizens have equal opportunity at success. Meritocracy suggests that success comes by participating in the U.S. capitalistic economy, cultivated by individualism, working hard, and pulling oneself up by the bootstraps (Vaught & Castagno, 2008; Yosso, 2002; Zamudio et al. 2010). Meritocracy is a delusion because all American citizens are not constructed as equal. For example, educational institutions make claims all the time about equal opportunity, yet, their constituents (students, staff, faculty) often face intersectional discrimination (Solórzano & Yosso, 2002); thus the color blind claims "just act as a camouflage for the self-interest, power, and privilege of dominant groups in U.S. society" (p. 26). For at least 500 years, Black people were legally only considered three-fifths of the value of Whites (Feagin, 2010). Even after the 13th Amendment abolished legal slavery, Jim Crow laws and Black Codes significantly limited Blacks from voting and participating in society as free citizens (Browne-Marshall, 2016). In a Washington Post interview, Bryan Stevenson, Executive Director of the Equal Justice Institute (as cited in Johnson, 2015) stated the following, which elevates the myth of meritocracy:

> We devastated the ability of African Americans in this country to do what other immigrant populations had done, which is to work hard and acquire wealth. Black people worked hard and they were lynched for it. They worked hard and they were forced to leave for it. They worked hard and they were disenfranchised and humiliated for it.

Consequently, Stevenson's comment demonstrates how it is a fallacy to think that if one just works hard, they will be rewarded, adding context to the fact that this reality has never been true for Black people in the United States. All things have never been equal. Therefore, CRT in education works to disrupt the myth of equal opportunity and consequently the myth of meritocracy.

Interest Convergence

The final CRT tenet we use in this analysis is the interest convergence principle (Bell, 1980, 2005a; Delgado & Stefancic, 2001; Ladson-Billings, 2004). The interest convergence principle posits that all social advances that appear to support greater racial equality eventually work to benefit the powerful and maintain the social order. Initially offered by Bell (2004) in his criticism of the result of the 1954 *Brown versus Board of Education* decision, he argues that "[B]lacks' rights are recognized and protected when and only so long as policy makers perceive that such advances will further interests that are their [Whites'] primary concern" (2004, p. 49). As a tenet, interest convergence is used to illustrate how policies and practices are employed to serve the interests of Whites and ultimately maintain a racial hierarchy.

CRT in Mathematics Education

Although CRT has been applied to general educational contexts examining Black students' experiences overall, CRT has a shorter history in mathematics education. Tate (1993) offered one of the first critical race analyses of the testing of Black students in underserved communities to illuminate standardized testing's influence in reinforcing the racial hierarchies that exist in society. Due to the fact that the results of these exams were largely a function of treatment and not knowledge, Tate argued that the aim of standardized testing was to create the justification for sorting and selecting students into specific mathematics programs.

Ladson Billings and Tate (1995) extended this argument in their seminal essay on CRT in education by proclaiming that success in U.S. schools reflects a form of "intellectual property" that is unequally distributed along racial lines (see Figure 8.2). Moreover, they state that real property (computers, science labs, and high-quality teachers) supports intellectual property. This foundational principle is central to the educational experiences of Black people throughout the history of the United States. For countless generations, the property right of education has been something that Black students have never been equally provided. This began with the anti-literacy laws that emerged from chattel slavery. It was then followed by the between school segregation that occurred during reconstruction (Williams, 2009; Woodson, 1919/2013) and continued through the *Brown* decision. Despite being over a half century removed from this landmark decision, exclusionary practices in schools are still maintained through curricular tracking decisions that occur in schools across the nation (Oakes, 1990).

Perhaps no content area in the educational curriculum is more prone to the practice of exclusion than mathematics. Due to its hierarchical structure that requires topics to be "mastered" prior to learning those that are more rigorous (Clements & Samara, 2004), classroom teachers have extreme discretion in determining the subsequent mathematics experiences to which students will be exposed. Ladson-Billings (1998), in her critique of mathematics assessments, shared a story of how a teacher suggested that a young Black girl could not do fourth grade mathematics, even though her full engagement with adulting (budgeting/paying bills) proved otherwise. With mathematics holding a cultural stigma of ability rooted in elitism, teachers are then permitted to ration the privileged knowledge based upon their assumptions about student intelligence. Oftentimes when Black students attend the schools where rigorous coursework is offered, they are still more likely to be relegated into basic mathematics courses (Oakes, 1990; Oakes, Joseph, & Muir, 2004); however, for those Black students in advanced mathematics classes, evidence suggests they face microaggressions and other assaults rooted in White supremacy (Battey & Leyva, 2016). This student tracking process starts in elementary school, continuing in middle and high school, thus setting a mathematics trajectory for the remainder of a student's mathematical career. This pathway sets up students for standardized assessments that are ultimately connected to college access. Again, Figure 8.2 shows that coursework and instruction are key to scoring high on mathematics assessments.

Lattimore (2001, 2003, 2005) wrote extensively about how Black students view mathematics assessments as barriers to graduation. In his work on examining the Ohio Proficiency Test, Black students had to pass this test to graduate, and his analysis found that while student motivation and attitude were important components of positive mathematics test performance, ineffective teacher pedagogy played a significant role. Ladson-Billings (1998) emphatically stated that "in the classroom, a dysfunctional curriculum coupled with a lack of instructional innovation (or persistence) adds up to poor performance on traditional assessment measures" (p. 20). Therefore, it is clear that mathematics curricula and pedagogy play an important role for preparing Black students to be successful on college access standardized assessments.

Overall, what CRT in mathematics education helps the field to understand about mathematics standardized assessment is that when race, racism, meritocracy, and Whiteness are not centered in the analysis of Black students' mathematics experiences, it can lead many to believe that the disparities in standardized testing for mathematics are attributable to limited intelligence and deficiency, rather than the structural practices that lead to significant disproportionality and unequal access to the advanced mathematics courses that matter. In the next section, we add to previous studies by applying CRT's tenets to three examples of Black students' experiences in schools related to the pathway of mathematics assessment—teacher quality, teacher bias, and tracking.

Racial Inequality and Standardized Mathematics Assessment: Black Students' Distinct Schooling Experiences

Example 1: Teacher Quality

During the 2015–2016 academic year, Calculus was offered at only 38% of high schools with large minoritized[2] populations (i.e. Asians, Blacks, Hispanics, American Indians, and Native Hawaiians), compared to all schools at 50% (Office of Civil Rights, 2018). Among the reasons this occurs is that schools with larger percentages of minoritized populations are less likely to have mathematics teachers of equal depth of mathematical content knowledge to those that are in suburban neighborhoods (Akiba, Letendre, & Scribner, 2007; Ingersoll & Perda, 2010; Peske & Haycock, 2006). Moreover, Ingersoll and May (2012) have found that schools with minoritized populations have high turnover rates of mathematics and science teachers since qualified teachers in these content areas are in such high demand. This turnover suggests that even when Black students in high minority schools gain access to a qualified mathematics teacher, they are less likely to have one the following year. Therefore, the opportunity for Black students who attend such schools to have a teacher who is qualified to teach Calculus, for example, is limited when compared to those who attend schools in suburban neighborhoods.

As mentioned previously, Black students are more likely to attend low resourced schools and are less likely to have curricular experiences that include high level mathematics courses (Oakes, Joseph, & Muir, 2004). What is disheartening is that in the early 1990s, Tate (1993) argued that Black students in urban schools were often taught by less qualified mathematics teachers. Now, over 25 years later, Davis (2014) also found that Black students continue to be taught by less qualified mathematics teachers and that the type of instruction students receive is test-driven, not focused on problem-based and conceptual thinking, which ultimately contributes to Black students' oppression (Davis & Martin, 2008). This lack of qualification greatly affects students' ability to fully understand the information as well as students' probability of passing mathematics standardized assessments. From a CRT perspective, this speaks to an example of how the myth of meritocracy shows up in the ways schools distribute teachers. Highly qualified mathematics teachers are not equally distributed across all schools.

Part of the solution to increasing highly qualified mathematics teachers for Black students is de-tracking; however, many mathematics [White] teachers oppose de-tracking (Oakes, Joseph, & Muir, 2004). Low track courses are routinely filled with students perceived to be difficult to teach and unmotivated to learn (Hallinan, 2011) thus making teaching low track courses an experience that is less desirable than teaching advanced courses (Kelly & Price, 2007). Teachers who have been given the opportunity to teach advanced courses are deeply resistant to integration thereby relegating these opportunities to teachers with less experience (Burris & Garrity, 2008; Kelly, 2004; Welner & Burris, 2006). The practice of teacher tracking "exacerbates the inequalities in opportunity to learn...by matching the teachers who are most likely to be successful in the classroom with the students who already occupy a privileged position" (Kelly, 2009, p. 454).

We know that teacher quality has been consistently identified as the most important school-based factor in student achievement (McCaffrey, Lockwood, Koretz, & Hamilton, 2003; Rowan, Correnti, & Miller, 2002), and that teacher effects on student learning have been found to be cumulative and long-lasting (McCaffrey et al., 2003). Consequently, we see over and over again that Black students continue to be relegated to low-quality mathematics teachers without systemic push back from decision-makers, such as district superintendents, directors, principals, mathematics teachers, and even Black parents. Black students not receiving high-quality instruction over decades of time is an example of how they are denied the right of high-quality mathematics curricula and instruction, which ultimately suggests that antiBlackness is in the air.

From a CRT perspective, this example provides a practical application of the interest convergence tenet. The practice of keeping the most qualified teachers with the most successful students ensures that the power dynamic that has been constructed throughout history remains unchanged. Black students simply are not often granted the same access to quality instruction as other students, mainly White and certain Asians who have been privileged in our mathematics educational system. Thus, it should come as no surprise that performance rates on standardized exams like the ACT are delineated along racial lines since the playing field is not equal in K–12 mathematics classrooms and never has been. The racial realism tenet of CRT would suggest that this phenomenon is predictable because after all racial discrimination is normal.

Example 2: Teacher Bias in Mathematics Course Placement Decisions

When Black students attend schools where advanced mathematics coursework is offered, unequal access to rigorous mathematics content still occurs (Oakes, Joseph, & Muir, 2004). One of the key barriers to their access is the perception bias often found in teachers when making placement decisions. While many teachers would argue that their placement decisions for students are based on performance and unbiased, teachers are often unable to set their biases aside when making placement decisions (Faulkner et al., 2014). Faulkner and colleagues found that Black students, in particular, only had a two-thirds chance of placement in an eighth grade Algebra class compared to White students. As a result, even when Black students perform equally to their White counterparts, bias prevents them from being given an opportunity to access the higher-level courses necessary for success on standardized exams, such as the ACT. CRT views such actions as illustrative of race and racism because even in the face of empirical data, White teachers and counselors (and even Black teachers who buy into similar ideas) refuse to make ethical decisions that position Black students in pathways that increase their access and likelihood of performing well on mathematics standardized assessments.

This idea of teacher discretion and disproportionality has also been studied in gifted education programs. Grisson and Redding (2015) found that Black students, with high standardized test scores, are less likely to be assigned by teachers to gifted services in mathematics, a pattern that persists when controlling for other background factors, such as health and socioeconomic status, and characteristics of classrooms and schools. This research literature substantiates that teachers perceive potential giftedness differently in students who are not White because of differences in backgrounds or biases in their judgments or expectations (Gershenson, Holt, & Papageorge, 2016; Grissom & Redding, 2015). For example, what a teacher may attribute precocity for one student may be considered disruptive behavior for another (Ferguson, 1998). Birthed out of the deficit thinking that has dominated American history, educators implicitly believe that Black students are undeserving of equal access to gifted spaces. The frequency of these antiBlack practices are common because far too many fail to challenge the social construction of race. Race is viewed as biological instead of the socially constructed phenomena that it is.

While teachers are the ones who make the primary decisions about course placement, parents can play a role in the decision-making process as well. Many Black parents, who do not come from a history of privilege, may be unaware of the relationship between standardized test scores and student placement (Berry & Bol, 2005). Therefore, some Black parents might unwittingly fail to challenge their children's placement in mathematics courses that are presumably easier in hopes of their children securing a high grade. This act of earning a high grade in a less challenging mathematics course will not support their children's efforts to pass the mathematics section of college admission standardized assessments. Therefore, the biases that teachers maintain about the capabilities of Black students can have far reaching effects, especially when they fail to problematize the social construction of race.

Example 3: Tracking Up: Effective Maintained Inequality

One seemingly obvious suggestion to this problem of access to advanced coursework would be for educators to only offer mathematics pathways that are predictive of success on college entrance exams, similar to what was found in the Algebra for all movement in California (Domina et al., 2016). Through this policy, middle and high school professionals worked collaboratively to require that all students be enrolled in at least Algebra I by eighth grade to allow the opportunity for them be eligible to enroll in Calculus and other advanced courses during their 11th and 12th grade years. A policy requirement such as this would presumably allow greater opportunities for Black students the opportunity to experience rigorous mathematics content since the course pathways are drastically reduced. However, simply labeling a course Algebra does not guarantee the content of the course. The second author of this chapter has lived this first hand. Through his 13 years of experience as both a building administrator and district curriculum director, he observed that principals and teachers both resist this policy by teaching students content that is below the Algebra I level despite the title of the course. Thus, students and parents are led to believe that the content to which they are being exposed is equivalent to that of their peers when in truth the coursework is equivalent to Pre-Algebra or perhaps lower.

From a CRT and antiBlackness perspective, educators' practices in this district suggest they do not care about Black children's mathematics outcomes. Educators often rely on some Black parents' limited understanding about the deep connections and consequences between mathematics course enrollment and college access. These same educators keep Black parents thinking the problem is their children, not the system. Martin (2000) discussed that Black parents themselves have had negative mathematics experiences complicated by a collection of socioeconomic and educational experiences that dramatically affected their own mathematics identities and expectations of themselves and their children. Thus, it is not unlikely, that the parents in the second author's school district rarely resisted.

Moreover, Domina et al. (2016) found that even when these policy prescriptions are deployed, parents of privilege mitigated these efforts by tracking their children up to the next level course (i.e. Geometry) to ensure that their students maintained a mathematics experience beyond that of the "average" student. Mathematics as a right to exclude is applicable in this case because mainly [White] parents are allowed to "track up" their students so as to view the Black body as something they want their children to have nothing to do with. This brings us back to the interest convergence tenet that was also displayed in the example with qualified teachers and assumptions about the social construction of race. Stated differently, the presence of Black bodies presumes a dilution of rigor of the mathematics. Lucas (2001) has termed this phenomenon as the *theory of effectively maintained inequality* whereby parents of privilege maintain the social hierarchy by ensuring their children have experiences that are separate and distinct. Overall, what we notice is that these inequalities make it more difficult for Black students to win, no matter what they do or how hard they try, which suggests to us a notion of antiBlackness in the air of our education system, especially with respect to mathematics education.

Conclusion

This chapter aimed to shed light on many Black students' mathematics education experiences and to nuance and elevate the antiBlackness associated with their pathways from mathematics curriculum to mathematics standardized assessments. Using complementary tenets of CRT, the analysis demonstrated that Black students' experiences in schools related to mathematics education is complicated by issues of race, racism, the deep belief in meritocracy, and the efforts made to influence stakeholders that Black students are worthy of being in advanced mathematics courses. The social construction of race, racial realism, interest convergence, and the myth of meritocracy all offer a critical way of calling into question the ways Black students experience mathematics curricular content and pathways to college readiness standardized assessments. These complementary tenets of CRT give us a way to contextualize Black students' mathematics experiences because pointing out how the national discourse about their performance on standardized assessments falls prey to myths about meritocracy, rather than innate ability provides a more complex picture of their experiences.

Doing such analysis aids in changing what the mathematics education field knows about Black students' curricula and standardized assessments experiences. We contend that when Black students do not have access to mathematics content that is assessed on standardized tests, the likelihood of them passing significantly decreases. While that assertion seems simple, the consequences for Black students can be far reaching and pernicious. The three concrete examples illuminate that unequal mathematics curricular access and assumptions about Black intelligence in mathematics represents social viciousness that works to support undemocratic goals.

Implications of this analysis suggest that there is a continued need to address the structural, social, and cultural differences in access to advanced mathematics and high-quality instruction for Black students. Teachers have long legitimized the myth of meritocracy through their course placement practices assuming that these decisions are fair and made without bias. However, within our mathematics education system, there are no real consequences in place for teachers who regularly limit Black students' opportunities to take advanced mathematics courses; thus, these practices and inequities remain. Consequently, racial realists equate this experience to the constant struggle for overall racial justice for Black people. Our experiences have also shown that even when individual schools or districts aim to implement policies, such as detracking in mathematics, many White parents consistently resist. What happens as a result of White parent resistant is that equity-minded educators, who promote Black excellence, often have to engage in interest convergence to convince parents and other stakeholders that including Black children in higher level mathematics courses is beneficial for all. Furthermore, these findings reveal the falsehood of meritocracy that all students are treated equally in the mathematics course placement process. We have argued that race, racism, and Whiteness have played significant roles in shaping Black students' unequal access to mathematics content.

We close this chapter by challenging our colleagues in mathematics education to engage in truth-telling. Why? The reason is because truth promotes respect for individuals and groups, and supports their autonomy. We challenge mathematics educators to tell the truth about the relationship between standardized exams, course placements and the ways in which Black students experience these pathways. We challenge mathematics educators to tell the truth about the long-term ramifications Black students and their families may experience when they have a desire to attend college, but have been counseled or guided into mathematics courses that do not support such aspirations. Finally, we wish for mathematics educators to engage in truth-telling that supports the discontinuance of the belief that the performance of Black students is a result of their pathology, rendering them deficient, and point to the systemic ways in which schools restrict opportunities to learn.

Kendi (2016) reminds us that "Black Americans' history of oppression has made Black opportunities—not Black people—inferior" (p. 11). We have seen this repeatedly revealed throughout history in countless ways despite Black peoples' constant attempts to assert that they are equally capable, intelligent, and worthy of dignity and humanity. If education reform leaders are serious about dismantling oppressive structures and focusing on mathematics learning as a human right, they must move beyond gap-gazing and first contend with the U.S.' historical and contemporary issues of race. Anything short of this will only serve to keep the status quo in place, and legitimize the myths that far too many have about Black intelligence because after all, "when you truly believe that the racial groups are equal, then you also believe that racial disparities must be the result of racial discrimination" (Kendi, 2016, p. 11).

Notes

1 Black refers to individuals who are multigenerationally born and raised in the United States; a group of people whose families identified themselves as African American for generations and for whom that identification is a crucial part of their sense of themselves, their families, and their communities. Black people have a distinct identity that has been shaped in large measure by a common history of slavery and by the political struggle of the Civil Rights Movement. Multigenerational African Americans have been

enculturated in how race and ethnicity are socially constructed in the United States (Clark, 2010).

2 According to Chase et al. (2014), the term minoritized refers to both the objective outcomes resulting from the historical and contemporary practices of racial-ethnic exclusion as well as the continued social, political, and economic existence of marginality and discrimination, though compositional racial-ethnic parity may have been achieved in particular contexts.

References

ACT. (2005). *Courses count: Preparing students for postsecondary success.* Iowa City, IA: ACT Policy Report.

ACT. (2017a). *Mathematics college and career readiness standards.* Retrieved from www.act.org/content/act/en/college-and-career-readiness/standards/mathematics-standards.html.

ACT. (2017b). *Profile report—national—graduating class of 2017.* Retrieved from https://docs.google.com/viewer?url=https%3A%2F%2Fwww.act.org%2Fcontent%2Fdam%2Fact%2Funsecured%2Fdocuments%2Fccr2017%2FP_99_999999_N_S_N00_ACT-GCPR_National.pdf.

ACT. (2017c). *The condition of college and career readiness.* Retrieved from https://docs.google.com/viewer?url=http%3A%2F%2Fwww.act.org%2Fcontent%2Fdam%2Fact%2Funsecured%2Fdocuments%2Fccr2017%2FCCCR_National_2017.pdf.

Akiba, M., LeTendre, G. K., & Scribner, J. P. (2007). Teacher quality, opportunity gap, and national achievement in 46 countries. *Educational Researcher, 36*(7), 369–387.

Anderson, N. (2017) We didn't know it was this bad: New ACT scores show huge achievement gaps. *The Washington Post.* Retrieved from https://www.washingtonpost.com/local/education/we-didnt-know-it-was-this-bad-new-act-scores-show-huge-achievement-gaps/2017/09/06/c6397f36-9279-11e7-aace-04b862b2b3f3_story.html.

Battey, D., & Leyva, L. A. (2016). A framework for understanding Whiteness in mathematics education. *Journal of Urban Mathematics Education, 9*(2), 49–80.

Bell, D. (1980). *Brown v. Board of Education* and the interest-convergence dilemma. *Harvard Law Review,* 518–533.

Bell, D. (2004). *Silent covenants: Brown v. Board of Education and the unfulfilled hopes for racial reform.* New York, NY: Oxford University Press.

Bell, D. (2005a). Economic determinism and interest convergence. In R. Delgado & J. Stefancic (Eds.), *The Derrick Bell Reader* (pp. 25–54). New York, NY: New York University Press.

Bell, D. (2005b). Racial Realism. In R. Delgado & J. Stefancic (Eds.), *The Derrick Bell reader* (pp. 73–77). New York, NY: New York University Press.

Bell, D. (2005c). Racism is here to stay now what? In R. Delgado & J. Stefancic (Eds.), *The Derrick Bell Reader* (pp. 85–90). New York, NY: New York University Press.

Berry, R. Q., & Bol, L. (2005). Perceptions of the mathematics achievement gap: A survey of the NCTM membership. In G. M. Lloyd, M. Wilson, J. L. M. Wilkins, & S. L. Behm (Eds.), *Proceedings of the 27th annual meeting of the North American Chapter of the International Group for the Psychology of Mathematics Education* (pp. 1–3). Roanoke, VA.

Berry, R. Q., Ellis, M., & Hughes, S. (2014). Examining a history of failed reforms and recent stories of success: Mathematics education and Black learners of mathematics in the United States. *Race Ethnicity and Education, 17*(4), 540–568.

Boykin, A. W., & Noguera, P. (2011). *Creating the opportunity to learn: Moving from research to practice to close the achievement gap.* Alexandria, VA: Association for Supervision & Curriculum Development.

Browne-Marshall, G. (2016). *The voting rights war: The NAACP and the ongoing struggle for justice.* Lanham, MD: Rowman & Littlefield.

Burris, C. C., & Garrity, D. T. (2008). *Detracking for excellence and equity.* Alexandria, VA: Association for Supervision & Curriculum Development.

Chase, M. M., Dowd, A. C., Pazich, L. B., & Bensimon, E. M. (2014). Transfer equity for "minoritized" students: A critical policy analysis of seven states. *Educational Policy*, 28(5), 669–717.

Clark, H. D. (2010). *We are the same but different: Navigating African American and death cultural identities* (Doctoral dissertation). Retrieved from ProQuest Dissertations and Theses Global (Accession Order No. 3421743).

Clements, D. H., & Sarama, J. (2004). Learning trajectories in mathematics education. *Mathematical Thinking and Learning*, 6(2), 81–89.

Clinedinst, M. & Koranteng, A. (2018). *2017 state of college admission.* Arlington, VA: National Association for College Admissions Counseling.

Cobb, F. (2012). *It's about access: How the curricular system and unequal learning opportunities predict the racial test score gap in mathematics* (Unpublished doctoral dissertation). University of Denver, Denver, CO.

Cobb, F. (Forthcoming). Leading against antiBlackness. In S. Alexander, S. Emanual, L. Scott, J. Alston, & L. Yates (Eds.), *Change agents: P–12 leaders of color tell their stories.* Charlotte, NC: Information Age.

Cobb, F., & Russell, N. M. (2015). Meritocracy or complexity: Problematizing racial disparities in mathematics assessment within the context of curricular structures, practices, and discourse. *Journal of Education Policy*, 30(5), 631–649.

Davis, J. (2014). The mathematical experiences of Black males in a predominantly Black urban middle school and community. *International Journal of Education in Mathematics, Science and Technology*, 2(3), 206–222.

Davis, J., & Martin, D. B. (2008). Racism, assessment, and instructional practice: Implications for mathematics teachers of African American students. *Journal of Urban Mathematics Education*, 1(1), 10–34.

Delgado, R., & Stefancic, J. (2001). *Critical race theory: An introduction.* New York, NY: New York University Press.

Dixson, A. D., & Rousseau, C. K. (2005). And we are still not saved: Critical race theory in education ten years later. *Race Ethnicity and Education*, 8(1), 7–27.

Domina, T., Hanselman, P., Hwang, N. & McEachin, A. (2016). Detracking and tracking up: Mathematics course placement in California middle schools, 2003–2013. *American Educational Research Journal*, 53(4), 1229–1266.

Dumas, M. J. (2014). Losing an arm: Schooling as a cite of Black suffering. *Race Ethnicity and Education*, 17(1), 1–29.

Dumas, M. J. (2016). Against the dark: AntiBlackness in education policy and discourse. *Theory Into Practice*, 55(1), 11–19.

Dumas, M. J., & ross, K. M. (2016). "Be real Black for me": Imagining BlackCrit in education. *Urban Education*, 51(4), 415–442.

ESSA. (2015). *Every Student Succeeds Act of 2015.* Retrieved from https://docs.google.com/viewer?url=https%3A%2F%2Fwww2.ed.gov%2Fpolicy%2Felsec%2Fleg%2Fessa%2Fessaassessmentfactsheet1207.pdf.

Faulkner, V. N., Stiff, L. V., Marshall, P. L., Crossland, C., & Nietfeld, J. (2014) The impact of race and teacher perceptions as predictors of Algebra placement. *Journal for Research in Mathematics Education*, 45(3), 288–311.

Feagin, J. R. (2010). *Racist America: Roots, current realities, and future reparations.* New York, NY: Routledge.

Ferguson, R. F. (1998). Teachers' perceptions and expectations and the Black–White test score gap. In C. Jencks & M. Phillips (Eds.), *The Black–White test score gap* (pp. 217–317). Washington, DC: Brookings Institution.

Gershenson, S., Holt, S. B., & Papageorge, N. W. (2016). Who believes in me? The effect of student–teacher demographic match on teacher expectations. *Economics of Education Review, 52,* 209–224.

Gewertz, C. (2017). Which states require students to take the SAT or ACT? *Education Week.* Retrieved from https://www.edweek.org/ew/section/multimedia/states-require-students-take-sat-or-act.html.

Giroux, H. A., Lankshear, C., McLaren, P., & Peters, M. (2013). *Counternarratives: Cultural studies and critical pedagogies in postmodern spaces.* New York, NY: Routledge.

Grissom, J. A., & Redding, C. (2015). Discretion and disproportionality: Explaining the underrepresentation of high-achieving students of color in gifted programs. *Aera Open, 2*(1), 1–25.

Gutiérrez, R. (2008). A "gap-gazing" fetish in mathematics education? Problematizing research on the achievement gap. *Journal for Research in Mathematics Education, 39*(4), 357–364.

Hallinan, M. (2011). Tracking: From theory to practice. In R. Arum, I. Beattie, & K. Ford (Eds.), *The structure of schooling: Readings in the sociology of education* (pp. 188–192). Newbury Park, CA: Pine Forge.

Harris, C. I. (1993). Whiteness as property. *Harvard Law Review, 106*(8), 1707–1791.

Harwell, M., Moreno, M., & Post, T. (2016). A study of the relationship between the ACT college mathematics readiness standard and college mathematics achievement. *Journal of Psychoeducational Assessment, 34*(3), 269–281.

Herrnstein, R. & Murray, C., (1994). *The bell curve: Intelligence and class structure in American life.* New York, NY: Free Press.

Hilliard, A. G. (2003). No mystery: Closing the achievement gap between Africans and excellence. In T. Perry, C. Steele, & A. Hilliard (Eds.), *Young gifted and Black: Promoting high achievement among African Americans* (pp. 131–165). Boston, MA: Beacon.

Ingersoll, R. M., & May, H. (2012). The magnitude, destinations, and determinants of mathematics and science teacher turnover. *Educational Evaluation and Policy Analysis, 34*(4), 435–464.

Ingersoll, R. M., & Perda, D. (2010). Is the supply of mathematics and science teachers sufficient? *American Educational Research Journal, 47*(3), 563–594.

Irvine, J. J. (2010). Culturally relevant pedagogy. *The Education Digest, 75*(8), 57.

Jensen, A. R. (1969). How much can we boost IQ and scholastic achievement? *Harvard Educational Review, 39*(1), 1–23.

Johnson, T. R. (2015). We used to count Black Americans as 3/5 of a person. For reparations, give them 5/3 of a vote. *The Washington Post.* Retrieved from https://www.washingtonpost.com/posteverything/wp/2015/08/21/we-used-to-count-black-americans-as-35-of-a-person-instead-of-reparations-give-them-53-of-a-vote/?noredirect=on&utm_term=.2b53a2f9c997.

Joseph, N. M., Haynes, C. M., & Cobb, F. (Eds.). (2016). *Interrogating Whiteness and relinquishing power: White faculty's commitment to racial consciousness in STEM classrooms.* New York, NY: Peter Lang.

Kelly, S. (2004). Are teachers tracked? On what basis and with what consequences. *Social Psychology of Education, 7*(1), 55–72.

Kelly, S. (2009). The Black-White gap in mathematics course taking. *Sociology of Education*, 82(1), 47–69.

Kelly, S., & Price, H. (2007). The correlates of tracking policy: Opportunity hoarding, status competition, or a technical-functional explanation? *American Educational Research Journal*, 48(3), 560–585.

Kendi, I. X. (2016). *Stamped from the beginning: The definitive history of racist ideas in America.* New York, NY: Nation Books.

Ladson-Billings, G. (1997). It doesn't add up: African American students' mathematics achievement. *Journal for Research in Mathematics Education*, 28(6), 697–709.

Ladson-Billings, G. (1998). Just what is critical race theory and what's it doing in a nice field like education? *International Journal of Qualitative Studies in Education*, 11(1), 7–24.

Ladson-Billings, G. (2004). Landing on the wrong note: The price we paid for Brown. *Educational Researcher*, 33(7), 3–13.

Ladson-Billings, G. (2006). From the achievement gap to the education debt: Understanding achievement in US schools. *Educational Researcher*, 35(7), 3–12.

Ladson-Billings, G., & Tate, W. F. (1995). Toward a critical race theory of education. *Teachers College Record*, 97(1), 47–68.

Lattimore, R. (2001). The wrath of high-stakes tests. *The Urban Review*, 33(1), 57–67.

Lattimore, R. (2003). African-American students struggle on Ohio's high-stakes test. *Western Journal of Black Studies*, 27(2), 118–126.

Lattimore, R. (2005). African American students' perceptions of their preparation for a high-stakes mathematics test. *Negro Educational Review*, 56(2/3), 135–146.

Lucas, S. R. (2001). Effectively maintained inequality: Education transitions, track mobility, and social background effects. *American Journal of Sociology*, 106(6), 1642–1690.

Martin, D. B. (2000). *Mathematics success and failure among African-American youth: The roles of sociohistorical context, community forces, school influence, and individual agency.* New York, NY: Routledge.

Martin, D. B. (2008). E(race)ing race from a national conversation on mathematics teaching and learning: The national mathematics advisory panel as White institutional space. *The Mathematics Enthusiast*, 5(2), 387–398.

Martin, D. B. (2018). *Refusing systemic violence against Black children: Toward a Black liberatory mathematics education.* A paper presented at annual meeting of the American Education Research Association, New York.

McCaffrey, J. R., Lockwood, D. F., Koretz, D. M., & Hamilton, L. S. (2003). *Evaluating value added models for teacher accountability* [Monograph]. Santa Monica, CA: RAND. Retrieved from http://www.rand.org/pubs/monographs/2004/RAND_MG158.pdf.

McGee Banks, C. A., & Banks, J. A. (1995). Equity pedagogy: An essential component of multicultural education. *Theory Into Practice*, 34(3), 152–158.

Milner, H. (2012). Beyond a test score: Explaining opportunity gaps in educational practice. *Journal of Black Studies*, 43(6), 693–718.

Morial, M. (2014a, February 26). National urban league endorses Common Core State Standards—Here's why: Part one. *The Huffington Post*. Retrieved from https://www.huffingtonpost.com/marc-h-morial/national-urban-league-end_b_4858809.html.

Morial, M. (2014b, November 27). National urban league finds Black parents support Common Core State Standards. *Minnesota Spokesman-Recorder*. Retrieved from http://spokesman-recorder.com/2014/11/27/national-urban-league-finds-black-parents-support-common-core-state-standards/.

Myrdal, G. (1944). *An American dilemma: The Negro problem and modern democracy (Vol. 2)*. Oxford, UK: Transaction.

Oakes, J. (1990). *Multiplying inequalities: The effects of race, social class, and tracking on opportunities to learn mathematics and science*. Santa Monica, CA: RAND.

Oakes, J., Joseph, R., & Muir, K. (2004). Access and achievement in mathematics. In J. A. Banks & C. A. M. Banks (Eds.), *Handbook of research on multicultural education* (pp. 69–90). San Francisco, CA: Jossey-Bass.

Office of Civil Rights (2018). *STEM course taking*. Retrieved from https://www2.ed.gov/a bout/offices/list/ocr/docs/crdc-2015-16.html.

Omi, M., & Winant, H. (2014). *Racial formation in the United States*. New York, NY: Routledge.

Painter, N. I. (2010). *The history of White people*. New York, NY: W. W. Norton & Company.

Peske, H. G., & Haycock, K. (2006). *How poor and minority students are shortchanged on teacher quality*. Washington, DC: The Education Trust.

Reeves, R. & Halikias, D. (2017, February 1). Race gaps in SAT scores highlight inequality and hinder upward mobility. *The Brookings Institution*. Retrieved from https://www.brookings.edu/research/race-gaps-in-sat-scores-highlight-inequality-and-hinder-up ward-mobility/.

Rowan, B., Correnti, R., & Miller, R. J. (2002). What large-scale, survey research tells us about teacher effects on student achievement: Insights from the prospectus study of elementary schools. *CPRE Research Reports*. Retrieved from http://repository.upenn. edu/cpre_researchreports/31.

Schmidt, W., & McKnight, C. (2012). *Inequality for all. The challenge for unequal opportunity in American schools*. New York, NY: Teachers College Press.

Solórzano, D. G., & Yosso, T. J. (2002). Critical race methodology: Counter-storytelling as an analytical framework for education research. *Qualitative Inquiry*, 8(1), 23–44.

Stinson, D. W. (2006). African American male adolescents, schooling (and mathematics): Deficiency, rejection, and achievement. *Review of Educational Research*, 76(4), 477–506.

Stinson, D. W., & Bullock, E. C. (2012). Critical postmodern theory in mathematics education research: A praxis of uncertainty. *Educational Studies in Mathematics*, 80 (1–2), 41–55.

Tate, W. F. (1993). Advocacy versus economics: A critical race analysis of the proposed national assessment in mathematics. *Thresholds in Education*, 19(1), 16–22.

Taylor, E. (2006). A critical race analysis of the achievement gap in the United States: Politics, reality and hope. *Leadership and Policy in Schools*, 5(1), 71–87.

Thrush, G., & Haberman, M. (2017). Trump gives White supremacists an unequivocal boost. *The New York Times*. Retrieved from https://www.nytimes.com/2017/08/15/ us/politics/trump-charlottesville-white-nationalists.html.

Valencia, R. R. (Ed.). (2012). *The evolution of deficit thinking: Educational thought and practice*. New York, NY: Routledge.

Vaught, S. E., & Castagno, A. E. (2008). "I don't think I'm a racist": Critical race theory, teacher attitudes, and structural racism. *Race Ethnicity and Education*, 11(2), 95–113.

Welner, K., & Burris, C. (2006). Alternative approaches to the politics of detracking. *Theory Into Practice*, 45(1), 90–99.

Williams, H. A. (2009). *Self-taught: African American education in slavery and freedom*. Chapel Hill: University of North Carolina Press.

Woodson, C. G. (2013). *The Education of the Negro prior to 1861: A history of the education of the colored people of the United States from the beginning of slavery to the Civil War.* Los Angeles, CA: Hard Press. (Original work published in 1919).

Yosso, T. (2002). Toward a critical race curriculum. *Equity & Excellence in Education, 35*(2), 93–107.

Zamudio, M., Russell, C., Rios, F., & Bridgeman, J. L. (2010). *Critical race theory matters: Education and ideology.* New York, NY: Routledge.

9

USING PERSONAL NARRATIVES TO ELUCIDATE MY CRT(ME) JOURNEY

Christopher C. Jett

Introduction

One privilege of being a mathematics education researcher is attending conferences and other specialized meetings. Conferences are a nice way to learn of the latest developments in the field, to connect with other scholars in different settings, and to generate fresh ideas for research collaborations and the like. In addition, conferences can be a nice way to explore different locales and enjoy the sceneries of those new places. In this vein, I was excited to attend a mathematics education conference in Houston, Texas in the spring of 2018. During the previous fall, the city had gone through a tumultuous time as residents had been impacted by Hurricane Harvey. Because of the catastrophic rainfall and subsequent flooding, it was uncertain whether the conference would even proceed in that city or if measures would have to be put in place to secure another location for the annual meeting. The weather conditions allowed for the conference be held there, so I looked forward to visiting the city for the first time, seeing the progress the city had made, and observing the resiliency of the city's people.

This conference meeting space was attached to Houston Galleria, a mall with anchor stores such as Neiman Marcus and Nordstrom. While walking through the mall area, one of the mall security officers stopped me. I was somewhat taken aback because I knew that I was simply going about shopping as usual, and one might think that the fancy mall would attract people with a certain type of racial and economic make-up, read as White and middle-class. The mall security officer informed me that I could not wear a hoodie in the mall. As one known to display various facial expressions, I am pretty sure that I looked somewhat astonished or puzzled by the request. The mall security officer added that it was the mall's policy. One nearby shopper who witnessed the exchange told me the hoodie is used as the signifier of folks who might steal, rob, or perform some other illegal activities in the mall. This racism woven into the fabric of a mall policy is a reflection of what happens in mathematics classrooms for those who enter with the wrong garment(s) and skin pigmentation. Stated differently, just as mall security officers anticipate criminal behavior with Black men in hoodies, mathematics teachers often equate Black students in urban attire with mathematics failure.

One point in opening with this personal story is to expose the threat of being Black and male within society. Thoughts about the murder of Trayvon Martin ran through my head, and I realized that the same type of racial profiling is responsible for the deaths of countless African American adults and children. As such, my background thinking constantly tells me, as a Black man, to make it out of these encounters alive. Another point is to demonstrate that we, as Blacks, are always under surveillance even in fancy malls with White folks with terminal degrees in our disciplinary field. In other words, while White mathematics educators can attend to business as usual, Black mathematics educators *always* have to consider racial dynamics no matter the setting where we reside. This heightened racial visibility adds an additional layer in that we have to navigate these racially antagonistic spaces as Black scholars both inside and outside conference spaces.

An important point in opening with this particular story is to bring attention to critical race theory (CRT) as both a theoretical framework for research and a way for me to make sense of my life as a Black mathematics education researcher. CRT places value on experiential knowledge through the use of personal narratives and storytelling (Lynn & Adams, 2002; Parker, 1998). These narratives allow CRT scholars to situate the theorizing of race within the context of their everyday experiences with racism (Lynn & Adams, 2002; Tate, 1997). They "illustrate, from a critical perspective, the historical and current connections and effects of racial issues and concerns" (Parker, 1998, p. 50). Thus, the aforementioned encounter reifies the current racial constructions of what a hoodie constitutes in relation to Black boys and men.

In this CRT tradition, I share this mall experience to make visible the racial differences, privileges, and microaggressions that reside in these spaces. "Racial microaggressions are brief and commonplace daily verbal, behavioral, or environmental indignities, whether intentional or unintentional, that communicate hostile, derogatory, or negative racial slights and insults toward people of color" (Sue et al., 2007, p. 271), and Solórzano (2018) argues that racial microaggressions are symptoms of White supremacy. I would categorize this experience as such. My experiences with racial microaggressions are too numerous to include within this chapter as they occur in mathematics education settings, in my institutional context, and in my day-to-day interactions. Hence, the racial climate within our society substantiates CRT's primary tenet that race is endemic in our society (Delgado & Stefancic, 2000).

In this chapter, I unearth my researcher positionality by sharing information about my childhood by honing in on my grandfather's influence on me. Then, I share information about my doctoral experiences at Georgia State University (GSU), the place where I began to engage with the CRT scholarly literature. Further on, I offer some thoughts about what CRT contributes to mathematics education scholarship in general and to my research with Black male students in particular. I conclude the chapter by challenging other mathematics education researchers to use this theoretical construct to work toward racial justice. On another note, it is important to point out that I use Black and African American interchangeably throughout this chapter. Furthermore, it is important to note that my aim in this chapter is not to essentialize or signify that my voice speaks for all Black men (Dixson & Rousseau, 2005). Rather, this chapter literally presents the "me" on my quest to explore CRT in mathematics education (*CRT(ME)*).

C is for Charlie: My Positionality

My grandfather—I called him "Daddy"—was influential in my upbringing, and he had a very strong position on race. I cannot recall the specific circumstances, but I remember him coming to live with us when I was a small child. Although he could not read and only possessed a first grade education, he was adamant about ensuring that my siblings and I received an education. I recall a phone conversation at home as we were preparing for my family to travel from Memphis to Nashville to attend my undergraduate commencement ceremony at Tennessee State University (TSU), a Historically Black College/University (HBCU). We were unsure exactly how all of my family members would travel to attend. Daddy grabbed the phone from my mother and boldly told me, "I'll be there if I have to walk!" Although I knew that there was no way that he could walk 200 miles to the event, I also knew that he was serious about making sure that he was there for this momentous occasion. There was nothing that he wanted more. Daddy passed away before the graduation happened. I was devastated that he was not able to witness the collegiate celebration here in the Earth realm.

I mention Daddy not only to highlight his influence on my life, but also because his name was Charlie Jett; he was named after his grandfather. My name is Christopher Charlie Jett. I am honored to carry their name, and I use my middle initial professionally as a tribute to them and as a demonstration of the familial capital associated with the name. Ironically, many of my college friends referred to me as granddaddy. My nickname was granddaddy because I was an "old soul" trapped in a young body. Apparently, my mannerisms, sayings, and words of wisdom resembled that of an old man... a granddaddy... my granddaddy... Daddy... Charlie. When my peers learned that my middle name is Charlie and that I shared the name with Daddy, it was like a light bulb went off in their brains and it all made sense to them. Fundamentally, my name represented a multi-generational legacy of Black wisdom present among a group of Generation X college students. Therefore, in my close circle of friends, I became affectionately known as Christopher Charlie.

Daddy was a rather slim man who was deeply committed to his family. Surprisingly, I have a similar build as he did, and my family members often joke that I was given the correct middle name given how much I resemble him. He told us stories about the racial injustices he experienced during his upbringing, the most memorable being that he had to quit going to school in the second grade largely because of a White man's non-negotiable "suggestion" for him to work instead. This story and the dynamic between Daddy and this White man have puzzled me since childhood. He also shared how he had to routinely fight against racist inequalities. I can imagine that his grandfather may have told him similar stories. Racial struggle is a part of the heritage of our shared name. As a result, he wanted us, especially his grandchildren, to take advantage of the educational opportunities available to us as he expressed that an education would yield a better life for us.

I engage in my CRT work with the spirit of Charlie. The good thing about this spirit is that it transcends time and place as his spirit resides in me whenever I engage in antiracist scholarship and activism. It stands to reason that Daddy would be so racially conscious with me given the subsequent conversations about the tapestry of racism with his children—my aunts and uncles—who have shared stories of being discouraged from pursuing a science degree by a White male science professor (which resulted in dropping out of college after only attending for a few weeks), getting into a heated verbal exchange with a White woman erroneously suspecting that something was stolen from a retail store, and being accused by a White supervisor of lying about taking a day off to attend my doctoral hooding ceremony. Thus, my familial upbringing coupled with my own racialized experiences have significantly influenced how I engage in research, teaching, service, and leadership efforts in mathematics education. I have written about how a White teacher tried to force me into special education during my first grade year of elementary school, how some non-Black mathematics professors at TSU attempted to dehumanize our mathematics experiences as African American students, how a history of mathematics professor dismissed my request to do a paper on an African American mathematician, and how I have dealt with racial slights as a mathematics education professional (Jett, 2009, 2013, 2016a). It should then come as no surprise that I would seek out doctoral programs to engage in such work.

Mathematics Education Doctoral Experiences

While researching doctoral programs, I was initially conflicted between pursuing a doctorate in mathematics or in mathematics education. I applied to programs in both disciplines and was leaning more heavily toward mathematics at first. My mathematics professors at TSU encouraged me to go the mathematics route given my previous successes and genuine interests in the subject, with many of them championing the institutions where they earned their doctorates. As fate would have it, I followed my passions and opted to go the mathematics education route. I did so because I was interested in conducting research on, for, and with African

American students to counter the disparaging racialized rhetoric about their mathematics abilities.

After applying to a few mathematics education doctoral programs, I elected to go to GSU for several reasons. At the time, there was a critical mass of Black women on the mathematics education faculty there. Drs. Christine Thomas, Pier Junor-Clarke, and Clara Okoka as well as then Ph.D. students Desha Williams and Becky Patterson's academic profiles were all displayed on the department's homepage. I vividly remember the natural hairstyles and African-themed attire on many of their photos. The unapologetically Black images depicted them in their true cultural selves and positioned this mathematics education doctoral program as one that could be affirming to me as a Black man. Fortuitously, a Black man, Dr. Lou Matthews, joined the mathematics education faculty and later served on my dissertation committee. Another primary attraction to this institution was my interest in Dr. David Stinson's research area. I found and read his dissertation on mathematically successful African American male secondary students and was excited about the possibility of establishing a similar research line in the undergraduate realm (Stinson, 2004). He would become my advisor/major professor. A final reason why GSU appealed to me was because of the urban education-focused college mission, and the affirming photos of Black students on the website solidified the idea that I would feel welcome there. Unlike some institutions that use images of Black students to promote an illusion of racial diversity, this photo op was actually representative of the racial atmosphere at GSU.

As a doctoral student, I was hungry for literature that centered the mathematics experiences of African American students. Among the first texts I read were Martin's (2000) *Mathematics Success and Failure among African-American Youth: The Roles of Sociohistorical Context, Community Forces, School Influence, and Individual Agency,* Moses and Cobb's (2002) *Radical Equations: Civil Rights from Mississippi to the Algebra Project,* and Strutchens, Johnson, and Tate's (2000) edited volume, *Changing the Faces of Mathematics: Perspectives on African Americans.* Through these books and additional articles, I was introduced to scholarship from other researchers concerning African American students' mathematics education experiences. Even at the time, it was apparent that this work was rare. It is encouraging, however, to see the recent proliferation of work from an up-and-coming group of mathematics education researchers who are filling in some of the critical shortages in the literature. Also, although these texts did not use CRT to frame their studies and primary arguments per se, they were instrumental in my exposure to what scholarship could look like with respect to my people. It also showed me that race matters (West, 2001). And if race matters in our society as West expounded upon in his treatise, then it stands to reason that race matters in mathematics education. Taken together though, these readings served as the beginning of my racialized turn in mathematics education.

As mentioned previously, I began to explore CRT more deeply while completing my mathematics education doctoral studies at GSU. Dr. Joyce E. King, also a member of my dissertation committee, was the most influential in my thinking about race and the use of CRT in my work. I was honored to have this Black education powerhouse on my committee to provide sage counsel about doing race work in mathematics education. I grappled with her concept of "dysconscious racism" (King, 1991) since I first read it. Plus, I had the pleasure of taking a couple of doctoral seminars from her—one in which we read and synthesized her *Black Education* edited text (King, 2005). I must add that her classes were the most liberating experience throughout my educational career. In practice, they offered an opportunity to initiate and strengthen an individualized transformative vision for Black (mathematics) education research.

During my time at GSU, there was not a CRT in education course offering for graduate students. Of course, I am not arguing that a single CRT course can solve all of the racial ills in (mathematics) education research as I posit that the entire curriculum should address issues of race and racism. However, I was able to write some final course papers on race-related topics, and I took a course in African American Studies to supplement what I learned about race in the College of Education (COE). Since that time, there have been courses in CRT in GSU's COE. This example demonstrates the traction CRT is gaining in institutional and programmatic spaces, and it shows that additional efforts are being exerted to produce researchers and practitioners who are more equipped to think analytically about race and racism.

Notwithstanding, I was drawn to CRT because it provided a heightened and more nuanced examination of race and racism and sharpened my racial consciousness. Like many others who begin to explore the CRT literature in education, one of the first CRT articles I read was the seminal piece, "Toward a Critical Race Theory in Education," by Ladson-Billings and Tate (1995). Once I began reading the CRT literature, I immersed myself in that body of scholarship as it resonated with my personal experiences and provided me with diverse viewpoints concerning race. Given CRT's genesis in legal scholarship, I read scholarship in law journals (e.g., Bell, 1989; Crenshaw, 1988; Delgado, 1989). I also read about the experiences of Latino/a through the form of Latino/a CRT (LatCrit; e.g., Bernal, 2002; Fernández, 2002; Villapando, 2003), indigenous people through the form of TribalCrit (e.g., Brayboy, 2005; Castagno & Lee, 2007), and other marginalized and stigmatized groups using CRT as a tool for analysis (e.g., Duncan, 2002; Solórzano, 1998). I read these articles critically, combed through the reference pages, and requested more articles from GSU's library to expand my knowledge base on the theory and its associated tenets—a practice I still employ today through my institutional library account. Throughout my doctoral journey, however, I began to formulate the words and ideas to "walk the walk" and "talk the talk" regarding CRT scholarship, especially as it pertains to its connections to mathematics education research.

What CRT Offers to Mathematics Education Scholarship

CRT was established through the work of legal scholars such as Alan Freeman, Richard Delgado, and Derrick Bell, the father of CRT (Delgado & Stefancic, 2001), and this theoretical construct has expanded to education research (Ladson-Billings & Tate, 1995). Lynn and Adams (2002) argue that "education continues to be one of the key arenas where the impact of racism is felt most" (p. 87), and I extend this argument to the mathematics education terrain. However, mathematics education is generally framed as an intellectual discipline that is racially neutral. Like other Black critical mathematics education scholars (Martin & Gholson, 2012), I posit that mathematics education is a highly racialized enterprise. Martin (2009) even highlights the racialized institutional culture of the discipline and argues that mathematics (education) serves as an institutional space of Whiteness. Other mathematics educators have made similar arguments relating to how various educational efforts, policies, and initiatives center the ideals, interests and values of Whites (e.g., Berry, 2018; Bullock, 2017; Martin, Rousseau Anderson, & Shah, 2017). We learn from this body of work that mathematics education operates under a White-normed paradigm. Therefore, what is needed in mathematics education is a "racecentricity—an explicitly race conscious approach to education" (Carbado, 2002, p. 181), and CRT is a solution to this perennial problem in the field.

Given this assertion and the United States' troubling racialized history, African Americans have suffered the most at the palm of racism's exploitative and oppressive hand. In this regard, Black students often deal with racial assaults, discriminatory acts, stereotypes, and other forms of racialization that pervade mathematics education spaces (Jett, 2012; McGee, 2015). The literature suggests that the constant grappling with such race-related incidents contributes to racial battle fatigue (RBF), which Smith, Allen, and Danley (2007) define as "the result of constant psychological, cultural, and emotional coping with racial microaggressions in less-than-ideal and racially hostile or unsupportive environments" (p. 555). On the other hand, DiAngelo (2011) argues that "White people in North America live in a social environment that protects and insulates them from race-based stress" (p. 54). And by extension, "using their White racial identity to feign innocence and victimization becomes a process that maintains White supremacy" (Matias, 2016, p. 36). Many of the perpetrators of racial microaggressions are our mathematics education colleagues, and many of them sit in our conference sessions where we, as Black mathematics educators, share race-related work. Interestingly, some of them claim to be allies and nod their heads in agreement when valid points are being made about racial insensitivities as if they can spot such behaviors among others, but not among themselves.

For mathematics education scholars who wish to investigate and dismantle White norms, CRT is a theoretical framework that explores the role of race and racism when investigating the mathematical schooling experiences of racialized students (DeCuir & Dixson, 2004). Ledesma and Calderón (2015) remind us that CRT scholarship does more than point to race: "it requires an engagement and articulation with the material, structural, and ideological mechanisms of White supremacy" (p. 206). Unfortunately, in our society "White supremacy was [is] the law, and Blackness was [is] a crime" (Abu-Jamal, 2017, p. 22). Relatedly, hooks (1995) declares that "racial hatred is real" (p. 17), and these ideologies become manifest via White supremacists' superiority infused mantras, robocalls, and death threats.

Theoretically, CRT renders many tenets to address these issues and advance mathematics education research—racial normalcy (e.g., Delgado & Stefancic, 2000), interest convergence (e.g., Delgado & Stefancic, 2001), race as a social construction (e.g., Ladson-Billings, 2013), intersectionality (e.g., Crenshaw, 1991), and experiential knowledge through voice as counter-narrative (e.g., Solórzano & Yosso, 2002). Many contributors to this edited volume have unpacked these tenets and others with respect to our disciplinary field. CRT also allows me to be a co-learner with research participants and for participants to raise important, race-related questions to me (Ladson-Billings, 1999). Moreover, it allows me to engage in critical reflexivity or self-reflexivity as a qualitative researcher (Ladson-Billings, 2000; Tracy, 2010). Importantly, employing CRT allows mathematics education researchers to explore the racial climate of K–12 and higher education institutions, explore the nature of racist acts, behaviors, and/or utterances to African American students, and examine the disciplinary acts of those who engage in these offensive racial undertakings (DeCuir & Dixson, 2004). In sum, a critical race lens offers mathematics education researchers an opportunity to examine and act to eradicate, to the fullest extent possible, racial inequalities and injustices (Parker & Stovall, 2004).

With regard to methodology, CRT's methodologies challenge Eurocentric paradigms and offer a liberatory embodiment of education research (Parker & Lynn, 2002; Tate, 1994). The most utilized CRT methodological aspect occurs through voice in qualitative research, whereby marginalized voices serve as counter-narratives to dominant racially denigrating discourses, and CRT has been underutilized with quantitative research (Delgado, 1989; Sablan, 2019). However, a significant finding across both the quantitative and qualitative research literature is the minimal treatment of race with these methodological approaches (Parker & Lynn, 2002; Sablan, 2018). The good news is that there are some innovative methodological advancements to address this shortcoming. For instance, "a very new development for CRT is critical race theory and empirical methods (eCRT) … by those, including many junior scholars, who believed that scholarship on race could benefit from intersecting sophisticated social science research methods with CRT" (Wing, 2016, p. 52). eCRT scholarship is interdisciplinary in nature and leverages the methodological fruitfulness from social science research.

What is less common in CRT work is the use of mixed-methods and quantitative methods (DeCuir-Gunby & Walker-DeVose, 2013; Sablan, 2019). QuantCrit is designed to use CRT to unmask racist paradigms associated with quantitative objectivity, and Gillborn, Warmington, and Demack (2018) offer five tenets of QuantCrit to assist with analysis of quantitative data. To address quantitative methods' foundations in White supremacy and to counter the proclamation, "let the numbers speak for themselves," Covarrubias and Velez (2013) propose a critical race quantitative intersectionality (CRQI). A CRQI, they argue, expands the functionality of CRT and simultaneously magnifies the impact of intersectionality. Mathematics education researchers are encouraged to engage in this literature as these examples show that CRT holds extraordinary potential to enrich qualitative, quantitative, and mixed-methods methodological approaches for the field.

Regarding pedagogy, mathematics (teacher) educators should continue to address issues of race and racism in their instructional practices. Critical race counter-stories, allegories, and revisionist histories can be taught in tandem with mathematics standards (Bell, 1989; Tate, 1994). Additionally, mathematics educators, researchers, and students should conduct critical race analyses of mathematics curricula to unearth, synthesize, and counter the hidden racial messages underlying these documents. For example, my colleagues and I use CRT to expose the blind spots of teaching/learning mathematics for social justice regarding race, racism, and racialization (Larnell, Bullock, & Jett, 2016). Johnson (2017) utilizes a racial storytelling assignment to critically examine how previous racial encounters situate themselves in today's context, and Gillborn (2016) has teachers create "*new* rules of racial standing" (p. 103). Mathematics educators could adapt these ideas to catapult their learning outcomes with respect to race. Further, Wing (2016) advocates for building critical race coalitions to bridge the gap between theory and practice. These coalitions could not only address ways to infuse CRT in our individual pedagogical practices, but they could also facilitate critical race mathematics teacher circles, critical race mathematics education research affinity groups, and so on to engage with and spur action grounded in CRT's principles. In sync with these ideas, a *CRT(ME)* course is a practical implication from this work that could be powerful in terms of sharpening mathematics constituents' critical race outlooks.

Here, I offer some guiding questions to invigorate CRT's utility for the mathematics education community. These include: How might CRT and mathematics education combine with other disciplines to further showcase the interdisciplarity of CRT? How might CRT be employed to thwart the racially motivated crimes that happen to Lesbian, Gay, Bisexual, Transgender, and Queer (LGBTQ+) individuals, especially in mathematics enclaves? In what ways might we employ CRT to better account for marginalized students' experiences, realities, and needs in mathematics education policies and reforms (Berry, 2018; Berry, Ellis, & Hughes, 2014)? In what ways might we use CRT's tenets to produce new (mathematics) knowledge in service to community-based racial knowledge? How might CRT start a movement in mathematics education whereby researchers and practitioners transition from being nonracist to becoming antiracist (Bonilla-Silva, 2014)? And given the growing interest in race, equity, social justice, diversity, and inclusion among mathematics educators, how might CRT help mathematics education researchers and practitioners to not work in favor of White supremacy?

Unequivocally, as mathematics education professionals, we still have much work to do related to utilizing CRT to advance theoretically-driven research projects critical in nature, extend the use of race-conscious methodological approaches, and infuse critical pedagogical practices in our work. In this section, I have only offered a snapshot of what is possible when conjoining CRT with mathematics education ideals. What is clear is that when mathematics education researchers weave the discipline together with CRT in unique ways, the epistemological limits are boundless. And yet again, I challenge mathematics education scholars to join me at "the critical race table to problematize, challenge, deconstruct, and work to eradicate issues of race and racism" (Jett, 2012, p. 27). I now turn my discussion to CRT with respect to my research agenda.

CRT with Black Male Students: Excavating My Research Agenda

Earlier, I discussed the wealth of knowledge I accumulated from Daddy concerning race and racism; however, I became keenly aware of how racism functioned with Black boys and men as a young teenager. Sadly, I, too, had an encounter with two White male police officers as a teen while playing on the front porch of our home. The police officers received a call about a man named Chris who was accused of attempting to rape a woman; he was reported to be on the block where I lived. When they approached our home looking for the man, the officers asked me my name. Of course, I replied "Chris," and I was immediately jacked up, slammed to the front door, and placed in handcuffs. My mother came running and yelling at the officers to let me go. She grabbed one of them, exclaiming that I was just a child. Her yelling drew the neighbors in our close-knit, family-like community from their homes. The neighbor who called the police even came forth to verify that I was not the one who attempted to rape her. The police officers let me go, and I was left in tears to sort through this trauma.

Even though Daddy shared stories of racism, this experience of being hand-cuffed served as a racial awakening for me. More specifically, it served as a Black male awakening whereby if you are in a Black male body, then get ready to "assume the position because you fit the description" (Smith, Allen, & Danley, 2007) without regard for age, stature, or any other childlike or innocent characteristic. If my police encounter would have occurred in today's technologically savvy times, my situation could have potentially been captured on film and posted to various social media outlets. It could have been equated to 10-year old

Michael Thomas Jr.'s viral video that sparked outrage. In it, this Black boy wet himself after police officers placed him in handcuffs because he "matched the description" of someone with a gun (Levy, 2018). While every experience is not exactly the same, the point is that these events occur time and time again among Black boys and that they leave us with unresolved trauma that we carry throughout our lifetimes.

Many of the racial challenges I see thrust upon Black children, youth, and adults that go viral through various social media outlets are not new to me as I have witnessed similar scenarios in my hometown of Memphis. The city is plagued with issues of police brutality, and it could be the home of the next uprising that receives national attention when city residents reach a boiling point as it relates to police brutality. Abu-Jamal (2017) writes about this issue of police brutality in the South and argues:

> But where once Whites killed and terrorized from beneath a KKK hood, now they did so openly from behind a little badge. And while it may seem like a leap to associate the historical White terrorism of the South with the impunity with which police kill in Black communities today, it is really not so great of a leap because both demonstrate a purpose of containment, repression, and the diminution of Black hope, Black aspirations, and Black life.
>
> (p. 9)

Abu-Jamal's argument is in parallel to Anderson's (2016) White rage thesis that Black achievement is the inevitable tripper for White rage. She writes:

> Black respectability or "appropriate" behavior doesn't seem to matter. If anything, Black achievement, Black aspirations, and Black success are construed as direct threats. Obama's presidency made that clear. Aspirations and the achievement of these aspirations provide no protection. Not even to the God-fearing.
>
> (p. 159)

Similar to Abu-Jamal, Anderson argues that "White rage doesn't have to wear sheets, burn crosses, or take to the streets. Working the halls of power, it can achieve its ends far more effectively, far more destructively" (p. 3). Both of these authors make the case that the underlying agenda with these establishments founded upon White supremacist logic is the devaluation of Black achievements and ultimately Black life. In this country, navigating the White space engorged with racial abhorrence against Black people results in such practices to halt Black life (hooks, 1995). Essentially, this logic system infiltrates mathematics education whereby Black students often lose mathematics-related aspirations, and this reduction of mathematics achievement is exacerbated in urban areas such as in my hometown of Memphis.

I recall this childhood incident in Memphis as well as the opening story to illustrate how I have continued to develop a critical race eye (Bell, 1992). I also share these examples to showcase that Black boys with academic promise and Black men with doctorates are not exempt from the racial stereotypes attempting to position us as criminals and sexual predators, among other negative portrayals (Bell, 1987; Dixson & Rousseau, 2005). What is more distressing is the fact that I have experienced racial microaggressions, degradations, and assaults from students, peers, and colleagues alike, namely, in institutions, professional association meetings, and research settings that have largely co-opted race-related mission statements, strategic plans, and other antiracist practices and policies. As a Black man, I am attempting to make sense of these racial contradictions, and I am continuously grappling with making sense of my ongoing racial struggles at the time of this writing.

Because of my upbringing in the city of Memphis and my past educational experiences, I have been led to this particular line of scholarly inquiry—the racialized experiences of African American male students. I am not attempting to position my work as a form of tokenism as there is a growing body of work using CRT with Black men (Duncan, 2002; Hotchkins, 2016; Howard & Reynolds, 2013; Johnson & Bryan, 2017) as well as a growing volume of research by mathematics education researchers who have used CRT with Black male students (Berry, 2008; Davis, 2014; Jett, 2011, 2016b, in press; Stinson, 2008; Terry, 2011). While engaging in this work, it is important to note that my research is not in opposition to feminist scholarship. In fact, I borrow from feminist theories such as FemCrit to inform my scholarship and expand my breadth and depth of knowledge concerning gender-specific race relations. In doing so, I draw from the body of knowledge using CRT to explore and examine the experiences of Black women (Caldwell, 2000; Crenshaw, 1991; Gregory, 2017; Joseph, Hailu, & Boston, 2017; Wilson, 2018). DeCuir and Dixson (2004) stress that: "Given the insidious and often subtle way in which race and racism operate, it is imperative that educational researchers explore the role of race when examining the educational experiences of African-American students" (p. 26). These realities guide my own thinking and action items as a mathematics education researcher, and this critical body of research informs my scholarly agenda.

To date, I would consider my most noteworthy accomplishment being the use of CRT to frame and guide my National Science Foundation (NSF) Early Career Faculty Development (CAREER) proposal. Constructs such as brilliant, mathematically resilient, and other strengths-based phrases govern my epistemological orientation and research agenda, so it should be expected that such ideologies would run rampant in my grant proposal. A few scholars were shocked to learn that my research regarding high-achieving African American male students was able to garner a CAREER award. Also, being that I am a faculty member at a primarily undergraduate teaching institution, I had to make a somewhat stronger case for being someone who could build a CAREER worthy profile during my negotiations. However, the CAREER grant has provided me with release time to devote to my scholarship, resources to engage in a humanistic research project, and professional development opportunities to grow as a scholar. I am in the midst of using this project to learn more about innovative qualitative research methods, explore Science, Technology, Engineering, and Mathematics (STEM) education vis-á-vis a national context, and meet others who are working to ensure that efforts are equitably tailored to meet the needs of African American (male) students. Because of these advantages, I have faith that the CAREER work will yield even more fruitful results concerning my research and scholarship.

On the cusp of my first decade as a mathematics education researcher, I realize that CRT has helped my work with Black male students to evolve. This theory has resulted in me thinking more deeply about institutionalized racism, White supremacy, and Whiteness scholarship. Whiteness scholarship privileges, centers, and reifies. White norms in unprecedented ways (Leonardo, 2013; Mathias, 2016). I concur with Matias who declares: "The term non-White or normalizing Whiteness as 'not different' places Whiteness at the center and all others in a 'non' category" (p. 32). However, CRT has allowed me to examine how White supremacists' stances are sanctioned with respect to Black men in my research. It has also planted seeds to think of ways to conjoin with Black masculinity theory to contribute to the burgeoning body of critical race masculinism work (Delgado & Stefancic, 2001). In this regard, CRT has caused me to begin to think about the macro-level racial injustices Black men experience in diverse contexts as there is a lot to be gleaned from the intersection of those racialized and gendered experiences. In addition, CRT has caused me to think about the impact of doing race work on scholars' mental psyches, including my own, in addition to adaptive coping strategies to withstand race-related stress (McGee & Stovall, 2015).

Concluding Thoughts

In this chapter, I have used personal narratives across my life as a point of entry to my racialized experiences as a Black man and to suggest, in many ways, that I have always drawn from critical race theoretical presuppositions to inform my perspective. These personal narratives elucidate my ongoing critical race journey and illustrate that racism persists. Delgado (1989) asserts that "storytelling emboldens the hearer, who may have had the same thoughts and experiences the storyteller describes, but hesitated to give them voice. Having heard another express them, he or she realizes, I am not alone" (p. 2437), so I hope that my personal narratives might empower those grappling with various racial frustrations and disappointments to write and act to bring about more awareness and change. This chapter was also designed to show how CRT can be useful for mathematics education researchers while simultaneously showcasing how this theory has informed my research agenda. As a Black mathematics education researcher, I know that I stand on the shoulders of many others who came before me, especially my family members. I am not attempting to compare my experiences with the horrific racial hurdles they had to jump during that time. Rather, I aim to show how my own racialized experiences build on this racialized continuum and serve as motivation for my research interests.

On an individual level, CRT has caused me to find my voice as a Black male academic. I have been told on a few occasions that I can be perceived as a somewhat quiet, timid guy in academic spaces, so it has given me the fortitude to unearth my race-oriented epistemologies. CRT has also forced me to realize that a racialized experience is not a single event and that all institutions are also implicated because of the permanence and operationalization of racism "at many different levels—individual, institutional, and structural" (Martin, Rousseau Anderson, & Shah, 2017, p. 611). In other words, it has taught me that racial experiences are multiplicitous, complex, and ubiquitous. As it pertains to my work, CRT has propelled me to expose and disrupt the degrading racial patterns with respect to Black (male) students. On a disciplinary level, it allows opportunities for mathematics education researchers to resist and transform the mathematics education enterprise. I am hopeful that it can, too, allow people to change their actions to produce healthy race-related outcomes for Blacks writ large.

As it stands, this country has been and continues to be plagued by racial tensions. These racial tensions have become heightened during this racist and xenophobic political climate. Notwithstanding, race relations are ongoing and the implications of such are widespread. Of course, these race-specific implications infiltrate mathematics education spaces, and one can argue that they will be with us in the future. And while I have advocated for the use of CRT with mathematics education research, I also understand that CRT is not the be-all and end-all of theoretical frameworks as other theoretical frameworks, lenses, and paradigms can be applied in conjunction with CRT to enrich our racial, mathematics-related understandings.

What is most clear across the aforementioned volume of work is that CRT offers theoretical, methodological, and pedagogical tools to analyze and change the racialized systems of domination, oppression, and exclusion in mathematics education. If we are serious about racial progress and wish to move beyond the lip service espoused in much of the social justice rhetoric, then we must engage in a systematic and more sophisticated treatment of race and racism as mathematics education researchers. In closing, I borrow from Hilliard's (1995) discussion about *a will to excellence*. In order to reach that destination, he argues that "not only must we change from the slow lane to the fast lane, we must change highways. Perhaps we need to abandon the highways altogether and take flight" (p. 206). Viewed in this light, CRT offers a robust theoretical voyage for us to take flight in our fight toward racial justice in mathematics education, and I hope that my journey might have inspired a renewed sense of commitment to advancing CRT in mathematics education scholarship.

References

Abu-Jamal, M. (2017). *Have Black lives ever mattered?* San Francisco, CA: City Lights Bookstore.

Anderson, C. (2016). *White rage: The unspoken truth of the racial divide.* New York, NY: Bloomsbury.

Bell, D. (1987). *And we are not saved: The elusive quest for racial justice.* New York, NY: Basic Books.

Bell, D. (1989). The final report: Harvard's affirmative action allegory. *Michigan Law Review,* 87, 2382–2410.

Bell, D. (1992). *Faces at the bottom of the well: The permanence of racism.* New York, NY: Basic Books.

Bernal, D. D. (2002). Critical race theory, Latino critical theory and critical raced-gendered epistemologies: Recognizing students of color as holders and creators of knowledge. *Qualitative Inquiry,* 8(1), 105–126.

Berry, R. Q. (2008). Access to upper-level mathematics: The stories of successful African American middle school boys. *Journal for Research in Mathematics Education,* 39 (5), 464–488.

Berry, R. Q. (2018). Disrupting policies and reforms in mathematics education to address the needs of marginalized learners. In T. G. Bartell (Ed.), *Toward equity and social justice in mathematics education* (pp. 3–20). New York, NY: Springer.

Berry, R. Q., Ellis, M., & Hughes, S. (2014). Examining a history of failed reforms and recent stories of success: Mathematics education and Black learners of mathematics in the United States. *Race Ethnicity and Education,* 17(4), 540–568.

Bonilla-Silva, E. (2014). *Racism without racists: Color-blind racism and the persistence of racial inequality in America* (4th ed.). Lanham, MD: Rowman & Littlefield.

Brayboy, B. (2005). Towards a tribal critical race theory in education. *The Urban Review,* 37(5), 425–446.

Bullock, E. C. (2017). Only STEM can save us? Examining race, place, and STEM education as property. *Educational Studies,* 53(6), 628–641.

Caldwell, P. M. (2000). A hair piece: Perspectives on the intersection of race and gender. In R. Delgado & J. Stefancic (Eds.), *Critical race theory: The cutting edge* (2nd ed., pp. 275–285). Philadelphia, PA: Temple University Press.

Carbado, D. W. (2002). Afterword: (E)racing education. *Equity & Excellence in Education,* 35(2), 181–194.

Castagno, A. E., & Lee, S. J. (2007). Native mascots and ethnic fraud in higher education: Using tribal critical race theory and the interest convergence principle as an analytical tool. *Equity & Excellence in Education,* 40(1), 3–13.

Covarrubias, A., & Velez, V. (2013). Critical race quantitative intersectionality: An anti-racist research paradigm that refuses to "let the numbers speak for themselves". In M. Lynn & A. D. Dixson (Eds.), *The handbook of critical race theory in education* (pp. 270–285). New York, NY: Routledge.

Crenshaw, K. W. (1988). Race, reform, and retrenchment: Transformation and legitimation in antidiscrimination law. *Harvard Law Review,* 101(7), 1331–1387.

Crenshaw, K. W. (1991). Mapping the margins: Intersectionality, identity politics, and violence against women of color. *Stanford Law Review,* 43(6), 1241–1299.

Davis, J. (2014). The mathematical experiences of Black males in a predominately Black urban middle school and community. *International Journal of Education in Mathematics, Science, and Technology,* 2(3), 206–222.

DeCuir, J. T., & Dixson, A. D. (2004). "So when it comes out, they aren't surprised that it is there": Using critical race theory as a tool of analysis of race and racism in education. *Educational Researcher*, 33(5), 26–31.

DeCuir-Gunby, J. T., & Walker-DeVose, D. C. (2013). Expanding the counterstory: The potential for critical race mixed methods studies in education. In M. Lynn & A. D. Dixson (Eds.), *The handbook of critical race theory in education* (pp. 248–259). New York, NY: Routledge.

Delgado, R. (1989). Storytelling for oppositionist and others: A plea for narrative. *Michigan Law Review*, 87(8), 2411–2441.

Delgado, R., & Stefancic, J. (2000). Introduction. In R. Delgado & J. Stefancic (Eds.), *Critical race theory: The cutting edge* (2nd ed., pp. xv–xix). Philadelphia, PA: Temple University Press.

Delgado, R., & Stefancic, J. (2001). *Critical race theory: An introduction*. New York, NY: New York University Press.

DiAngelo, R. (2011). White fragility. *International Journal of Critical Pedagogy*, 3(3), 54–70.

Dixson, A., & Rousseau, C. K. (2005). And we are still not saved: Critical race theory in education ten years later. *Race Ethnicity and Education*, 8(1), 7–27.

Duncan, G. A. (2002). Beyond love: A critical race ethnography of the schooling of adolescent Black males. *Equity & Excellence in Education*, 35(2), 131–143.

Fernández, L. (2002). Telling stories about school: Using critical race and Latino critical theories to document Latina/Latino education and resistance. *Qualitative Inquiry*, 8(1), 45–65.

Gillborn, D. (2016). The rules of racial standing: Critical race theory for analysis, activism, and pedagogy. In G. Ladson-Billings & W. Tate (Eds.), *"Covenant keeper": Derrick Bell's enduring education legacy* (pp. 91–109). New York, NY: Peter Lang.

Gillborn, D., Warmington, P., & Demack, S. (2018). QuantCrit: Education, policy, "big data" and principles for a critical race theory of statistics. *Race Ethnicity and Education*, 21(2), 158–179.

Gregory, S. L. (2017). Bruised but not broken: African-American women's persistence in engineering degree programs in spite of stereotype threat. In S. Marx (Ed.), *Qualitative research in STEM: Studies of equity, access, and innovation* (pp. 85–118). New York, NY: Routledge.

Hilliard, A. G. (1995). *The maroon within us: Selected essays on African American community socialization*. Baltimore, MD: Black Classic Press.

hooks, b. (1995). *Killing rage: Ending racism*. New York, NY: Holt Paperbacks.

Hotchkins, B. K. (2016). African American males navigate racial microaggressions. *Teachers College Record*, 118(6), 1–36.

Howard, T. C., & Reynolds, R. (2013). Examining Black male identity through a raced, classed, and gendered lens: Critical race theory and the intersectionality of the Black male experience. In M. Lynn & A. D. Dixson (Eds.), *Handbook of Critical Race Theory in Education* (pp. 232–247). New York, NY: Routledge.

Jett, C. C. (2009). *African American men and college mathematics: Gaining access and attaining success* (Unpublished doctoral dissertation). Georgia State University, Atlanta, GA.

Jett, C. C. (2011). "I once was lost, but now am found": The mathematics journey of an African American male mathematics doctoral student. *Journal of Black Studies*, 42(7), 1125–1147.

Jett, C. C. (2012). Critical race theory interwoven with mathematics education research. *Journal of Urban Mathematics Education*, 5(1), 21–30.

Jett, C. C. (2013). Culturally responsive collegiate mathematics education: Implications for African American students. *Interdisciplinary Journal of Teaching and Learning*, 3(2), 102–116.

Jett, C. C. (2016a). Building on our mathematical legacy of brilliance: A critical race reflective narrative. In B. L. McGowan, R. T. Palmer, J. L. Wood, & D. F. Hibbler (Eds.), *Black men in the academy: Narratives of resiliency, achievement, and success* (pp. 77–91). New York, NY: Palgrave Macmillan.

Jett, C. C. (2016b). Ivy League bound: A case study of a brilliant African American male mathematics major. *Spectrum: A Journal on Black Men*, 4(2), 83–97.

Jett, C. C. (in press). Mathematical persistence among four African American male graduate students: A critical race analysis of their experiences. *Journal for Research in Mathematics Education*.

Johnson, L. (2017). The racial hauntings of one Black male professor and the disturbance of the self(ves): Self-actualization and racial storytelling as pedagogical practices. *Journal of Literacy Research*, 49(4), 476–502.

Johnson, L., & Bryan, N. (2017). Using our voices, losing our bodies: Michael Brown, Trayvon Martin, and the spirit murders of Black male professors in the academy. *Race Ethnicity and Education*, 20(2), 163–177.

Joseph, N. M., Hailu, M., & Boston, D. L. (2017). Black girls' and women's persistence in the P–20 mathematics pipeline: Two decades of children, youth, and adult education research. *Review of Research in Education*, 41(1), 203–227.

King, J. E. (1991). Dysconsious racism: Ideology, identity, and the miseducation of teachers. *The Journal of Negro Education*, 60(2), 133–146.

King, J. E. (Ed.). (2005). *Black education: A transformative research and action agenda for the new century*. Mahwah, NJ: Lawrence Erlbaum Associates.

Ladson-Billings, G. (1999). Just what is critical race theory and what's it doing in a nice field like education? In L. Parker, D. Deyhle, & S. Villenas (Eds.), *Race is ... race isn't: Critical race theory and qualitative studies in education* (pp. 181–204). Boulder, CO: Westview Press.

Ladson-Billings, G. (2000). Racialized discourses and ethnic epistemologies. In N. Denzin & Y. Lincoln (Eds.), *The sage handbook of qualitative research* (2nd ed., pp. 257–277). Thousand Oaks, CA: Sage.

Ladson-Billings, G. (2013). Critical race theory—What it is not! In M. Lynn & A. D. Dixson (Eds.), *Handbook of critical race theory in education* (pp. 34–47). New York, NY: Routledge.

Ladson-Billings, G., & Tate, W. (1995). Toward a critical race theory in education. *Teachers College Record*, 97(1), 47–68.

Larnell, G. V., Bullock, E. C., & Jett, C. C. (2016). Mathematics, social justice, and race: A critical race analysis of teaching mathematics for social justice. *Journal of Education*, 196(1), 19–29.

Ledesma, M. C., & Calderón, D. (2015). Critical race theory in education: A review of past literature and a look to the future. *Qualitative Inquiry*, 21(3), 206–222.

Leonardo, Z. (2013). *Race frameworks: A multidimensional theory of racism and education*. New York, NY: Teachers College Press.

Levy, L. (2018). *Terrified fourth-grader handcuffed after officers mistake him for someone else*. Retrieved from: http://thestir.cafemom.com/parenting_news/212572/video-chicago-police-handcuffing-boy.

Lynn, M., & Adams, M. (2002). Introductory overview to the special issue critical race theory and education: Recent developments in the field. *Equity & Excellence in Education*, 35(2), 87–92.

Martin, D. B. (2000). *Mathematics success and failure among African-American youth: The roles of sociohistorical context, community forces, school influence, and individual agency*. Mahwah, NJ: Lawrence Erlbaum Associates.

Martin, D. B. (2009). Researching race in mathematics education. *Teachers College Record*, 111(2), 295–338.

Martin, D. B., & Gholson, M. (2012). On becoming and being a critical Black scholar in mathematics education: The politics of race and identity. In O. Skovsmose & B. Greer (Eds.), *Opening the cage: Critique and politics of mathematics education* (pp. 203–222). Rotterdam, The Netherlands: Sense.

Martin, D. B., Rousseau Anderson, C. R., & Shah, N. (2017). Race and mathematics. In J. Cai (Ed.), *The compendium for research in mathematics education* (pp. 607–636). Reston, VA: National Council of Teachers of Mathematics.

Matias, C. E. (2016). *Feeling White: Whiteness, emotionality, and education*. Rotterdam, The Netherlands: Sense.

McGee, E. O. (2015). Robust and fragile mathematical identities: A framework for exploring racialized experiences and high achievement among Black college students. *Journal for Research in Mathematics Education*, 46(5), 599–625.

McGee, E. O., & Stovall, D. (2015). Reimagining critical race theory in education: Mental health, healing, and the pathway to liberatory praxis. *Educational Theory*, 65(5), 491–511.

Moses, R. P., & Cobb, C. E. (2002). *Radical equations: Civil rights from Mississippi to The Algebra Project*. Boston, MA: Beacon Press.

Parker, L. (1998). "Race is … race ain't": An exploration of the utility of critical race theory in qualitative research in education. *Qualitative Studies in Education*, 11(1), 43–55.

Parker, L., & Lynn, M. (2002). What's race got to do with it? Critical race theory's conflicts with connections to qualitative research methodology and epistemology. *Qualitative Inquiry*, 8(1), 7–22.

Parker, L., & Stovall, D. O. (2004). Actions following words: Critical race theory connects to critical pedagogy. *Educational Philosophy and Theory*, 36(2), 167–183.

Sablan, J. R. (2019). Can you really measure that? Combining critical race theory and quantitative methods. *American Educational Research Journal*, 56(1), 178–203.

Smith, W. A., Allen, W. R., & Danley, L. L. (2007). "Assume the position … you fit the description": Psychosocial experiences and racial battle fatigue among African American male college students. *American Behavioral Scientist*, 51(4), 551–578.

Solórzano, D. G. (1998). Critical race theory, race and gender microaggressions, and the experience of Chicana and Chicano scholars. *Qualitative Studies in Education*, 11(1), 121–136.

Solórzano, D. G. (2018). Why racial microaggressions matter: How I came to answer that question and why I do the work I do. In L. W. Perna (Ed.), *Taking it to the streets: The role of scholarship in advocacy and advocacy in scholarship* (pp. 92–99). Baltimore, MD: John Hopkins University Press.

Solórzano, D. G., & Yosso, T. J. (2002). Critical race methodology: Counter-storytelling as an analytical framework for education research. *Qualitative Inquiry*, 8(1), 23–44.

Stinson, D. W. (2004). African American male students and achievement in school mathematics: A critical postmodern analysis of agency. *Dissertations Abstract International*, 66(12). (UMI No. doi:3194548).

Stinson, D. W. (2008). Negotiating sociocultural discourses: The counter-storytelling of academically (and mathematically) successful African American male students. *American Educational Research Journal*, 45(4), 975–1010.

Strutchens, M. E., Johnson, M. L., & Tate, W. F. (Eds.). (2000). *Changing the faces of mathematics: Perspectives on African Americans*. Reston, VA: National Council of Teachers of Mathematics.

Sue, D. W., Capodilupo, C. M., Torino, G. C., Bucceri, J. M., Holder, A. M. B., Nadal, K. L., & Esquilin, M. (2007). Racial microaggressions in everyday life: Implications for clinical practice. *American Psychologist*, 62(4), 271–286.

Tate, W. F. (1994). From inner city to ivory tower: Does my voice matter in the academy? *Urban Education*, 29(3), 245–269.

Tate, W. F. (1997). Critical race theory and education: History, theory, and implications. *Review of Research in Education*, 22(1), 195–247.

Terry, C. L. (2011). Mathematical counterstory and African American male students: Urban mathematics education from a critical race theory perspective. *Journal of Urban Mathematics Education*, 4(1), 23–49.

Tracy, S. J. (2010). Qualitative quality: Eight "big-tent" criteria for excellent qualitative research. *Qualitative Inquiry*, 16(10), 837–851.

Villapando, O. (2003). Self-segregation or self-preservation? A critical race theory and Latina/o critical theory analysis of Chicana/o college students. *Qualitative Studies in Education*, 16(5), 619–646.

West, C. (2001). *Race matters*. New York, NY: Vintage Books.

Wilson, J. A. (2018). *"Ain't I a woman?": Black women negotiate and resist systemic oppression in undergraduate engineering and mathematics disciplines* (Unpublished doctoral dissertation). University of South Florida, Tampa, FL.

Wing, A. K. (2016). Is there a future for critical race theory? *Journal of Legal Education*, 66(1), 44–54.

10

USING CRITICAL RACE THEORY AS A PEDAGOGICAL, THEORETICAL, METHODOLOGICAL, AND ANALYTICAL TOOL IN MATHEMATICS EDUCATION FOR BLACK STUDENTS IN URBAN AREAS

Julius Davis

Trina, a Black female high school senior, described her views on mathematics and racism. She stated, "Math is a way of life, kind of sort of like how racism takes place in life.... You're going to always have to deal with math in life.... You're going to always have to deal with racism in life." As Trina asserted, racism is so embedded in all aspects of life that Black adults and children will always have to deal with it. She compared racism to mathematics, a comparison many people find hard to believe given that mathematics is often perceived as an objective, neutral, culture-free subject area. Schools and mathematics classrooms, however, are not exempt from the ubiquitous impact of racism. What is most interesting about Trina's statement is that, as a high school senior, she has come to understand the omnipresence of racism and mathematics.

While racism is pervasive throughout all aspects of life, schooling, and mathematics experiences, many people find it challenging to identify the effects of racism beyond individual, blatant acts committed by a White person. Such people find it difficult to understand how the systematic effects of racism impact all areas of people activity (Welsing, 1991). The lack of understanding of racism is exacerbated when considering the lived realities, schooling, and mathematics experiences of Black students (and adults) in urban communities. The dominant narrative in society, school systems, and mathematics spaces is to blame Black adults and children for the dilapidated conditions of their communities, schools, and mathematics classrooms without considering the impact of systemic racism and, consequently, racist laws, policies, and acts committed by people and institutions to produce those conditions. Critical race theory (CRT), a legal and educational analytical framework, provides useful tools for mathematics education researchers, theoreticians, and practitioners to understand how racism affects Black adults' and students' lived realities, schooling, and mathematics education.

In this chapter, I illustrate how CRT can be useful for mathematics education researchers, theoreticians, and practitioners who seek to understand how racism affects the lived realities, schooling, and mathematics education of Black students in urban communities, schools, and mathematics classrooms. To start, I discuss important precursors of using CRT as a tool in mathematics education. Afterward, I provide a brief overview of the development of CRT in education and mathematics education. Then, I explain how the CRT concepts of counter-stories and mathematical counter-stories, intellectual property, Whiteness as property, and interest convergence principle can be used as pedagogical, theoretical, methodological, or analytical tools in mathematics education.

The Precursor for Using CRT in Mathematics Education

Before using CRT as a tool to understand Black students' lived realities, schooling, and mathematics education, stakeholders must have an operationalized definition of race and racism, a critical perspective of Black adults and students' lived experiences in urban spaces, a sociohistorical context in analyzing race and racism, and a sociopolitical perspective. In the next section, I expand on these ideas and why they are important for mathematics educators using CRT.

Operationalized Definition of Race and Racism

To understand how racism operates in mathematics education, stakeholders must understand how racism works in the larger society. The racism that functions in mathematics education is a microcosm of the racism that functions globally. I agree with Larnell et al. (2016) that "race and racism are operating whether their roles are central, peripheral, or otherwise not rendered visible with respect to the objective of the task or study" (p. 24). In my review of the literature, there is no set definition of racism that all critical race theorists or mathematics educators use in their work. Some mathematics educators who mention or discuss racism do not provide a definition that describes their understanding of the construct. It is my firm belief that to use CRT properly, mathematics educators should have their own perspective and operationalized definition and understanding of race and racism.

My discussion of race and racism will primarily focus on the White–Black binary (Tate, 1997) given that issues of race and racism have historically revolved around the relationship between Whites and Blacks. I operate from the assumption that race is a social and ideological construct and provide a basic perspective on how racism functions. Given that Whites legitimize their position using an ideology of superiority, racism is the ideological and social construct that justifies their beliefs, assumptions, and social, educational, and mathematical arrangements. I operate from the position that racism is not stagnated but is always changing. I agree with the assertion that, "If you do not understand White supremacy (racism)—what it is, and how it works—everything else that you understand, will only confuse you" (Fuller, 1971, p. A).

Like many other CRT scholars, I operate from the premise that racism is omnipresent and intransigent in the lives of Black adults and students. I define racism by adhering to the CRT tradition of crossing disciplinary boundaries to make use of definitions taken from different scholars' work in psychology, sociology, history, political science, and grassroots political activists (Ture & Hamilton, 1992; Welsing, 1991; Wright, 1984).

I agree with Welsing's (1991) definition of racism as:

> A local and global power system structured and maintained by persons who classify themselves as White, whether consciously or subconsciously determined; this system consists of patterns of perception, logic, symbol formation, thought, speech, action and emotional response, as conducted simultaneously in all areas of people activity (economics, entertainment, health, labor, law, politics, religion, sex and war).
>
> *(p. ii)*

Racism is both overt and covert. It takes:

> Individual Whites acting against individual Blacks and acts by the total White community against the Black community. We call these *individual racism* and *institutional racism*. The first consists of overt acts by individuals…. The second type is less overt, far more subtle, less identifiable in terms of specific individuals committing the acts. But it is no less destructive of human life. The second type originates in the operation of established and respected forces in society, and thus receives far less public condemnation than the first type.
>
> *(Ture & Hamilton, 1992, p. 4)*

Using these definitions, it is clear that Blacks cannot be racists. I concur with Fuller (1971), Welsing (1991), and Wright (1984), who argue that Black people do not have the ability to be racist given that they collectively lack the power to oppress any group locally or globally. In essence, White supremacy is the only functioning racism (Fuller, 1971; Welsing, 1991). This means all truly racist acts maintain White supremacy, regardless of the race of the actor.

Taken together, these definitions form the basis for how I have conceptualized and defined racism. It is a local and global power system consisting of individual acts and institutional practices that oppress and exploit Black people by maintaining the social order of White supremacy in all areas of people activity (Welsing, 1991). The assumptions and beliefs guiding racism imply Black people are lazy, undeserving, uncivilized, criminal, and intellectually inferior while White people are diligent, deserving, civilized, lawful, and intellectually superior (Gardner, 1995;

Gould, 1981, 1995; Tate, 1997). Essentially, racist assumptions suggest Black people are intellectually inferior and White people are intellectually superior (Gardner, 1995; Gould, 1981, 1995; Tate, 1997).

I agree with Welsing (1991), who argues that White people have created an evolving system based on White supremacy that is maintained by social, economic, educational, and political structures to support the myth of Black inferiority. Because Whites control the world's resources (Fuller, 1971; Welsing, 1991), they have access to social, economic, educational, and political capital that allows them to shape the discourse and structure of society, schools, and mathematics education in America and around the world. These definitions, assumptions, and beliefs guide my use of CRT and help me explore how race and racism shape Black adults' and students' lived realities, schooling, and mathematics education in urban spaces.

Critical Perspectives of Black Adults' and Students' Lived Realities, Schooling, and Mathematics Education in Urban Areas

My critical perspectives of Black adults' and students' lived realities, schooling, and mathematics education emerged from my own experiences in urban communities. Growing up and attending schools in predominantly Black urban communities in Baltimore, Maryland shaped my perspectives of race, racism, classism, and other forms of oppression. I started eighth grade back in Baltimore with my father, his wife, and my little sister. We lived in Chester Heights, a poor and working-class, drug-infested community. I attended Park Middle School and met a young man named John Beckford, also known as Boo. We connected instantly and developed a good relationship. Boo lived with his grandmother because his mother and father were addicted to drugs and alcohol, respectively.

One day in class, Boo pulled a few valves of crack cocaine out of his shoe to show me in class. I was shocked. I knew he sold drugs in our neighborhood, but I never expected him to bring them to school. As I reflect on my experiences with Boo, I realize that our relationship exposed me to his lived realities in and out of school, which subsequently shaped my own. When I spent time together with Boo, his family and friends became my friends, and his habits became mine, too.

Later in the academic year, I was moved to another class, away from Boo and our friends. I was also moved into an algebra class since I did well in mathematics. I remember coming into the new algebra class and immediately sitting down, quietly, to do the drill from the board. This was the routine in this class. The students did their work, so I joined in. After drills, Mrs. Earl would lecture. They were always boring, but the class would sit quietly. We would then do board work and worksheets. My homeroom teacher was Mrs. Coleman. I remember her announcing to the class that I had passed the mathematics portion of the Maryland Standardized Test. "Julius, I knew you could do it [pass the test] if we moved you out that class!" she said. I did not really know what that meant at the time, but I was happy I passed the test.

My academic success in mathematics continued in high school. I did well in all my mathematics courses. In fact, I did well academically in all subject areas. I was also actively involved in extracurricular activities (e.g., student government, class officer, etc.). I also participated in a law program that examined problems (e.g., drugs, vacant homes, liquors, etc.) plaguing my community. We presented the results of our investigation to the community association. Initially, I thought these efforts were going to help change the conditions of my community, but I soon realized that they would not.

I graduated from high school as the valedictorian of my class and with a desire to give back to my community. My desire led me to teach in the middle and high schools I attended as a student. I also conducted research on Black students in my community because I wanted to understand how racism (White supremacy) impacted our lived realities, schooling, and mathematics education. I wanted to be a change agent and improve the conditions of my community by providing students with a liberatory mathematics education to help them change our lived experiences. It was through these experiences that I became more aware and knowledgeable of how racism (White supremacy) impacted our lived realities, schooling, and mathematics education. As I reflected on my racialized experiences in these settings, participation in the law program, and teaching experiences, I realized that my perspectives were aligned with a CRT in (mathematics) education framework.

Sociohistorical Context Matters in Analyzing Race and Racism

I believe sociohistorical context is important in theorizing and analyzing race and racism. I used Bell's (2005) notion of revisionist history to "reexamine America's historical record, replacing comforting majoritarian interpretations of events with ones that square more accurately with" (Delgado & Stefancic, 2001, p. 20) Black adults and children lived realities in Chester Heights, where I lived for much of my youth. Here, I cite the references used to discuss my community to maintain anonymity (McDougall, 1993; Orr, 1999). At its onset, in the 1930s, Chester Heights was a predominantly White community with most of the housing units being owner-occupied. By the 1950s, more Whites had settled in Chester Heights, accounting for 95% of the population by 1960.

However, during the 1960s, a population shift occurred swiftly for various social, economic, racial, and political reasons. A substantial part of the White community began leaving as Blacks started moving in. Before moving into Chester Heights, many Blacks were homeowners, but they were forced to become renters because of redlining practices, where they were systematically denied bank loans. As Blacks moved in and Whites funneled out, Black renters became the dominant racial group in Chester Heights by the 1970s. Most Whites left Chester Heights because they did not want to live in the same community with Blacks. In more recent times, Chester Heights had more than 2,000 vacant houses, lots and/ or buildings in the community as a result of redlining.

The economic problems Blacks experienced historically and contemporarily in Chester Heights have contributed to the dilapidation of the community, which now has high rates of poverty. When I lived in Chester Heights, it was predominantly Black and one of the most deprived communities in Baltimore, with a population of more than 40,000 residents. Over 56% of the residents over the age of 16 were unemployed, and 49.1% were not in the labor force. Many residences received governmental housing assistance. Chester Heights had 50 times more children living in poverty than any other community. The juvenile arrest rate was 56% higher than the citywide average. One-third of the juvenile arrests were for drug-related offenses. The juvenile arrest rate for Black children with at least one prior offense was 75%.

When Chester Heights was predominantly White, the local businesses provided jobs for the community. Residents benefited from jobs in lumber yards, metal fabrications companies, framing plants, and bottling companies. When Black residents began to move in, those companies moved away, leaving the new residents with few nearby job opportunities. This led to the abandonment and underutilization of the area.

Before Black adults and children were able to live in Chester Heights, most of the community resources were "used-up." Wright's (1984) perspective helps explain what happened. He states:

> [Whites] never accept blame for Blacks' environmental conditions which are clearly the result of White oppression. On the contrary, Blacks are held responsible for the deterioration of their communities even though all the property is White-controlled. In addition, municipal services are withdrawn from Black communities and most of these communities have been "used-up" before Blacks are allowed to move into them.
>
> *(p. 7)*

According to Cadwallader (1995), the poverty that Blacks experience in Black communities like Chester Heights is a result of not being able to find employment or being excessively underpaid. Wilson (1998) contends that "many of today's problems in the inner-city ghetto neighborhoods—crime, family dissolution, welfare, low levels of social organization and so on—are the fundamental consequence of the disappearance of work" (p. 90). The sociohistorical context of Chester Heights helps critical race theorists see how issues of race and racism impacted Black people historically to produce contemporary rundown urban communities with dilapidated housing, high rates of un- and under- employment, and crime.

Sociohistorical context is essential to understanding how race and racism operate in and out of mathematics education (Martin, 2000). There is a tendency to conduct research and create policy documents without situating Black students' experiences, participation, and performance in mathematics into a sociohistorical context (Martin, 2003, 2007; Tate, 1997). Most qualitative and quantitative research and policy documents fail to situate Black students' schooling and mathematics education in a sociohistorical context that helps us understand how: (a) historical events shape their contemporary life, and educational and mathematics experiences; (b) race and racism shape their existing experiences, participation, and performance in and out of schooling and mathematics contexts; and (c) the conditions they experience in society, school, and mathematics settings are linked and further evince the effects of social constructions of race and racism.

Mathematics education researchers Snipes (1997) and Stinson (2004) situate Black students' mathematical experiences in a sociohistorical context. Socio-historical context helps us better understand how the laws, policies, social customs, and social constructions of race and racism in and out of mathematics education help to shape Black adults' and children's lived realities, schooling, and mathematics education.

Sociopolitical Perspective

My experiences in urban communities and schools have contributed significantly to my sociopolitical perspective, specifically, why things are the way they are for Blacks in society, Black communities, school systems, schools, and mathematics classrooms. My sociopolitical perspective informs my conceptualization and understanding of various social phenomena historically, economically, politically, and culturally. My views and understanding of race, racism, and classism are why my work focuses on Black students' lived realities, schooling, and mathematics education in urban communities. I strongly believe racism is responsible for the poor conditions of the Black communities I lived in and the schools I attended, and I believe they were intentionally designed to be that way.

Unfortunately, racism is rarely viewed as omnipresent in the daily lives of Black people. It is typically only viewed through the lens of the individual actions of White people, so few explore or understand how it operates on a macro level. For example, the continued isolation of Blacks into drug-infested, poor and working-class racially segregated communities with dilapidated housing, high rates of un- and under- employment, crime, and rundown schools with inadequate resources would never be considered a function of the system of racism (White supremacy; Ture & Hamilton, 1995). In my view, this is a function of the system of racism (White supremacy) because it maintains the subordination, oppression, and exploitation of Black adults and children. I agree with Welsing (1991) who proclaims:

> Drugs are placed deliberately in the Black community. The drugs are then used to "street-treat" Black male frustration and depression. The high prices for which drugs are sold provide the Black male population with the illusion that finally they are beginning to make some money and share in the

"American Dream." Guns are then placed at the disposal of the same Black male persons, supposedly to aid them in enforcing payment for drug sales. More important, the strategy is for Black males to kill and destroy one another and then carry the blame. (It must be realized that no Black males manufacture the chemicals for drug use, nor do any Black males manufacture guns).

(p. v)

The blame is most comfortably placed on the Black victims of racism living in urban environments (Bell, 1992; Ryan, 1976).

In American society, racism is generally perceived as irrational acts committed by an individual in a neutral, rational, and just society (Lopez, 2003). Individual acts of racism are rarely contextualized as an outgrowth of an American society that is not just, rational, or neutral, but instead built on the uncivilized behavior of Whites who lynched, enslaved, and brutalized Black adults and children (Lopez, 2003). In other words, the individual acts of racism performed by Whites have been reduced to broad generalizations about another group based on their race, instead of a functioning system (Lopez, 2003). Viewing racism only through the lens of personal and individual acts—as opposed to a systemic issue—is not only shortsighted, but it reinforces the notion that racism is a personal, irrational act conducted by only a few Whites and ignores its presence as a functioning system in American society, educational institutions, particularly in the area of mathematics education:

> Racism is much more than having an unfavorable impression of members of other groups. For realists, racism is a means by which society allocates privilege and status. Racial hierarchies determine who gets tangible benefits, including the best jobs, the best schools, and invitations to parties in people's homes.
>
> *(Delgado & Stefancic, 2001, p. 17)*

In mathematics education, Martin (2009a) describes racial hierarchies as a method for characterizing the mathematical ability of Black students, who are seen as intellectually inferior to White students who are characterized as being mathematically superior. Martin argues that systems of White privilege maintain this racial hierarchy of mathematical ability. The dominant narrative about Black students' performance revolves around international, national, and state standardized test results in mathematics (Davis, 2014). These results are often framed as a racial achievement gap and widely accepted as factual and indisputable evidence that Black students are intellectually inferior to White students in mathematics (Martin, 2009a). The so-called racialized achievement gap highlights the "adverse conditions under which some children are often forced to learn, the privileged conditions afforded to others, and how forces like racism are used to position students in a racial hierarchy" (Martin, 2009a, p. 300).

Tate (1993) makes a similar argument that "standardized tests do not measure the commitment of the Black student who must venture through streets inflicted with crime, drugs, and other artifacts of urban neglect and decay to attend a school that is staffed with less qualified teachers, fewer resources, and poorer facilities" (p. 16). Tate further argues that the schooling Black students receive in mathematics is intended to reproduce their home lives, community conditions, and replace their parents and community members in and out of the job market. In my view, the poor schooling of Black students in mathematics is intentional, a function and goal of racism (White supremacy) and intended to reproduce their lived realities.

I believe Black people living in communities and attending schools in urban areas did not create these conditions nor do they want to live in and attend poorly maintained schools. As a mathematics educator who uses CRT, experiences and perspectives are important to grounding my research, theorizing, teaching, and analysis of race, racism, poverty, and other forms of oppression. Teachers and researchers must have a culturally grounded, asset- and strength-based perspective and know how racism impacts Black students and adults around the world, not just in their locale. They must also have a perspective, ideology, and philosophy that guides them to seek liberatory outcomes for the collective problems Black people face. These are important precursors for using CRT in mathematics education. Simply using CRT to research a Black population or because race is mentioned is not enough (Ladson-Billings, 2013; Larnell et al., 2016; Lynn & Dixson, 2013). Mathematics education researchers who use CRT must have a critical perspective of race, racism, classism, Black people and other forms of oppression to ground their theorizing, teaching, research, and approaches to achieving liberatory and social justice outcomes.

CRT in Mathematics Education

CRT emerged out of the Critical Legal Studies (CLS) movement and discourse. In the late 1970s, the CLS movement was developed to reevaluate "the merits of the realist tradition of legal discourse" (Tate, 1997, p. 207). CLS scholars have designed a movement aimed at analyzing "legal ideology and discourse as a mechanism that functions to re-create and legitimatize social structures in the United States" (Tate, 1997, p. 207). Although CRT was born out of the CLS movement, it is a separate entity from the earlier CLS movement and discourse (Ladson-Billings, 1999). CRT is an outgrowth of discontent with CLS scholars' failure to address racism. CRT operates from the presumption that racism is a deeply rooted, permanent fixture in American society. In other words, racism has never ceased to exist. It has simply shifted over time from more overt and blatant forms of racism, as seen in old television footage, to more "subtle, hidden, and often insidious forms of racism that operate at a deeper, more systematic level" (Lopez, 2003, p. 70). Racism is seldom contextualized as deeply rooted in the fabric of American institutions (e.g. schools, government, etc.) and connected to inequities or a larger system where individual acts and institutions function as a system.

Given its legal roots, CRT has expanded into the field of education (Ladson-Billings & Tate, 1995) and mathematics education (Tate, 1993). Although Ladson-Billings and Tate (1995) are credited with introducing CRT in education over 20 years ago, Tate (1993) used CRT in mathematics education before they collaboratively laid out the theoretical constructs of the framework. Solórzano and Yosso (2002) state that CRT in education provides a "framework or set of basic insights, perspectives, methods, and pedagogy that seeks to identify, analyze, and transform those structural and cultural aspects of education that maintain subordinate and dominant racial positions in and out of the classroom" (p. 25). Ladson-Billings and Tate (1995) provide propositions for examining how race and property rights provide an analytical tool for understanding social and school inequity. The three central propositions are:

1. Race continues to be a significant factor in determining inequity in the United States.
2. U.S. society is based on property rights.
3. The intersection of race and property creates an analytic tool through which we can understand social (and, consequently, school) inequity (p. 48).

In my view, the point at which race and property intersect allows one to understand how racism functions to produce longstanding and persistent social, educational, and mathematical inequities. CRT has emerged as a powerful pedagogical, theoretical, methodological, and analytical framework in education, specifically mathematics education. The foundational components of CRT in education (Solórzano & Yosso, 2002) that have relevance to mathematics education are:

a   Racism is an endemic and permanent feature of American society, schools, mathematics spaces, and structures.
b   CRT challenges dominant ideologies, paradigms, research findings, theories, methodologies and texts about Black adults and students used to blame them for the conditions of their communities, families, schooling, and mathematics education.
c   CRT centralizes the racialized, gendered, classed, and mathematical experiences of Black adults and students.
d   CRT uses an interdisciplinary approach and knowledge to better understand race, racism, sexism, classism, life, and mathematical experiences of Black adults and students in and out of mathematics spaces.
e   CRT is committed to achieving liberatory and social justice outcomes for Black adults and students in society, schools, and mathematics spaces.

In the area of education, scholars have yet to fully realize the contributions or connections of CRT in mathematics education (Jett, 2012; Larnell, Bullock & Jett, 2016). "Too often, race, racism, and social justice are relegated as issues not appropriate for mathematics education when actually these issues are central to the learning and teaching of mathematics for all students" (Berry, 2005, p. 2). Many mathematics education researchers have used CRT (Berry, 2008; Davis, 2014; Jett, 2011; McGee & Martin, 2011; Terry & McGee, 2012). However, there are also other tenets that can be used in mathematics education. The purpose of this chapter is to discuss the uses of CRT for mathematics education scholars, practitioners, theoreticians, and researchers as it is a powerful pedagogical, theoretical, methodological, and analytical framework for the field.

Useful CRT Tenets in Mathematics Education

There are many tenets of CRT that mathematics education stakeholders can use to shape pedagogy, theory, research, methodology, and data analysis. In this chapter, I use the following CRT tenets to provide a roadmap on how stakeholders can use this tool: (a) counter-stories and mathematical counter-stories (Solórzano & Yosso, 2002; Terry, 2011); (b) intellectual property (Ladson-Billings & Tate, 1995); (c) Whiteness as property (Harris, 1993); (d) interest convergence principle (Bell, 1980); and (e) achieving liberatory and social justice outcomes (Solórzano & Yosso, 2002).

CRT Counter-stories and Mathematical Counter-stories

Counter-stories are methods of telling "the stories of those people whose experiences were not often told (i.e., those on the margins of society)" (Solórzano & Yosso, 2002, p. 32). Counter-stories are created using "(a) the data gathered from the research process itself, (b) the existing literature on topic(s), (c) … one's own professional experiences, and (d) … one's own personal experiences" (Solórzano & Yosso, 2002, p. 34). I use counter-stories in the following ways: (a) to examine experiences and perspectives of Trina and Michael, two Black high school seniors from Chester Heights; (b) to use scholarly literature; and (c) to reflect on my personal and professional experiences to articulate CRT's notion of counter-stories. Michael's voice is more prominent throughout the chapter because he had more to say racial issues from his lived experiences and schooling. I describe the usefulness of CRT tenets to mathematics education as well as how race, racism, and classism function in the lives, schooling, and mathematics education of Black adults and youth. According to Solórzano and Yosso (2002), counter-stories "recount the racialized, sexualized, and classed experiences of people of color" (p. 33). Counter-stories are grounded in the reality and experiences of Black adults and youth using stories, data, and literature that are contextualized in social, political, and historical situations (Solórzano & Yosso, 2002).

Counter-stories are a CRT methodology that many researchers and practitioners have not found relevance for in mathematics education (Terry, 2011). Counter-stories provide research and pedagogical possibilities for mathematics educators. Few mathematics educators have used CRT counter-stories as a method to conduct research of Black students (Stinson, 2004). Mathematics educators should continue to use counter-story methodology to tell the racialized, gendered, classed, and mathematical stories of Black students. There is a growing body of research focused on successful and high-achieving Black students in mathematics education being developed by Black researchers to counter the dominant narrative focused on failure and supposed lack of mathematical ability (Ellington, 2006; Moody, 2003; Sheppard, 2006; Thompson & Davis, 2013; Thompson & Lewis, 2005). These studies do not employ CRT's counter-story-telling methodology, but they challenge the dominant narrative about Black students' mathematical ability. However, some of the researchers miss opportunities to center the race, gender, and class in the experiences of Black students in mathematics and school contexts.

Terry (2011) expanded the use of counter-stories to a pedagogical approach in mathematics education. He introduced the concept of mathematical counter-stories as a pedagogical strategy "for developing productive curricular and instructional interventions in urban mathematics classrooms" (p. 25). He uses mathematical counter-stories focused on Black males. Terry contends that mathematical counter-stories allow educators to address missed opportunities to re-orient Black males to the usefulness of mathematics. He encourages mathematics educators to "look for mathematics" in interesting and engaging spaces and mathematize situations that are significant to African American students.

While Terry (2011) uses mathematical counter-stories as a pedagogical approach, I contend that they can serve methodological purposes in mathematics education. Mathematical counter-stories can be used to tell the stories of Black adults' and children's mathematical experiences, which are not often told in the field or larger society. Similar to CRT counter-stories in education, mathematical counter-stories can use research data, mathematics education literature, and researchers' personal and professional experiences, as I do in this chapter. Mathematics counter-stories can be used to narrate the racialized, sexualized, classed, and mathematical experiences of Black students. Counter-stories and mathematics counter-stories provide researchers and practitioners with methodological and pedagogical practices to advance the understanding of Black students in urban spaces.

Intellectual Property in Mathematics Education

Ladson-Billings and Tate (1995) underscore the usefulness of race and property to mathematics in their articulation of intellectual property. They argue, "The quality and quantity of the curriculum varies with the 'property values' of the school" (Ladson-Billings & Tate, 1995, p. 54). Ladson-Billings and Tate articulate the notion of intellectual property through the counter-stories of two boys preparing to attend high school. A modified version of the story is presented:

> The boys excitedly poured over course offerings in their respective school catalogues. One boy was planning on attending school in an upper-middle-class White community. The other would be attending school in an urban, largely African-American district. The difference between the course offerings as specified in the catalogues was striking. The boy attending the White, middle-class school had his choice of … mathematics [course] offerings, included algebra, geometry, trigonometry, calculus, statistics, general math, and business math. The science department at this school offered biology, chemistry, physics, geology, science in society, biochemistry, and general science. The other boy's curriculum choices were not nearly as broad. His mathematics choices were general math, business math, and algebra (there were no geometry or trig[onometry] classes offered). His science choices were general science, life science, biology, and physical science.
>
> (p. 54)

This story highlights the different types of intellectual property in the form of mathematics and science curriculum and course offerings at an upper-middle-class White school and predominantly Black urban school. These differences shape the students' opportunity to learn (OTL) mathematics. Ladson-Billings and Tate (1995) argue mathematics curriculum detailing what students should know and be able to do must be accompanied by material resources and real property (e.g., certified and prepared teachers) to support their learning.

The reality for many Black students' learning mathematics in urban schools like the one described by Ladson-Billings and Tate (1995) indicates that their OTL mathematics is delimited by a lack of material resources and real property in the form of teachers, curriculum, and course offerings. In a similar vein, I used CRT's notion of intellectual property to examine the mathematical experiences of Black boys in an urban middle school (Davis, 2014). In so doing, I found that the students had unqualified and unprepared mathematics teachers, below-standard mathematics curriculum shaped by remediation and high-stakes testing, and poorly managed classrooms that interfered with learning. This type of instruction restricted their ability to develop conceptual understanding and procedural fluency in mathematics. I also found that the focus of Black male students' mathematics education was on getting their performance to the level of White students.

To further describe the analytical use of intellectual property, I share Michael's mathematical counter-story. Michael's experiences help illuminate how his OTL mathematics was limited by a coach who served as a mathematics teacher but did not know how to do mathematics. He started experiencing difficulty with mathematics since he was being taught by a teacher who had no background in the subject area. Michael shared:

> When I got to the 9th grade, I started failing [math], so during high school it really wasn't a good one, like something I could be proud of.... I got to high school and then it was nobody to help you 'cause nobody really understood the math.... We had Coach D in the 9th grade. He was a breeze. Like, in 9th grade, like, we ain't do no work in his class. I don't even count him as a math teacher.... In Coach D class, it was an all-boys class, so we did whatever we wanted to do. If you talked about sports to him, it was a wrap for the day. He would go on and on about sports instead of learning. And so, he didn't know the math 'cause we had another 9th-grade teacher, Mrs. P, who used to come in there and try to assist him [Coach D] and everything he used to do was wrong. Like, so, she came in there to help and whatnot.... Coach D was the worst. Everything was mostly chaos at Public High School (PHS)... 9th grade year my average was an 85, but I ain't do no work. He just passed everybody.

Michael indicated that not only did Coach D not have a background in mathematics, but he experienced difficulties doing the mathematics himself and facilitating student learning. The teacher needed just as much assistance as the students. Michael stated that Coach D was the worst teacher he had in mathematics at PHS.

In his next mathematics class, Michael's OTL was restricted by a mathematics teacher that provided him with inadequate instruction and left him ill-prepared for the Scholastic Aptitude Test (SAT). He explained:

> I had this math teacher named Mr. G. He was fun 'cause, like, he helped you. He helped you so much it was like he was doing your work for you. So, you weren't really learning. So, it did not really get me nowhere. Like, if I had to do some math right now, I would probably fail. If you asked him a question, he'd come and actually break the whole thing down and there go your answer. He'd walk you through the whole problem, the whole problem.... He was basically doing the work. So like, when SAT time came around, I ain't understand it cause I ain't really do it myself.

When Michael went to geometry, he experienced problems learning the material because of his previous instruction. He elaborated on his experience:

> I ain't understand it cause I ain't really do it myself. Like, I seen him do it, but I ain't do it for myself. So, it was difficult. Especially going from him, to Mrs. R, 'cause she didn't do nothing for you. Like, she showed you one thing and that was all. So, it was kind of hard.

In the 10th grade, Michael took geometry with Mrs. R, but she left the school because of a death in her family. A substitute teacher covered the class. He explained what he experienced in her absence:

In geometry … it was kind of boring. Like, I really didn't want to listen 'cause I didn't think you need it. So, it was kind of tough. But, I don't know, I think that if I would have listened I probably would have understood more, but I didn't. But my experience, it wasn't a good one, I know that. It was horrible when I look back on it…. I passed, but like with a 70 and I barely passed 'cause the teacher, she was out for most of the time 'cause her son passed away and whatnot, so she was out during most of the year and we had a substitute.

Centering race and property rights in Michael's mathematical counter-story helps mathematics educators to see how CRT's notion of intellectual property can be to understand how long standing inequities in mathematics are maintained. Michael and the other Black students in his mathematics classes OTL was delimited by having unqualified mathematics and substitute teachers lacking in mathematical knowledge to teach the content and they were not able to help him learn mathematical content and concepts. From a CRT perspective, the type of mathematics instruction, teacher quality, or learning experiences met by Michael and other Black students in his classes would not knowingly be allowed for White students.

Whiteness as Property In and Out of Mathematics Education

To further articulate the analytical usefulness of CRT in mathematics education, I turn my discussion to the counter-stories of Michael and Trina and mathematics education literature to describe Whiteness as property. Harris (1993) describes four main property functions of Whiteness: (a) rights of dispositions; (b) rights to use and enjoyment; (c) reputation and status property; and (d) the absolute right to exclude. The right to disposition contends that property rights are fully transferable to students who conform to White norms or sanctioned cultural practices. The right to use and enjoyment asserts that having white skin allows them to use and enjoy properties of Whiteness legally and socially without question. The status and reputation of schools and programs in the field of education in general and mathematics, in particular, diminish when Whites are not associated with them. The absolute right to exclude is socially constructed as the absence of Blackness in schools, mathematics programs, and higher-level mathematics courses.

In discussions of race and his mathematical experiences, Michael shared his views of the world, race, and his city, which help illuminate Whiteness as property. He stated:

I think it's a White world and we [Black people] are living in it. If you honestly look at things, the richest people are White…. Like, even though I want to go to the pros [pro football], the person who is going to be signing my check is going to be White. The people that own the teams are White, White, White. The people that own McDonald's are [mainly] White. There is a lot of Black people working there. There is a lot Black managers, but it is like it is kind of hard to come up, especially coming from here because it is Baltimore.

Michael's thoughts help us understand how Whiteness functions at a societal and global level. His thoughts about White people specifically (e.g., White men controlling the world resources) are very well documented and are connected to the history of race relations in America and around the world (Delgado & Stefancic, 2001). His views suggest that Whiteness functions at a privileged level whereas Blackness functions at a level subordinate to and oppressed by Whiteness. Michael expound on his thoughts more in the following statement:

We [Black people in his community] are in poverty if you look at all the vacant houses for miles and miles, and miles and miles, all the drugs for miles and the jailhouses and then us being Black, it's like everything is against us and people expect us to fail.

Michael thinks the problems in his community are intentional and his failure is expected. He has spent a lot of time thinking about Whiteness, comparing it to Blackness through his social and educational lens. He understands how it affects his community. In discussions of his schooling, Michael stated:

The education system is the worst. Like, it is hard.... The odds are against you coming from PHS and Baltimore.... People look at you like you are a murderer. It's either you are a drug dealer, or you do drugs, or you do crime.... It is more of them [Whites] going on to graduating and going to college than Black people finishing high school.

Michael is not the only student who shares views about the status of Whiteness and Blackness as it relates to going to college. Trina stated, "In the Caucasian society, it is not a question of kids going to college. It's where you're going. [Black] students are questioning graduating from high school."

Ladson-Billings and Tate (1995) argue that the functions and attributes of Whiteness have historically been deployed in the service of establishing Whiteness as a form of property in social, educational, and mathematics spaces. Martin (2008) argues that Black students are learning mathematics in what he calls a White institutional space. He asserts:

One can also understand mathematics education as White institutional space by considering who is allowed to speak on issues of teaching, learning, curriculum, and assessment and who dominates positions of power in research and policy contexts. In each instance, White scholars disproportionately fill these roles, an important signifier of White institutional space.

(p. 390)

Not only do White scholars fill important research and policy roles of power in mathematics education, but White mathematics teachers are the main teachers of Black students. This fact represents another indicator of White institutional space. The incorrect notion that White men created mathematics is another example of the White institutional space. "The decision to define some groups' knowledge as the most legitimate, as official knowledge, while other groups' knowledge hardly sees the light of day, says something extremely important about who has power in society" (Apple, 1993, p. 222). Martin's argument about White institutional space elucidates the analytical power of Whiteness as property in mathematics education. This approach to mathematics serves the interests of Whites and does not lead to liberatory outcomes for Black people.

The White institutional space proposition helps mathematics education researchers understand how White students almost exclusively enjoy and benefit from high quality, rigorous mathematics curriculum. Researchers have reported findings that demonstrate how several Black students have been excluded access to high quality, rigorous mathematics curriculum (McGlamery & Mitchell, 2000; Polite, 1999). Scholars have also noted that tracking, policies, teacher practices and recommendations, and perspectives have played a major role in excluding large numbers of Black students from honors, gifted and talented, and advanced mathematics courses and programs (Berry, 2008; McGlamery & Mitchell, 2000; Oakes, 2005). In predominantly White, Black and mixed-race school settings, some Black students gain access to these specialized mathematics courses and programs but are often forced to conform to the standard of Whiteness; are treated unfairly by White students, teachers, and administrator; or are sometimes taught by subpar teachers (Berry, 2008; Moody, 2003; Thompson & Lewis, 2005). Black students tend to gain access to specialized mathematics courses and programs only if their access converges with the interests of Whites. Whiteness as property helps mathematics educators understand the analytical power in research, mathematics spaces, and curriculum. It also helps explain why a national or international effort has not been to change the White male-dominated narrative in mathematics curriculum, because doing so does not converge with the interests of Whites.

Interest Convergence Principle in Mathematics Spaces

The interest convergence principle hinges on the landmark 1954 Supreme Court legal case *Brown v. Board of Education* of Topeka, Kansas to end state-mandated racial segregation in schools (Bell, 1980, 1992). This principle serves dual purposes in Bell's scholarship (Tate, 1997). First, it contributes to the intellectual discourse on race in American society. Second, it promotes political activism to achieve racial justice. The interest convergence principle documented by Bell (1980, 1992) argues that progress for Blacks is only ascertained if the goals of Blacks converge with the needs of Whites. This principle also makes the case that Whites will not support policies that threaten their socially constructed status as racially superior.

This interest convergence principle suggests that perceived gains in civil rights should be approached with caution and not accepted at face value (Bell, 1980, 1992). For example, civil rights legislation conferred basic rights to Blacks, but it ultimately benefited Whites. These basic rights only came to Blacks who converged with the interests of Whites. Gains that coincide with the interest of Whites do not typically make substantial differences in the lives of the masses of Black people in education, mathematics education, or society. Ultimately, the limited and precarious gains of the *Brown* verdict resulted in a loss: dismissal of scores of Black teachers and administrators, school closings in Black neighborhoods, and restricted access to high-quality curricula in the form of tracking, honors and/or gifted programs, and other factors. This state of affairs has made the so-called gains questionable.

Martin's (2008) notion of White institutional space helps further elucidate the interest convergence principle. It is clear Whites hold all forms of power in mathematics education to control the direction of policy, research, curriculum, teaching, learning, and assessment. Any substantial change in the mathematical experiences of Black students will have to converge to benefit White constituents (students, families, teachers, etc.). Apple (1993) argues that dominant groups (i.e., Whites) "try to create situations where the compromises that are formed favor them" (p. 10). The interest of Whites in mathematics education is connected to their larger societal, governmental, political, and economic goals to maintain White superiority, international warfare, capitalism, and workforce participation (Apple, 1993; Martin, 2003). As an analytical tool, the interest convergence principle helps mathematics education researchers and policymakers understand that to improve the experiences of Black students, the interest of Whites will always supersede the goal of liberatory mathematics and must be realistically considered.

Achieving Liberatory and Social Justice Outcomes for Black Students in Mathematics Education and Beyond

Researchers, theoreticians, and practitioners who use CRT in mathematics education to address race, racism, and other forms of oppression must not forget the commitment to achieving liberatory and social justice outcomes for Black adults and students in society, schools, and mathematics spaces. Unbeknownst to many, there is a longstanding history of using mathematics to achieve liberatory, social justice, and culturally relevant outcomes for Black students (Larnell et al., 2016; Pitts Bannister et al., 2017). Some have argued that social justice should be a primary goal in mathematics education (de Freitas, 2008), but unfortunately, it is not. In mathematics education, Black scholars are advancing liberatory and social justice-oriented research as well as theoretical and pedagogical perspectives to improve outcomes for Black students (Martin, 2009b; Martin & McGee, 2009).

There is a developing movement of mathematics educators using CRT to achieve liberatory and social justice outcomes for Black students (Larnell et al., 2016; Terry, 2010, 2011). Larnell and associates (2016) used CRT to broaden their efforts at teaching and learning mathematics for social justice (TLMSJ). These scholars examined TLMSJ historically and contemporarily in mathematics education in search of figuring out if TLMSJ can address issues of racial justice. Bell (1980) argues that racial justice should be a priority for Black people. Larnell et al. used CRT tenets—racial realism, interest convergence, critique of liberalism, intersectionality, and counter-storytelling—to critically analyze TLMSJ, racial justice, and mathematical tasks that do not explicitly address race. Terry (2011) also grounded his notion of mathematical counter-stories in TLMSJ. He states "mathematical counter-storytelling can provide an important conceptual space… for math educators to begin synthesizing their math and social justice pedagogical goals" (Terry, 2010, p. 95). He views mathematical counter-stories as a tool to challenge dominant forces, narratives and structures that negatively shape the mathematics and schooling experiences of Black males. To achieve justice, Terry (2011) states, "Attention must be paid to the 'voice' of male African Americans and their narratives about (mathematics) learning" (p. 28).

Michael's counter-story and Chester Heights' sociohistorical and contemporary context help mathematics educators find topics to engage Black students in liberatory and social justice ways. Martin and McGee (2009) contend that "any relevant framing of mathematics education for African Americans must address both the historical oppression they have faced and the social realities they continue to face in contemporary times" (p. 210). To achieve liberatory and social justice outcomes for Black students in urban areas, they must engage TLMSJ with CRT. This conjoining must be a regular practice, but most teachers do not teach in these ways, even when they purport to teach mathematics for social justice (Larnell et al., 2016). Several mathematics educators have provided examples of how to engage students in mathematics that are related to issues/problems plaguing urban communities. They have connected mathematics to housing issues (Gutstein, 2004, 2013a; Heckman & Weissglass, 1994), liquor stores (Tate, 1994, 1995), economics (Dean, 2013; Frankenstein, 2013; Gutstein, 2013b; Hersh & Peterson, 2013), jails, incarceration, drugs (Terry, 2010, 2011). If you listen to Michael's voice as Terry (2011) calls mathematics educators to do, then you will see ways to connect mathematics to issues and problems impacting Black communities in urban areas.

CRT provides a lens to develop curricular and pedagogical tools to engage Black students in liberatory and social justice mathematics in urban spaces that are often missing critical perspectives of race and racism. I contend that in liberatory and social justice mathematics, Black students must impact real change in their personal and family lives and communities, and they must improve the lived realities and mathematics education of Black adults and children collectively. The mathematics Black students engage in must help them understand how issues of race and racism impact them, their families, Black communities, and the masses of Black people locally, nationally and internationally. The goal must be the collective betterment of Black adults' and children's lived realities and education, especially in mathematics.

Conclusion

Researchers, theoreticians, and practitioners who use CRT in mathematics education have many methodological, theoretical, pedagogical, and analytical tools at their dispositional. However, I argue that CRT is not a methodological, theoretical, pedagogical, or analytical tool for all mathematics educators. Stakeholders who use CRT in mathematics education must have operationalized definitions of race and racism, sociopolitical perspectives, sociohistorical context, and critical perspectives of Black adults' and children's lived realities, schooling, and mathematical experiences in urban spaces. The tenets of CRT provide a roadmap on how stakeholders can use: (a) counter-stories and mathematical counter-stories; (b) intellectual property in mathematics education; (c) Whiteness as property in and out of mathematics education; (d) interest convergence principle in mathematics spaces; and (e) achieving liberatory and social justice outcomes in mathematics education and beyond. CRT is useless unless it produces real and tangible outcomes for Black students in and out of mathematics education.

References

Apple, M. W. (1993). The politics of official knowledge: Does a national curriculum make sense? *Discourse*, 14(1), 1–16.

Bell, D. (1980). Brown and the interest-convergence dilemma. In D. Bell (Ed.), *New perspectives on school desegregation* (pp. 90–107). New York, NY: Teachers College Press.

Bell, D. (1992). *Faces at the bottom of the well: The permanence of racism.* New York, NY: Basic Books.

Bell, D. (2005). *The Derrick Bell reader.* New York, NY: New York University Press.

Berry, R. Q. (2005). Building an infrastructure for equity in mathematics education. *The High School Journal*, 88(4), 1–5.

Berry, R. Q. (2008). Access to upper-level mathematics: The stories of successful African American middle school boys. *Journal for Research in Mathematics Education*, 39(5), 464–488.

Cadwallader, M. (1995). *Urban geography: An analytical approach.* Upper Saddle River, NJ: Prentice Hall.

Davis, J. (2014). The mathematical experiences of Black males in a predominantly Black urban middle school and community. *International Journal of Education in Mathematics, Science and Technology*, 2(3), 206–222.

Dean, J. (2013). Living algebra, living wage: 8th graders learn some real-world math lessons. In E. Gutstein & B. Peterson (Eds.), *Rethinking mathematics: Teaching social justice by the numbers* (pp. 67–74). Milwaukee, WI: Rethinking Schools.

Delgado, R., & Stefancic, J. (2001). *Critical race theory: An introduction.* New York, NY: New York Press.

Ellington, R. (2006). *Having their say: High-achieving African-American mathematics majors discuss the family, educational, communal and personal factors that impacted their decision to succeed and persist in mathematics* (Unpublished doctoral dissertation). University of Maryland, College Park, MD.

Frankenstein, M. (2013). Using math to take a critical look at how the unemployment rate is determined. In E. Gutstein & B. Peterson (Eds.), *Rethinking mathematics: Teaching social justice by the numbers* (p. 34–77). Milwaukee, WI: Rethinking Schools.

de Freitas, E. (2008). Troubling teacher identity: Preparing mathematics teachers to teach for diversity. *Teaching Education,* 19(1), 43–55.

Fuller, N. (1971). *The united independent compensatory code/system/concept: A textbook/workbook for thought, speech and/or action for victims of racism (white supremacy).* Washington, DC: Neely Fuller Jr. Production.

Gardner, H. (1995). Cracking open the IQ box. In S. Fraser (Ed.), *The bell curve wars: Race, intelligence, and the future of America* (pp. 23–35). New York, NY: Basic Books.

Gould, S. J. (1981). *The mismeasure of man.* New York, NY: W. W. Norton & Company.

Gould, S. J. (1995). Curveball. In S. Fraser (Ed.), *The bell curve wars: Race, intelligence, and the future of America* (pp. 11–22). New York, NY: Basic Books.

Gutstein, E. (2004). Home buying while Brown or Black: Teaching mathematics for racial justice. *Learning and Teaching Mathematics,* 1(1), 31–34.

Gutstein, E. (2013a). "I can't survive on $8.25"—Using math to investigate minimum wage, CEO pay and more. In E. Gutstein & B. Peterson (Eds.), *Rethinking mathematics: Teaching social justice by the numbers* (pp. 75–77). Milwaukee, WI: Rethinking Schools.

Gutstein, E. (2013b). Whose community is this? The mathematics of neighborhood displacement. *Rethinking Schools,* 27(3), 11–17.

Harris, C. (1993). Whiteness as property. *Harvard Law Review,* 106(8), 1707–1791.

Heckman, P. E., & Weissglass, J. (1994). Contextualized mathematics instruction: Moving beyond recent proposals. *For the Learning of Mathematics,* 14(1), 29–33.

Jett, C. C. (2011). "I once was lost, but now am found": The mathematics journey of an African American male mathematics doctoral student. *Journal of Black Studies,* 42(7), 1125–1147.

Jett, C. C. (2012). Critical race theory interwoven with mathematics education research. *Journal of Urban Mathematics Education,* 5(1), 21–30.

Ladson-Billings, G. (1999). Just what is critical race theory, and what's it doing in a nice field like education? In L. Parker, D. Deyhle, & S. Villenas (Eds.), *Race is—race isn't: Critical race theory and qualitative studies in education* (pp. 7–30). Boulder, CO: Westview Press.

Ladson-Billings, G. (2013). Critical race theory—What it is not! In M. Lynn & A. Dixson (Eds.), *Handbook of critical race theory in education.* New York, NY: Routledge.

Ladson-Billings, G., & Tate, W. F. (1995). Towards a critical race theory of education. *Teachers College Record,* 97(1), 47–68.

Larnell, G. V., Bullock, E. C., & Jett, C. C. (2016). Rethinking teaching and learning mathematics for social justice from a critical race perspective. *Journal of Education,* 196(1), 19–29.

Lopez, G. R. (2003). The (racially neutral) politics of education: A critical race theory perspective. *Educational Administration Quarterly,* 39(1), 68–94.

Lynn, M., & Dixson, A. D. (Eds.). (2013). *Handbook of critical race theory in education.* New York, NY: Routledge.

Martin, D. B. (2000). *Mathematics success and failure among African American youth: The role of sociohistorical context, community forces, school influence, and individual agency.* Mahwah, NJ: Lawrence Erlbaum Associates.

Martin, D. B. (2003). Hidden assumptions and unaddressed questions in mathematics for all rhetoric. *The Mathematics Educator,* 13(2), 7–21.

Martin, D. B. (2007). Beyond missionaries or cannibals: Who should teach mathematics to African American children? *The High School Journal,* 91(1), 6–28.

Martin, D. B. (2008). E(race)ing race from a national conversation on mathematics teaching and learning: The national mathematics advisory panel as White institutional space. *The Montana Mathematics Enthusiast,* 5(2&3), 387–398.

Martin, D. B. (2009a). Researching race in mathematics education. *Teachers College Record,* 111(2), 295–338.

Martin, D. B. (Ed.). (2009b). *Mathematics teaching, learning, and liberation in the lives of Black children.* New York, NY: Routledge.

Martin, D. B., & McGee, E. (2009). Mathematics literacy for liberation: Reframing mathematics education for African-American children. In B. Greer, S. Mukhophadhay, S. Nelson-Barber, & A. Powell (Eds.), *Culturally responsive mathematics education* (pp. 207–238). New York, NY: Routledge.

McDougall, H. (1993). *Black Baltimore: A new theory of community.* Philadelphia, PA: Temple University Press.

McGee, E. O., & Martin, D. B. (2011). "You would not believe what I have to go through to prove my intellectual value!" Stereotype management among academically successful Black mathematics and engineering students. *American Educational Research Journal,* 48(6), 1347–1389.

McGlamery, S., & Mitchell, C. T. (2000). Recruitment and retention of African-American males in high school mathematics. *Journal of African-American Men,* 4(4), 73–87.

Moody, V. R. (2003). The ins and outs of succeeding in mathematics: African American students' notions and perceptions. *Multicultural Perspectives,* 5(1), 33–37.

Oakes, J. (2005). *Keeping track: How schools structure inequality.* New Haven, CT: Yale University Press.

Orr, M. (1999). *Black social capital: The politics of school reform in Baltimore, 1986–1998. Studies in government and public policy.* Lawrence: University Press of Kansas.

Pitts Bannister, V. R., Davis, J., Mutegi, J., Thompson, L., & Lewis, D. (2017). "Returning to the root" of the problem: Improving the social condition of African Americans through science and mathematics education. *In Catalyst: A Social Justice Forum,* 7(1), 5–14.

Polite, V. C. (1999). Combating educational neglect in suburbia: African American males and mathematics. In V. C. Polite & J. E. Davis (Eds.), *African American males in school and society: Practices and policies for effective education* (pp. 97–107). New York, NY: Teachers College Press.

Ryan, W. (1976). *Blaming the victim.* New York, NY: Vintage Books Edition.

Sheppard, P. (2006). Successful African-American mathematics students in academically unacceptable high schools. *Education,* 126(4), 609–625.

Snipes, V. (1997). *Examination of the mathematical education of African Americans in North Carolina and Louisiana utilizing critical race theory of education* (Unpublished doctoral dissertation). Florida State University, Tallahassee, FL.

Solórzano, D. G., & Yosso, T. J. (2002). Critical race methodology: Counter-storytelling as an analytical framework for educational research. *Qualitative Inquiry,* 8(1), 23–44.

Stinson, D. W. (2004). African American male students and achievement in school mathematics: A critical postmodern analysis of agency. *Dissertations Abstract International*, 66(12). (UMI No. doi:3194548).

Tate, W. F. (1993). Advocacy versus economics: A critical race analysis of the proposed national assessment in mathematics. *Thresholds in Education*, 19(1), 16–22.

Tate, W. F. (1997). Critical race theory and education: History, theory and implications. *Review of Research in Education*, 22(1), 195–247.

Terry, C. L. (2010). Prisons, pipelines, and the president: Developing critical math literacy through participatory action research. *Journal of African American Males in Education*, 1(2), 73–104.

Terry, C. L. (2011). Mathematical counterstory and African American male students: Urban mathematics education from a critical race theory perspective. *Journal of Urban Mathematics Education*, 4(1), 23–49.

Terry, C. L., & McGee, E. O. (2012). "I've come too far, I've worked too hard": Reinforcement of support structures among Black male mathematics students. *Journal of Mathematics Education at Teachers College*, 3(2), 73–85.

Thompson, L. R., & Davis, J. (2013). The meaning high-achieving African-American males in an urban high school ascribe to mathematics. *The Urban Review*, 45(4), 490–517.

Thompson, L. R., & Lewis, B. F. (2005). Shooting for the stars: A case study of the mathematics achievement and career attainment of an African-American male high school student. *The High School Journal*, 88(4), 6–18.

Ture, K., & Hamilton, C. V. (1992). *Black power: The politics of liberation in America*. New York, NY: Vintage Books.

Welsing, F. C. (1991). *The ISIS papers: The keys to the colors*. Chicago, IL: Third World Press.

Wilson, W. J. (1998). Jobless ghettos: The impact of the disappearance of work in segregated neighborhoods. In L. A. Daniels (Ed.), *The state of Black America* (pp. 89–107). New York, NY: National Urban League.

Wright, B. E. (1984). *The psychopathic racial personality*. Chicago, IL: Third World Press.

INDEX

Made in the USA
Middletown, DE
31 August 2021